USE-WEAR ANALYSIS OF FLAKED STONE TOOLS

Patrick C. Vaughan

THE UNIVERSITY OF ARIZONA PRESS / TUCSON, ARIZONA

ABOUT THE AUTHOR

Patrick C. Vaughan's fieldwork on prehistoric stone tools and the analysis of their uses has carried him to France, Greece, West Germany, Italy, Japan, Peru, and Pakistan since 1978. He has published widely on the subject of lithic microwear in journals such as *La Recherche*, the *Journal of Field Archaeology*, *Revista del Museo Nacional* (Lima), and *Germania*. The author, who received his Ph.D. from the University of Pennsylvania where he remains affiliated as a research fellow, has been engaged in use-wear research at the Laboratorium für Urgeschichte, Universität in Basel, Switzerland, since early 1985.

Respectfully dedicated to the memory of Professor François Bordes (1919–1981), lithic technologist, prehistorian, geologist, science-fiction author

THE UNIVERSITY OF ARIZONA PRESS

Library of Congress Cataloging in Publication Data
Vaughan, Patrick C.
    Use-wear analysis of flaked stone tools.

    1. Stone implements—Analysis. 2. Stone implements—
France—Analysis. 3. Cassegros Site (France)
4. Magdalenian culture. I. Title.
GN799.T6V38 1985   930.1'028'5   85-989
ISBN 0—8165—0861—5

Contents

Figures

Preface

This book is based on a program of research into the functional analysis of stone tools, undertaken between 1978 and 1981 at the University of Pennsylvania (Philadelphia), the Institut du Quaternaire, Université de Bordeaux (France), and the Archaeological Museum of Náfplion (Greece). The project was begun with the aim of combining and further developing the techniques of use-wear analysis which had been initiated by R. Tringham (the "low-power" method) and by L. Keeley (the "high-power" method) during the mid-1970s. In 1978 it was still necessary for each microwear researcher to undertake extensive lithic use-wear experimentation: Part I of this book describes the results of the experimental program designed to test on a systematic basis a wide range of cryptocrystalline silicates (flints) and contact materials. This experimental project, encompassing 249 tests with three varieties of flint, constitutes the largest set of use-wear experiments yet published in such detail. Obviously, every possible mode of tool utilization could not be tested (e.g., tests on ivory, shell, hafting mechanisms, and projectile points were not conducted). But the results presented here are certainly representative of the common usages of most chipped-stone implements from prehistoric periods. Part I, then, is intended as a reference for the use-wear specialist and may appear overly technical and detailed to the non-specialist.

Part II is of more general interest to anthropologists and prehistorians as a whole, for contained in this section is information on an application of the experimental use-wear data in a functional study of a Lower Magdalenian flint assemblage (ca. seventeenth millennium B.C.) from the cave of Cassegros in southwestern France. In addition to defining the functional composition of the cave's excavated stone-tool assemblage, the study investigates the relations between the discernible function and the typology, technology, and distribution of the prehistoric flints. Since the site and its stone-tool inventory are small, it was possible to analyze all chipped-stone material (larger than one cm) which had been excavated from 1973 to 1979. Use-wear analyses of truly representative samples of lithic artifacts from excavated sites are still the rare exception. It is hoped that the study presented here will act as an incentive toward more representative functional analyses, which will be of far greater benefit to other branches of anthropology and prehistory than studies of isolated tool groups. Though the field of use-wear analysis still has some 'growing-up' to do, we must not lose sight of the 'mature phase' which lies ahead: functional information on stone tools, gathered by reputable techniques and used to complement technological, paleoeconomic, and paleoecological studies intended to describe and explain prehistoric human behavior.

An extensive photodocumentation is presented here with the intent of sparing other archaeologists the time, expense, and trouble of undertaking as lengthy a program of tool-use experimentation as this one. However, a microanalyst would be heading for trouble if he undertook a functional study with only a 'photo manual' in hand. It is absolutely necessary that an analyst visually understand the stages of polish formation, the degrees of polish variability on a single edge, the areas of overlap between generally distinctive polishes, and the characteristic distributions of wear traces. Such an understanding comes only from careful experimental work. A beginning microanalyst would do well to undertake tool-use tests involving at least one longitudinal action (cutting, slicing, or sawing) and one transverse action (scraping, planing, or whittling) on the major varieties of substances available to prehistoric cultures (e.g., stone, bone, antler, wood, plants, hides, carcasses, etc.). Published use-wear micrographs would be of assistance both during the experiments and afterwards in the functional analysis of archaeological pieces. But two-dimensional pictures cannot replace the three-dimensional features which one must learn to interpret on prehistoric or ethnographic stone tools.

The reader should be aware of certain limitations to optical microphotography. Due to the shallow depth of focus at the higher magnifications employed in this study, it was often not possible to include all the relevant features within one focal plane, or even within one frame. One micrograph of a minute area on a utilized stone edge cannot possibly convey all the detailed use-wear information that is to be found along both sides of the edge. For example, given the enlargement ratios used in printing the micrographs taken at 280x, it would take a composite micrograph of *40 centimeters* in length to document the microwear that is present on only *one centimeter of one side* of a used edge. On a completely different level, the damage that is inflicted on the surfaces and edges of archaeological stone tools by natural and accidental ('nonuse') mechanisms can substantially alter prehistoric use-wear patterns and thus affect their characteristics as captured on only one micrograph of an entire used prehistoric stone edge. When viewing the micrographs, the reader is urged to concentrate on (a) the shapes and surface texture of use-wear features, and (b) subtle differences in the microtopography of the wear features and the unaltered tool surface. Even though important microwear phenomena such as polishes and some striations are easily distinguished in the microscope oculars by means of the intensity of the light which they reflect, it is not advisable to rely solely upon contrasts of darker and lighter grey-tones to compare features in or among the micrographs, as the general tone of a printed picture is subject to the vicissitudes of the printing process.

The research which culminated in this book benefited at many points along the way from the perceptive comments and sound advice of Jacques Bordaz, my advisor at the University of Pennsylvania. I am most grateful to Jean-Marie Le Tensorer (Seminar fuer Ur- und Fruehgeschichte der Universitaet Basel) for the opportunity to participate in the excavations at Cassegros and for access to the cave's lithic collections for use-wear analysis. Parts of the project would not have been possible without the assistance of the directors and of various members of the Institut du Quaternaire, Université de Bordeaux: the late François Bordes, Denise de Sonneville-Bordes, Michel Lenoir, Patricia Anderson-Gerfaud, Maria Estela Mansur-Franchomme. A special word of appreciation goes to Catherine Perlès (Université de Paris X - Nanterre) for helping me through difficult periods all throughout this research. My thanks also extend to Ruth Tringham (University of California, Berkeley) for her advice at the early stages of my interest in microwear studies.

The parts of the project conducted in Greece also benefited from the assistance of many people: Thomas Jacobsen, Curt Runnels, Priscilla Murray (Indiana University); the director and staff members of the Náfplion Museum; Alexandra Kurz and Dimitri and Sophia Orphanos of Asini.

The following individuals graciously provided help in various technical matters of the most diverse nature: M. Rothman, C. Liakouras, R. White, J. Adelman, A. Fahringer (University of Pennsylvania); G. Wrobleski and G. Seiter (Gordon Seiter Associates, Ft. Washington, Pennsylvania); G. Kourtessi-Philippakis (Université de Paris I); R. Herron (University of Indiana); W. Longacre (University of Arizona, Tucson); and Rev. P. Capitolo SJ (St. Ignatius College Preparatory, San Francisco).

This book is based in part upon work supported by the National Science Foundation under Grant No. BNS 7820669.

Finally, but most importantly, I am grateful to my parents for their understanding and constant support throughout all the years that I have been away pursuing a future in the past.

PATRICK C. VAUGHAN

Glossary

contact surface: the side of a stone edge (ventral or dorsal) which is held facing the object being worked.

degree of linkage: the proportion of flint surface in a used edge area which is actually covered with polish components, as opposed to unpolished dark areas such as *interstitial space*.

diffuse depressions: sunken areas in a polish surface which have poorly defined, sloping sides.

directional indicators: striationlike features within polish surfaces (e.g., *groove, troughs*), as opposed to "striations" which form on an unpolished flint surface.

edge band: a solid line of polish situated on the very crest of the *working edge*.

groove: striationlike feature in a polish surface whose sides are well defined (cf. *trough*).

immediate edge area: the one-tenth of a millimeter (0.1 mm) of surface area adjacent to the crest of the *working edge*.

independent use zone (IUZ): an edge or ridge used to accomplish a task, as defined by the motion, worked substance, and the contact angle of the stone edge to the object's surface.

interstitial spaces: dark, unpolished spots of unaltered flint surface showing between polish components.

longitudinal actions: motions such as sawing, cutting, slicing, where the movement runs parallel to the *working edge*.

microcraters: roundish depressions in polished areas which display well-defined sides and whose bottom surface usually exhibits a multicolored glittering aspect or what appears to be a silica grain.

micropit: a minute pinhole in a polish surface.

noncontact surface: the side of a stone edge (ventral or dorsal) which is facing away from the object being worked.

nonuse factors: natural or accidental causes of alterations to stone surfaces (e.g., solifluxion, subsoil compaction, trampling, dropping, etc.)

pit-depression: a hole with well-defined sides within a polish surface.

polish: an altered flint surface which reflects light and which cannot be removed by cleaning with acids, bases, and solvents.

reflectivity: the relative brilliance of light reflection off a polish surface (e.g., very bright, dull, etc.), as viewed at 280x magnification in this study.

surface features: any diagnostic traits which occur only in certain polishes, such as "comet-tails" in bone polish, *diffuse depressions* in smooth-type antler polish, etc.

surface texture: relative smoothness or roughness of the surface of a polish.

transverse actions: motions such as whittling, scraping, planing, chopping, where the movement runs perpendicular to the *working edge.*

troughs: striationlike features in a polish surface with sides that are sloping and less well defined than those found on *grooves.*

unspecified harder material (UHM): substances such as bone, antler, reeds, or perhaps hardened woods.

used edge or piece: a stone edge or tool which bears microscopically detectable traces produced by intentional utilization in prehistoric times.

volume: relative height of the polish surface above the surrounding flint surface (i.e., the thickness of the polish).

working edge: the very crest of a stone edge, defined as the intersecting line between the ventral and dorsal surface planes.

Use-Wear Analysis
of Flaked Stone Tools

From Analogies to Microscopes: An Introduction

The desire to reconstruct the uses of stone tools in ancient or prehistoric times dates to the early days of the fledgling discipline of Prehistoric Archaeology. Throughout the nineteenth century and even up until the 1960s prehistorians followed various avenues of inquiry in the pursuit of functional interpretations of a growing body of lithic material. These efforts coincided, most understandably, with the need to set the great mass of tool data into coherent chronological and geographical classifications. Ironically enough, until recently modern technology has not provided the physical capacity for proper viewing of the manufacture and use-wear traces left behind on the vestiges of prehistoric technology. Ethnology, on the other hand, made a substantial contribution to the interpretation of stone tools since it offered seemingly ready-made answers to the perplexing functional questions posed by the newly discovered remains of mankind's "antedeluvian" past. Nevertheless, certain astute macroscopic observations of wear traces and replicative use experimentation held some currency in the earlier days of lithic studies. But it was not until the publication of the English edition of Serge Semenov's *Prehistoric Technology* (1964) that functional studies—at least in the West—began to come of age. Only a brief outline of the trends leading to current techniques of use-wear research is presented here, given the availability of extensive reviews of the development of functional interpretation in lithic studies, such as those by Hayden and Kamminga (1979), L. Keeley (1974), G. Odell (1982b), D. Olausson (1980), Owen et al. (1982–1983), and P. Vaughan (1981b:2–76).

The usual method of assigning 'functional' names and qualities to prehistoric stone tools was basically that of untested analogy to known uses of similarly shaped tools. S. Nilsson (1838–1843) undertook the earliest systematic attempt at descriptive classification of stone tools by functional arrangement based on undeniable general resemblances between the shapes of some prehistoric tools and the forms of certain modern metal or wooden implements or of ethnographic stone tools (Daniel 1950:44,47; Olausson 1980:48). This "speculative functional approach" (Hayden and Kamminga 1979:3) was current during the last century and the early part of the twentieth century (e.g., Boucher de Perthes 1847–1864; Lartet and Christy 1864; Lubbock 1872; Evans 1872; Pfeiffer 1912, 1920). Since the basic goal of most early lithic studies was the ordering of prehistoric tools along chronological and geographical lines, the *precise* function of individual stone implements was not the principal concern at the time. Yet aspects of the speculative functional approach have continued up to the present day (e.g., Sankalia 1964; Mauser 1965; Hole and Flannery 1967:262–264; Hole, Flanner, Neeley 1969:76; Binford and Binford 1966; S. Binford 1968; and L. Binford 1973), even after the development of stone tool classifications which rely principally on morphological and technological criteria (e.g., Bordaz 1970; Bordes 1950a, 1961; Tixier 1963; Brézillon 1977:25–31).

Even prior to Semenov's influence in lithic studies, however, there were a number of archaeologists who realized the significance of wear traces for proper functional interpretation. S. Nilsson (1838–1843), for example, noted that "through carefully examining how tools were worn, one can often with certainty conclude how they were used" (translated in Olausson 1980:48). Not at all uncommon were reports of simple visual examination of the more heavily developed traces caused by tool utilization (e.g., Rau 1864; Greenwell 1865; Evans 1872; Mueller 1897; Stroebel 1939; Peyrony et al., 1949; Witthoft 1955; Tixier 1955) or by natural and accidental agencies (e.g., de Mortillet 1833; Moir 1912; Warren 1905, 1913, 1923a, b; Vayson 1920; Bordes 1950b; Tixier 1958–1959). During the nineteenth and first half of the twentieth centuries a large number of experiments were conducted with stone tools in order to test the capability of a given tool type in accomplishing the function(s) which had been attributed to it over the years. Although such 'efficiency studies' were instrumental in indicating certain functional possibilities of the tested stone implements, the formation of use-wear patterns was generally not studied at the same time (e.g., Rau 1869; Leguay 1877; Muller 1903; Pope 1923; Ray 1937; Steensberg 1934; Woodbury 1954). Another type of tool-use experimentation at the time consisted of "direct verification" (Keeley 1974: 329), in which the researcher conducts only such tests as are thought necessary to support or disprove a given functional hypothesis for a certain class of implements, with the major emphasis being placed on comparison of experimental and prehistoric use-wear patterns (e.g., Spurrel 1884; Warren 1914; Curwen 1941; Barnes 1932; Bruijn 1958–1959; Behm-Blancke 1962–1963; Sonnenfeld 1962). Still, tool-use experimentation and the observation of wear traces were for the most part unsystematic and of limited scope and scientific control. Furthermore, examination of use-wear remained essentially macroscopic, since a microscope was rarely applied to problems of functional interpretation (cf., Bordes 1950b; Witthoft 1955; Bruijn 1958–1959; Sonnenfeld 1962).

The appearance in 1964 of the English edition of S. Semenov's *Prehistoric Technology* had a substantial influence over the course of use-wear research in the West. Semenov's basic contribution was to demonstrate the necessity of systematic tool-use experimentation and microscopic examination of wear traces. Although Semenov clearly took into account all the traces of wear which result from manufacture, use, and natural agencies—polishes, striations, rounding, cracks, edge chipping—his traceological manual gave primary consideration to striation, in accord with his emphasis on reconstructing the "kinematics" (motions) of stone-tool use (Semenov 1964:3–4, 16–21).

But since Semenov's publications and those of his associates at the Leningrad Academy of Science are only rarely available in English or French (Semenov 1973; Korobkova 1980; see also Levitt 1979), very little is known about the actual procedures of their traceological method or about precise details of their experimental and archaeological analyses. This lack of available detail caused serious problems for analysts who tried to apply Semenov's method to experimental tools (e.g., Ahler 1971; Bordes 1971; Kantman 1970a), to ethnographic material (e.g., Gould et al. 1971), and to prehistoric collections (e.g., Feustel 1973, 1974; Gramsch 1966, 1973; MacDonald and Sanger 1968): "Disappointment and disillusionment followed as one investigator after another found Semenov's results impossible to substantiate" (Keeley 1977:108).

Since striations were not found to form on flint tools as often as one would be led to believe from Semenov's book, some researchers decided to turn to other types of use-wear for functional identification: edge chipping (Tringham et al. 1974; Odell 1975), polishes (Keeley 1976, 1977; Keeley and Newcomer 1977), and nonorganic residues (Anderson 1980a, b; Anderson-Gerfaud 1981). These major new trends in post-Semenov research on microwear are based on wide frameworks of tests designed to control a number of variables which influence the production of wear from use and nonuse factors. Moreover, the resulting microwear attributes—especially microchipping and polishes—have been analyzed and published in greater detail than was the case with the results of earlier wear studies. At the same time, the processes behind the formation of wear phenomena have also been investigated. Techniques of observing microwear have advanced considerably: the use of stereoscopic and compound microscopes has become routine, and the special capabilities of the scanning electron microscope have been enlisted.

Before outlining the newer methods of use-wear analysis, brief mention should be made of the large number of functional studies done since the mid-1960s which followed the various approaches current before the English publication of Semenov's text: functional classifications of prehistoric stone tools by analogy to modern tools or to ethnographically known stone-tool traditions (see p. 3); macroscopic or microscopic observation of wear traces without replicative tool-use experimentation (e.g., Bordes 1973, 1974a, b; Bosinski and Hahn 1972; Brézillon 1973; D'Aujourd'hui 1977b; Hester 1976; Hester and Green 1972; Kantman 1970a, b; Massaud 1972; Lenoir 1971, 1978; Pradel 1973a, b; Rosenfeld 1970; Seitzer 1977–1978); limited use-wear experimentation or direct verification testing, to compare with prehistoric use-wear patterns (e.g., Barton and Bergman 1982; Biberson and Aguirre 1965; Broadbent and Knutsson 1975; Crabtree 1973; D'Aujourd'hui 1977a; Fiedler 1979; Gould et al. 1971; Hayden 1979b; C. Keller 1966; Lawrence 1979; Ranere 1975); and efficiency studies designed to investigate the execution of a task but not the resulting microwear traces (e.g., Davois 1974; Jones 1980; Newcomer 1977; Poplin 1972; Rigaud 1972; Sollberger 1969; Walker 1978).

Recent Trends in Microwear Research

One of the most important developments in microwear research since the introduction of Semenov's work to the West has been the realization that use-wear experimentation must be conducted in a comprehensive, systematic fashion (Keeley 1974; Odell 1975; Odell et al. 1976). The functional analysis of a prehistoric assemblage cannot be based on a limited number of use-wear tests as is the case in the direct verification method of analysis. This means that an analyst must perform, or have access to the results of, a comprehensive framework of use-wear experiments.

> To avoid errors arising from the convergence of wear patterns of diverse origins, each hypothesis about utilization should be considered against a *framework* of experiments and/or ethnographic comparisons, in order to enable the investigator to say that certain implements have been used in a particular manner on a particular material, not merely because direct verification proved positive, but also because many other experiments or ethnographic comparisons have shown that no other use in any other manner or on any other material is capable of producing similar wear patterns (Keeley 1974:329).

Concurrent with the adoption of a wide range of use-wear tests has been an equally important change in functional research: the systematic and detailed *microscopic* analysis of wear patterns, mainly with respect to attributes of microchipping, polishes, and nonorganic residues.

R. Tringham and several of her students published the results of the first wide-ranging series of microwear tests (Tringham et al. 1974). The experiments controlled for the variables of lithic raw material, worked material (Table 1.1), use motion, nonuse damage, number of strokes, mode of prehension, intentional retouch, pressure, and the spine-plane angle. The experimental flint edges were examined under a stereoscopic microscope with "most useful viewing at 40-60x" (Tringham et al. 1974:185). Edge damage in the form of chipping or microscarring was the principal wear phenomenon recorded, according to the attributes of the distribution, size, shape, and sharpness of the edge of the microflake scars (Tringham et al., 1974:187–88). A number of high-quality micrographs of edge chipping also accompanied the presentation of a summary of the experimental results.

Tringham et al. (1974) concluded that there was sufficient patterning in the experimental edge-scarring results to warrant functional analyses of prehistoric stone-tool assemblages on the basis of microflaking attributes. Specifically, the prehistoric use motion (longitudinal, transverse, rotative) and the relative degree of hardness of the contact material (hard, medium, soft) could be interpreted from microscar patterns (Tringham et al. 1974:195). Functional analysis by low-power microscopic inspection of edge scarring involves uncomplicated equipment (a stereoscopic microscope) and can proceed at a relatively rapid pace once the analyst is experienced (Tringham et al. 1974:175). G. Odell has been most instrumental in further refining the microchipping or "low-power" method (Odell 1976, 1977, 1979, 1981a), in undertaking additional use-wear experimentation with the method (Odell 1977:645f, 1978, 1980b; Odell and Odell-Vereecken 1980), and in applying it to the analysis of archaeological material from a Dutch Mesolithic site (Odell 1977, 1980a, 1981b, 1982a; cf. Yacobaccio and Borrero 1982; Sabo 1982). Many of the papers presented at the first symposium on microwear topics (the Conference on Lithic Use-Wear, Vancouver, Canada, March 1977) dealt with various experimental aspects of the microflaking approach and the physical principles behind edge chipping on stone tools (Hayden 1979). Other archaeological applications of edge-chipping analysis include studies by E. Coqueugniot (1983), E. Elster (1976), B. Hayden (1979b), D. Olausson (1982–1983); Seitzer (1977–1978), R. Tringham [1971 and n.d. (a), (b)], and by S. Roy (1983). The scarring attributes and the experimental patterns of edge microchipping that have been published by Tringham and by Odell are discussed and evaluated in greater detail in chapter 2.

Likewise, L. Keeley conducted a wide range of use-wear experiments to test the variables of lithic material, worked material, action, use duration, edge angle, contact angle, and intentional retouch (Keeley 1976, 1977, 1978b, 1980; Keeley and Newcomer 1977). Keeley employed compound microscopes to view primarily micropolishes and striations at magnifications of up to 400x, but microphotography and identification were routinely carried out at 200x. Keeley's "high-power" approach to microwear analysis has concentrated on distinguishing among general categories of worked materials on the basis of the reflectivity, surface texture, topographical features, and distribution of the polishes which the contact materials produce on used flint edges. Similar high-power microwear experimentation has been conducted, for example, by P. Anderson-Gerfaud (1981), S. Beyries (1982), J. Gysels (1980, 1981), M. E. Mansur-Franchomme (1983a, b), E. Moss (1978, 1983a), H. Plisson (1979, 1982), and by the Tohoku University Microwear Research Team (Kajiwara and Akoshima 1981; Serizawa et al., 1982). There has been an overall high degree of replicability and agreement reported for the micropolishes resulting from these various experimental projects. Use polishes have been the principal topic of discussion at the most recent international symposia on microwear analysis: Conference on Microwear Analysis of Chipped-Stone Artefacts, Sheffield, England, November 1979; Recent Progress in Microwear Studies, Tervuren, Belgium, Spring 1980 and 1981 (Cahen 1982); Traces d'utilisation sur les outils néolithiques du Proche Orient, Lyon, France, June 1982 (Cauvin 1983); and the Fourth International Flint Symposium, Brighton, England, April 1983 (Sieveking and Newcomer, n.d.).

Interest in the polishes has stemmed from the demonstration that micropolishes are for the most part diagnostic of the category, not just the hardness of a material worked with a flint implement—i.e., stone, bone, antler, wood, hide, and plant. However, it has been pointed out that such a degree of precision is gained at the expense of costlier equipment and a slower speed of analysis than is reportedly the case with the low-power microchipping method, which determines only the relative hardness of the worked material (Odell and Odell-Vereecken 1980). Nonetheless, the consistent patterns of micropolishes obtained in repeated independent tests have established

the usefulness of the high-power approach in determining the modes of utilization of archaeological flint assemblages. The characteristics of micropolishes and the procedures involved in the high-power approach are discussed in detail in Chapters 1 and 2, and an outline of collections anlayzed by the polish method is presented in Table 4.42.

Most recently, P. Anderson-Gerfaud has expanded the polish method by using the scanning electron microscope up to 10,000x magnification to investigate structured nonorganic residues which are contained in the micropolishes formed on stone-tool edges used to work plant, arboreal, and animal substances (Anderson 1980a, b; Anderson-Gerfaud 1981, 1982; see also Mansur 1982, Mansur-Franchomme 1983a, b). Previously, the electron microscope had been used by a number of researchers to obtain better resolution of the features on worn tool surfaces than is possible under high magnification with optical microscopes (e.g., Brothwell 1969; Dauvois 1976; Hayden 1979:passim; Hayden and Kamminga 1973a; Kamminga 1977; Keeley 1977; Pant 1979a, b; Shiner and Porter 1974). These studies did not, however, reveal any new traces which were not already known from observation with light microscopes (Anderson-Gerfaud 1981:27).

P. Anderson-Gerfaud has demonstrated experimentally that plant and animal mineral residues which replicate cell membrane structure or cell shape become trapped into a layer of amorphous silica gel which forms in the working area of a stone edge as a result of the dissolution of silica in the tool surface during contact with the worked material. Since some durable residues (e.g., phytoliths) may retain their shapes and are comparable to the mineral components of modern samples, "these residues can therefore often give very precise identifications of the plant and wood types or animal tissues worked by prehistoric tools" (Anderson 1980a:190). The precision of such determinations is limited at present —for example, to subfamilies and tribes of grasses—by a scarcity of comparative botanical and zoological information. Undoubtedly, further research into structured residues will allow greater depth to lithic functional analyses and more specific paleoeconomic and paleoenvironmental reconstructions.

Part I

Experimental Bases
of Use-Wear Analysis

1 / Methodology

Scope of the Experimentation

It is now accepted as *sine qua non* that a functional analysis of prehistoric stone tools must be based on the experimental results of a wide framework of use-wear tests. At the time this microwear project commenced in the spring of 1978, summaries of the results of only two sets of wide-ranging wear experiments were available in the West: one from the Harvard group of R. Tringham and the other from L. Keeley. Although an informal framework of use-wear criteria had been established since the 1930s by Semenov and his associates through their experimental-traceological method, their experimental results per se had not been presented in comprehensive form. Although there was, in addition, a large body of functional tests published before the work of R. Tringham and that of L. Keeley (e.g., Curwen 1935; C. Keller 1966; Martin 1923:51−53), these are of very limited usefulness because of the generally restricted scope or lax methodologies of use-wear experimentation before the mid-1970s.

The focus of the present experimental project was two-fold at its start: (a) the systematic testing of a wide range of lithic and contact materials, and (b) a combination of the low-power and the high-power microwear approaches.

Both the Harvard group and L. Keeley had employed mainly British chalk flint in their tests, with the addition of Danish chalk flint by the Harvard group. It was unsound to assume at the time that the results of their experiments could be applied without reserve to other kinds of flints, let alone to other types of lithic raw materials (Odell et al. 1976). On the other hand, to avoid repeated use-wear testing on every known type of flint or lithic material, it was necessary to find some easily identifiable physical property of stone material which could serve as a reliable indicator of the potential for microwear formation. The need was especially acute in the case of the vast group known as cryptocrystalline silicates, or "flints" in the generic sense of the term (i.e., flint, chert, chalcedony, and jasper). Previous researchers had demonstrated to some extent that there seemed to be a consistent relationship between the grain-size or texture of a rock type and the formation of microwear traces (Curwen 1935:64−65; Kamminga 1977:206; Semenov 1964:11; Sonnenfeld 1962:61). It remained, however, to test the relation between granularity and microwear on a systematic basis in a more comprehensive experimental framework. Therefore, an experimental project was undertaken with the aim of using three varieties of limestone flint distinguished on the basis of grain-size. Obviously, other classes of lithic materials such as quartzite, volcanic rocks, and obsidian must be tested in a similar fashion (see Beyries 1982; Plisson 1982; Vaughan 1981a, 1981b:186-214).

In addition to a variety of lithic materials, the project encompassed a wide range of contact materials: stone, bone, antler, wood, reeds, plants, meat, carcasses, hide, grit, and soil. Where possible, each of these major categories was represented by two or more different varieties. Depending on the physical properties of the individual contact substance, the samples were worked in various states such as fresh, dried, and water-soaked. The worked materials represent virtually the entire range of common, naturally occurring substances which were at the disposal of Paleolithic and Mesolithic cultures in Europe. Furthermore, they are the materials tested by L. Keeley (1980), with the addition of reeds in the present experiments. Absent from the tests were projectile-point and hafting experiments, as were more unusual or difficult-to-obtain substances such as ivory, horn, shell, and fish scales.

The dichotomy between the low-power and the high-power microwear methods was a major issue in use-wear research at the time the present experimental project began (e.g., Keeley 1974; Keeley and Newcomer 1977:35−36; Odell 1975) and has continued to occupy researchers in recent years (e.g., Moss 1983b; Odell 1983). The distinction is based jointly on the magnification at which traces are viewed and on what classes of use-wear are taken into greatest consideration in the analyses. It was decided at the onset of the project that a combination of the two techniques was in order and would produce better results than choosing to rely on one approach alone *a priori*. Due to prohibitive costs of acquiring and transporting two sorts of microscopes (stereoscopic for examination of edge scarring and a compound microscope for the polishes), the study was conducted with one instrument, a WILD-M50 metallurgical microscope equipped with optics ranging from 34x to 560x. Thus, virtually the entire range of magnifications normally used in use-wear optical microscopy was available in one machine.

The framework of experiments was designed initially for a projected use-wear study of the Mesolithic assemblages of the Franchthi Cave in southern Greece (Jacobsen 1976, 1981; Perlès and Vaughan 1983). As a result of regional surveys and the water-sieving of cultural materials from the two major trenches inside the cave, a substantial corpus of paleoeconomic and paleoenvironmental data is available (Diamant 1979; Hansen 1978; Hansen and Renfrew 1978; Jacobsen and Van Horn 1974; Payne 1975; Perlès 1976a, b, 1979). The advantage for the microanalyst is that the kinds of animal, arboreal, and vegetal products likely to have been worked with stone tools are well documented. Similarly, there is reasonably good information on the most probable proveniences of the lithic materials used by the Franchthi inhabitants to make their stone implements. The remaining variables tested in the experiments were drawn mainly from the principal use-wear studies of both the low- and high-power approaches (Hayden 1979; Hayden and Kamminga 1973a, b; Keeley and Newcomer 1977; Odell 1977; Semenov 1964; Tringham et al. 1974). Ethnographic data on stone-tool use among groups at a basically Late Paleolithic-Mesolithic level of subsistence economy and technology were also taken into consideration (e.g., Driver 1961; Kroeber 1925; Mason 1891; McGrath 1970). In addition, it was necessary to make certain assumptions and face limitations with respect to some variables in the experimental design. For example, it was not possible to obtain freshly shed antler; and the degree of pressure to be exerted on a tool during use was standardized to the amount of pressure necessary to execute the task in an efficient, nonexerting manner. It was thus possible to construct a reasonably comprehensive and realistic framework of use-wear tests whose results could be applied without much difficulty to most Stone Age assemblages composed of flint tools.

The actual number of tests conducted per each category of worked material is presented in Table 1.1, along with comparative data on previously published experimental programs. In all, 249 tests with three flint varieties were performed. This figure represents over 2.5 times the number of experiments reported in the original article by the Harvard group and substantially more than the tests outlined in other previous publications on experimental use-wear analysis by L. Keeley (1980) and P. Anderson-Gerfaud (1981). The following two chapters contain summaries of the analysis of the test data resulting from the present experimental project. The data which could be collected in coded form have been presented in full elsewhere (Vaughan 1981b:327−345).

Classes of Microwear

Five categories of wear phenomena were studied on the experimental tools: microchipping, striations, rounding, micropolishes, and residues. The following sections present definitions and brief summaries of recent research for each class of wear traces.

Microchipping

The scars produced along an edge as the result of intentional utilization or nonuse damage mechanisms are variously known in English as "microflaking"

(Tringham et al. 1974:171), "edge scarring" (Odell 1975:229), "utilization damage" (Keeley and Newcomer 1977:35), "edge damage" (Keeley 1980:24), etc., and in French as *micro-esquillement* and *ébréchures* (Dauvois 1977:282, 285), *retouche d'utilisation* (Brézillon 1977:106), or *micro-écaillures* (Anderson-Gerfaud 1981:25). Even more diverse are the terms used to describe the various attributes and patterns of microchipping such as scar shape, size, distribution, cross-section, etc. (terms listed in Odell 1977:112−116, 1979:333−334; Hayden 1979:133−135). The terminological confusion is as much a reflection of the variability of the microscars and their patterning as it is of the diverse methods used in the past to view microchipping (simple visual inspection, hand lens, and various kinds of microscopes). Optimal viewing of microscars is obtained with a stereoscope of capabilities up to 100x, although normally only magnifications from 10x to 40x are employed (Odell and Odell-Vereecken 1980:90).

The great variability in scar attributes and patterns is the central issue in the debate over whether microchipping is a reliable indicator of the mode of utilization of a stone edge. Some researchers maintain that their experimental evidence establishes certain attributes and patterns of microchipping to be the result of the use action, and other patterns and attributes to be the function of the worked material (e.g., C. Keller 1966; Odell 1981a; Odell and Odell-Vereecken 1980; Ranere 1975; Tringham et al. 1974). The attribute of scar outline (e.g., scalar, trapezoidal, rectangular scars; Odell 1975:232) has been reevaluated recently and found to be a less reliable indicator than the cross-section of the flake scar at its initiation or proximal end and at the termination or distal end (Cotterell and Kamminga 1979; Lawrence 1979; Hayden 1979:133−135).

Other microanalysts, however, have experimented and found that many variables other than the use action and the worked material assert substantial influences over the formation of microchipping (e.g., Anderson-Gerfaud 1981; Keeley 1980; Keeley and Newcomer 1977; Moss 1983b). Edge angle, contact angle, pressure, and deliberate retouch are the principal 'extraneous' variables which have been known to come into play along with use motion and worked material to influence microchipping attributes and patterning. For example, numerous researchers have reported experimental and ethnographic evidence which indicates a major role for the edge angle in scar formation. Specifically, acute edges quite often scar differently from obtuse edges when all other major use variables in the tests are held constant (e.g., Del Bene

and Shelley 1979:254; Hayden and Kamminga 1973a:7; Keeley in Hayden 1979:140; Keeley 1980: 42, 49, 59−61; Lawrence 1979:119−120; Schousboe 1977:15−17; Tringham et al. 1974:180; White 1968b: 515). And for the case of detecting use microchipping on intentionally retouched edges, analysts have reported great difficulty in distinguishing the smaller scar components of deliberate retouch from the microscarring caused by a subsequent utilization of the retouched edge (e.g., Brink 1978a:57f; Fiedler 1979:69−70, 100, 107, 110; Kantman 1971; Keeley 1980:27−28; Keeley and Newcomer 1977:35; Odell 1977:204, 297, 300, 316, 382; Pradel 1973b:91; but cf. Odell 1977:148−151 and Tringham et al. 1974:181 for proposed relative distinctions).

A further consideration in recent years has been the microscarring that is caused by natural and accidental damage (see Moss 1983b; Vaughan 1981b: 67−71). Tringham et al. (1974:191−192) claimed that their nonuse tests involving trampling and the agitation of water, sand, stones, and flint flakes in a plastic container produced a random, nonlocalized distribution of scars along the flakes' perimeters, a random orientation to the scars, and no standardization of scar size or shape on each test flake. Flenniken and Haggarty (1979), on the other hand, reported that well-controlled trampling experiments with obsidian flakes resulted in a substantial degree of patterned macro- and microscopic edge chipping, as has also been shown for flint artifacts submitted to trampling tests (Bordes and Bourgon 1951:17; Keeley 1980:34; Mansur-Franchomme 1983a:179). D. Keller (1979) and R. Knudson (1979) both found that lithic material from surface sites known to have been subjected to accidental damage, particularly trampling by animals, exhibited microchipping which resembled edge-scarring patterns produced by intentional use of experimental tools. The effects of agricultural implements on stone tools in open-air sites have been shown to include the production of minor, unpatterned edge damage as well as extensive edge chipping which resembles that from utilization or intentional retouch (Betts 1978; Mallouf 1982). Hayden and Kamminga (1973a:4) observed among Australian aboriginals that handling and transport of unused adze flakes resulted in a good amount of edge scarring.

Thus, studies of experimental, archaeological, and ethnographic stone tools have reported *both* random and patterned aspects to the microchipping that is caused by nonuse factors. It should be recalled that edge damage from natural actions was the central issue in a long and acrimonious debate in the early 1900s over whether eoliths were the products of human or natural factors (references in Brézillon 1977:213; Hester and Heizer 1973:20-22; Johnson 1978:343–345; Vaughan 1981b:30–36). Careful study of experimental and archaeological material, particularly by S. Warren (1923a, b), H. Breuil (1910; Breuil and Lantier 1965) and F. Bordes (1951, 1957, 1961; Bordes and Bourgon 1950, 1951), finally led to a recognition of the most common types of 'pseudo-tools' which can be produced by natural and accidental edge scarring. The possibility that patterned edge flaking (macro- or microscopic) on archaeological stone tools is due to nonuse agencies and not necessarily to intentional utilization or retouch by humans is of significant import for any method of use-wear analysis which relies heavily on the attributes of edge scarring.

Striations

Linear indicators of the direction of use motion, simply known as striations, also suffer from a lack of standardized terminology. Striations exhibiting depth have been called scratches, grooved scratches, furrows, linear depressions, sleeks, and abrasion tracks; and striations of more superficial appearance have been termed chattermarks and abraded lines (Hayden 1979:192–193; Kamminga 1979:148; Keeley 1980: 23, 32, 43). The deep striations have been classified on the basis of morphology, specifically the width and definition of the sides of the groove (Dauvois 1977:283; Fredje 1979; Kamminga 1979:148; Keeley 1980: 23; Pant 1979a, b). More recent analysis of experimental and archaeological flints under high-power optical and electron microscopy has led to the first systematic classification of striations based on their morphology, width, depth, and quantity, in addition to information on the formation processes of striations according to the state of the stone-tool surface during usage or natural alteration (Mansur 1982).

S. Semenov (1964) relied heavily on striations for reconstructing the kinematics, or motions, of prehistoric stone tools. Much to their chagrin, subsequent researchers have found that striations on archaeological stone tools are not all that common, but this is also a question of the microscopic techniques employed (Keeley 1974:324–325; Odell 1975:229–230). Furthermore, experimental pieces do not always exhibit striations (e.g., Bordes 1971; Brink 1978a, b) even when viewed at magnifications of hundreds or thousands of diameters (Anderson-Gerfaud 1981; Keeley 1980). Thus, while striations have been shown to be a valuable indicator of use motion, their presence is somewhat fortuitous, depending on the inclusion of foreign particles or on auto-abrasion by microchips

embedded in the worked material (Mansur-Franchomme 1983b; Odell 1975:229; Semenov 1964:15; Witthoft 1955:20, 1967:384).

Rounding or Smoothing

The rounding of edges and ridges and the smoothing of adjacent surface areas of used stone edges constitute a phenomenon which has long been known by visual inspection of certain more extreme examples (e.g., Greenwell 1865; Evans 1872; Tixier 1958–1959; Bruijn 1958–1959; Hahn and Bosinski 1972; Rigaud 1977). Microscopic investigation has permitted a more accurate understanding of the variations in rounding and smoothing as caused principally by the contact material, especially if grit is present on the working surface, and by the use motion (e.g., Brink 1978a; Keeley 1980; Mansur-Franchomme 1983b; Shackley 1974). Different degrees of rounding on the ventral vs dorsal surfaces of a used edge can lead to an assessment of the kinematics involved, particularly in the case of transverse actions where the contact surface becomes more rounded than the noncontact surface of the same edge, under normal conditions (Anderson-Gerfaud 1981; Keeley 1980). There are differing opinions, however, as to the physical mechanisms responsible for the observed phenomena of rounding and smoothing: abrasion (Dauvois 1976; Diamond 1979), build-up of silica through frictional fusion (Witthoft 1955, 1967), or dissolution and reformation of the surface silica of the working edge (Anderson 1980a; Anderson-Gerfaud 1981, 1982; Mansur-Franchomme 1983a, b).

Micropolishes

The characterization of micropolishes produced by certain categories of worked or contacted materials was initiated in the mid-1970s by L. Keeley. Previous researchers had used the presence and localization of polishes on a macro- or microscopic scale as indicators of utilization but not of a specific category of worked material, except in the case of sickle gloss (e.g., Bordes 1971; Brink 1978a, b; Curwen 1930, 1935; Hayden and Kamminga 1973a; Kamminga 1977; Odell 1977, 1978; Ranere 1975; Semenov 1964). As pointed out by P. Anderson-Gerfaud (1981: 26–27), even scanning electron microscope investigations of polished stone-tool surfaces did not result in fine-scale distinctions between microwear polishes (e.g., Dauvois 1976; Kamminga 1977; Pant 1979a, b).

In his various publications, L. Keeley has stressed the need for viewing micropolishes at a minimum of 200x magnification for characterization, although initial scanning of the flint edges can be accomplished at around 100x. This effectively eliminates stereoscopes for distinguishing between microwear polishes, since the stereo optical system does not permit optimal resolution beyond 100x. It is, therefore, necessary to use compound microscopes (usually called "binocular" microscopes) with the light beam transmitted through the objective and onto the tool surface. In addition, Keeley has advocated thorough cleaning of experimental and archaeological stone tools before analysis, primarily in an acid (HCl) and a base (NaOH) (Keeley 1980:10–11).

The mechanical and/or chemical processes responsible for creating use-wear polishes have been much discussed. Interest in polish mechanisms was spawned by the sickle gloss controversy which began at the end of the last century (see Vaughan 1981b:23–27, 57–63). There are three major explanations at present for the formation of micropolishes regardless of the worked material involved. Most commonly accepted has been the *abrasion model* (e.g., Crabtree 1974; Dauvois 1977; Diamond 1979; Kamminga 1979; Masson et al., 1981; Meeks et al., 1982), which basically postulates that "polish is produced by the gradual loss of surficial material (wearing down) and smoothing of those surfaces" (Del Bene 1979:172). The polishing agent would be intrusive abrasive particles in the working area such as dust, sand, and microchips. But polished surfaces on flint tools cannot be resolved into fine striation patterns even at very high magnifications with the scanning electron microscope (Anderson 1980a:184; Anderson-Gerfaud 1981:103; del Bene 1979:173).

The second hypothesis of polish formation is the *frictional-fusion* theory (Witthoft 1955:23; 1967) which proposes melting or fusion of the silica comprising the tool surface as a result of the intense localized frictional heat generated in the contact area of a stone edge in use. However, there is some discussion as to whether "the heats generated by utilization are sufficient to melt the tool stone" (Del Bene 1979: 174; also Anderson-Gerfaud 1981:105). The third and most recent explanation of polish formation could be termed the *amorphous silica gel model* (Anderson-Gerfaud 1980a, 1982; Mansur-Franchomme 1983b; Unger-Hamilton 1984). It calls for the localized dissolution of silica in the tool surface and the subsequent formation of a layer of amorphous silica gel on the surface of the contact area of the stone implement. Several factors cause the silica concentration in water on the tool's working edge to rise above the critical level of 115 parts per million, thus bringing about dissolution of the silica of the tool surface in the contact area and then the precipitation of the silica gel in an amorphous state as a "polish." These factors include friction-induced heat, abrasion by intrusive particles, the structure and hardness of the tool material, water, extreme pH conditions, certain plant acids, colloidal silica, solid amorphous silica such as is found in plants, and nonsiliceous crystal substances like calcium oxalate (Anderson 1980a:184).

Given the yet unresolved situation concerning the nature of polishes, it is better to adopt here a definition which does not imply any process(es) of formation: "polish" is a surface which reflects light, whatever its origins may be (Anderson-Gerfaud 1981:33).

Residues

Under certain ideal conditions of preservation, organic residues such as vegetal fibers or amino acids may be left adhering to prehistoric stone tools and can be studied by relatively straight-forward methods of chemical or physical examination (e.g., Briuer 1976; Broderick 1979; Shafer and Holloway 1979). Where no such surface deposits have survived the post-depositional or post-excavation life cycles of the tools, P. Anderson-Gerfaud (1981; Anderson 1980a, b) and M. E. Mansur-Franchomme (1983a, b) have shown that it is possible to resort to very high magnification studies with the scanning electron microscope to locate and characterize nonorganic residue particles fused in the polish areas. The residues investigated in the present project are simply surface deposits visible in the light microscope (see Chapter 2).

Methods and Variables

The following sections outline the methods and variables used in this experimental project. Proveniences of the lithic raw materials and of the various worked materials are discussed, then descriptions of the procedures followed in conducting the tests, an outline of the variables and microwear attributes that were recorded in each experiment, and finally a discussion of the reliability test which was performed to check my capabilities in detecting microwear.

Materials

Lithic Materials. The flints were obtained from the general region of the Franchthi Cave in the southern

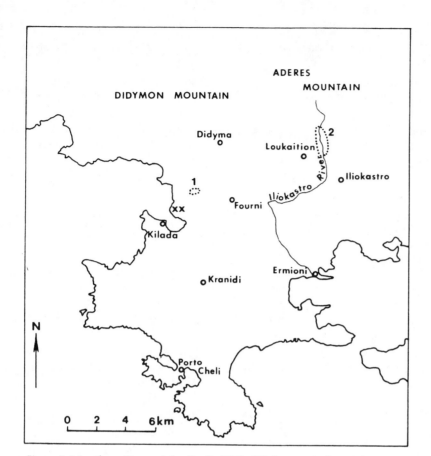

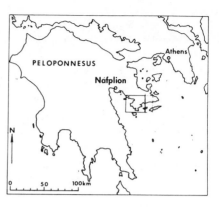

Figure 1.1 Southern Greece (after Perlès 1979: 82). Sources in the southern Argolid peninsula for the flint materials used in the microwear experiments. 1: Paliokastro source. 2: Upper Iliokastro River source. XX: Franchthi Cave.

part of the Argolid peninsula on the Peloponnese in southern Greece (Fig. 1.1). On a low hill known as Paliokastro, about 2 km northeast of Franchthi Cave, was found an abundant source of greyish-blue tabular limestone flint which is very fine-grained but contains cleavage planes, often with thin quartz inclusions, running perpendicular and parallel to the bedding. From the upper Iliokastro River area, 11 km northeast of the Cave, were collected large quantities of a 'medium-fine grained,' dark-brown flint and a 'medium-coarse grained,' dark-brown flint. These occurred as small-sized nodules, of 2 to 8 cm in diameter, in the seasonally dry bed of the Iliokastro River. They are transported there from an as yet unlocated source in the Aderes Mountain. Although many other kinds of flint were collected in various parts of the southern Argolid region, the three varieties of flint mentioned above were sufficient to represent most of the variability in grain-size which can occur in flints, for example, from very fine to coarse.

Worked Materials. The woods used in the tests came from around Náfplion, southern Greece, and were chosen to represent hardwoods (almond) and softwoods (cypress). They were worked when freshly cut, seasoned indoors for 8 months, and resoaked in water for a few days. The reeds came from both the Náfplion area (*Phragmites communis* Trin.) and from Philadelphia [*Pseudosasa japonica* (Sieb. & Zucc.) Makino]. They were worked principally in the fresh state, but also in a dried state after six months indoors. Reeds had been neglected in previous use-wear experimentation, despite the numerous uses to which they can be put: food, fuel, tools, containers, furniture, fishing poles, wattle-and-daub or other house construction (Forde 1963), shade roofs or lean-tos (Griffin and Estioko-Griffin 1978), small sailing rafts (Sordinas 1970: 31−34), the shafts of arrows and javelins (e.g., Pope 1918: 111, 1923: 333, 361; Horniman Museum 1929: 32, 37−38; McGrath 1970: 23, Table 6). Several kinds of nonwoody plants were cut with the experimental tools. Ripe domesticated barley (*Hordeum* sp.) was harvested in a field in Asini, southern Greece. Wild *Gramineae* in the green state were cut in an open field in Talence, France. Cattail (*Typha* sp.) from irrigation canals near Náfplion, southern Greece, were sliced diagonally along their entire length. And the green stems of very prolific marsh-elder (*Iva xanthifolia* Nutt.) from Philadelphia were cut.

The meat and bone tests used the ribs, vertebrae, and lower legs of cows (from the supermarket and slaughtering house), the carcasses of ether-dispatched rabbits from a medical research laboratory, and a blue fish from the market. Butchering was performed only on fresh animal products, while bone was worked in fresh, soaked, and dried-boiled states. Commercially available beef jerky was used to experiment with cutting dried beef. The antler, from a red deer, was easily worked after soaking in water for one to two weeks (see Clark and Thompson 1953:149).

The hide products worked in the fresh state (i.e., dehairing and defleshing) came from freshly slaughtered cows and ethered rabbits. As a substitute for drying fresh hides outdoors to produce dry hides, commercially tanned hides of deer, rabbit, and cow (both thick leather and supple suede) were worked in a dry state, slightly redampened, and with lard spread over the working area. Although untreated skins were often softened by scraping only after being left to dry (e.g., Mason 1891), it was also common for hides to be softened by scraping with stone tools only after they had been tanned in some natural solution such as deer brains (e.g., Hallock 1877: 656−657; McGrath 1970: 21). It is also the modern nonindustrial practice to soften hides with tools only after the tanning procedure (Grantz 1969:141−147).

Tool Knapping and Experimental Procedures

Flakes were struck from the flint nodules with a limestone hammerstone, but in the case of certain nodules of the medium-coarse grained flint, a metal hammer had to be used when the hammerstone proved ineffective in removing flakes. The knapping was carried out over a large leather pad, and the potentially usable flakes were placed in individual plastic bags. Edges were retouched when desired by pressure or percussion techniques with an antler tine, a dried bone point, a seasoned wooden point, or a hammerstone. After use, each test piece was numbered, inspected for use-wear, wrapped in tissue, and returned to its plastic bag.

Every attempt was made to execute the tests in as realistic a manner as possible. On the one hand, it was necessary for purposes of scientific control to impose arbitrary observation points, to maintain a certain degree of constancy in the way a tool was held or oriented, or to eliminate or add grit. On the other hand, meaningful use-wear traces intended for the functional analysis of prehistoric stone tools could only result from authentically re-created aboriginal conditions. By adopting an "as if" approach to the experimental tests, the tasks were conducted in a scientifically controlled manner which was still a reflection of realistic modes of using stone implements (Vaughan 1980). In other words, to carve a finished antler harpoon or to prepare a complete hide was not attempted. But the controlled, limited version of the aboriginal tasks was conducted with the same materials and motions *as* would be the case *if* the tasks were being performed 'for real' and not under 'laboratory conditions'. The experiments imparted the distinct impression that the mechanics of efficient stone-tool use are definitely an acquired art and differ considerably from the motor habits applicable to metal tools.

The motions employed were those commonly designated as the basic modes of utilizing tools (e.g., Leroi-Gourhan 1943:43−64; Tringham et al., 1974:181; Keeley 1980:17−19. Actions oriented perpendicularly to the working edge were designated *transverse actions* and included several variations— namely, whittling, planing, scraping, and chopping—that are based on differences in contact angle and/or the edge angle. Boring is a rotative action which could be assimilated into the group of transverse motion since resulting use striations are oriented perpendicularly to the side edges of used borers. Motions oriented parallel to the working edge were termed *longitudinal actions,* which also include a few variants such as cutting, sawing, slicing, and grooving. The precise motion (i.e., variant) was recorded at the time of each test, but the kinematic results of the experiments are summarized mainly in terms of transverse and longitudinal actions as general categories.

Each test was conducted for a predetermined duration and measured in both the number of strokes and the minutes elapsed, on a cumulative basis. The purpose of establishing arbitrary observation points such as 50, 200, 800, and 1600 strokes was to follow the major stages in the continuum of use-wear formation. Where possible, the first tests in a group of experiments included several observation points so that developmental patterns could be established. Once the formation patterns were documented, or if working conditions precluded repeated observations during such times as harvesting in a field, only one or two observations of wear formation were made per working edge. Within each class of experiments, however, several observations were made to document wear patterns that resulted from both very short use up to very extended use. The extended use of a stone tool depended greatly on the lithic material, the contact substance, the motion, and the angle of the working edge in the particular case. For example, an obtuse unretouched edge is effective for scraping bone or reeds, yet dulls relatively quickly, whereas an acute unretouched edge of fine-grained flint was still useful after three hours' harvesting of barley. Again, realistic modes of utilization were attempted within the bounds of controlled experimentation. As a result, it was possible to establish general guidelines for estimating use duration of an edge based on the lithic material involved and the degree of polish formation and edge rounding exhibited by the working edge.

At each observation point, the used edge was washed in warm soapy water, medicinal alcohol or acetone, and in some cases with dilute (15%) hydrochloric acid. Systematic use of the acid was avoided because it removed diagnostic residues, such as those from bone, antler, dried beef, and stone (see Chapter 2), and it destroyed the surface of flints in which there were even minute limestone impurities within the silicate matrix. When a used edge was reexamined after the experiment in which it was involved, finger grease was removed with alcohol or acetone.

Edges were examined before use and at the observation points on a WILD-M50 metallurgical microscope. The inverted stage of this type of microscope allows one to view tools of virtually any size and shape once they are properly and solidly positioned by means of a greaseless plastolene. The optimal magnification for critical distinction of the microwear polishes and striations was found to be 280x, whereas the lowest magnifications possible on the machine (34x, 56x) or a small hand lens (10x) were generally found best for viewing the edge microchipping. The lack of the three-dimensional aspect afforded by a stereoscopic microscope was initially troublesome for viewing the microflaking, but a mental adjustment to a two-dimensional viewing field was easily made and relative depths could be judged for operational purposes.

By substituting an ordinary 35mm single lens reflex camera fitted with a special microscope adaptor tube for one of the microscope oculars, and a similarly adapted light-meter probe for the other ocular, it was possible to take micrographs of the various use-wear patterns produced in the tests. Such micrographs are essential for standardizing the interpretive criteria used in the microwear analysis of prehistoric stone tools. Therefore, great efforts were expended to obtain micrographs which represent as accurately as possible the aspect, configuration, and minute details of the wear traces as seen through the microscope. The very fine-grained black-and-white film developed by

Kodak especially for micrography (Technical Pan, formerly SO-115) was found to give excellent results at 100 ASA. Equally important for obtaining good-quality photos was the powerful light source on the M50 (a 100-Watt halogen bulb), stopping down the microscope's field diaphragm to eliminate glare in the viewing area, and the occasional use of a polarizing filter to reduce excessive light refraction from white-patinated or light-colored stones. Synthetic replicas of tool edges and surfaces are also effective in eliminating troublesome light refraction (e.g., Beyries 1981; Plisson 1983b).

Variables and Data Analysis

Preliminary experiments (N = 26) were conducted with the three varieties of flint to work bone, antler, hard- and softwoods, reeds, green plants, hide, and meat. The exact results of these tests are not reported here since their purpose was only to become familiar with the range of possible wear patterns, particularly with respect to the micropolishes. The outcome of these initial tests served to establish which use-wear characteristics from among those noted in the recent literature were to be incorporated into the full-scale experimentation.

There was especially some question at the onset whether to use the microchipping attributes of scar outline as described by the Harvard group or the attributes of scar cross section as proposed by various other researchers, particularly at the 1977 Vancouver Lithics Use-Wear Conference (Cotterell and Kamminga 1979: 104–106; Hayden 1979:133–135; Hayden and Kamminga 1973a:7–8; Lawrence 1979:114–117). As a result of the preliminary tests, it was decided that microscar outline (e.g., scalar, trapezoidal, rectangular, irregular) was often too subjective and time-consuming to judge and seemed, moreover, very dependent upon the stone material. Therefore, the cross-sections of the microscars at their distal and proximal ends (see Figure 2.1, p. 21) were adopted for the full-scale experimentation. Specifically, the proximal scar cross-section could be shallow, break-shallow, steep, or a crescent break. The distal cross-section of the microscars could be a crescent break, feathered, or of the hinge or step varieties.

The 25 variables recorded for each test and each use-wear observation point consisted of information concerning:

(1) *The tool and the manner of use:* edge utilized, lithic material, retouch method, type of retouch, edge angle, action, contact surface, contact angle,

worked material, added grit, number of strokes, minutes, and ease of execution;

(2) *The attributes of resulting use-wear traces:* the predominant surface, distal and proximal cross-sections, relative size, distribution, and edge-row feature of the microchipping; the predominant surface, morphology, and orientation of the striations; surface and intensity of edge rounding; and the surface of greater degree of polish development.

Although the amount of pressure exerted during tool use is a factor in the production especially of microflaking along the working edge, the variable of pressure was held constant throughout the tests by attempting to exert only as much force onto the tool as was required to accomplish the task in an efficient, nonexerting manner.

Of the microchipping characteristics the variables of predominant surface, relative size, and distribution along the working edge were adopted from Odell's (1977:584–588) data recording scheme. As mentioned above, the scar cross-sections were drawn from various other publications. The 'edge row' attribute of microchipping refers to the row of small step- or hinge-type microscars which often occur within the proximal region of larger scars along a used or crushed edge (Plate 1). The edge-row attribute was the result of observations made during the initial experiments but is essentially the same phenomenon as reported by others (e.g., Hester et al. 1973:93; C. Keller 1966: 508; Rosenfeld 1970:178).

The attributes for striations and edge rounding were features seen in the preliminary test results or noted by previous analysts. Since use-wear polishes had only been described of recent date before the start of this project, the single polish attribute that was gathered in coded form dealt with the surface of greater degree of polish develoment—that is, which surface (ventral or dorsal) exhibits the more heavily developed manifestation of a use-wear polish found along the used edge. Otherwise, written descriptions were made of the polishes' reflectivity, surface texture, volume, surface features, degree of linkage, and their extension into the interior away from the crest of the edge. These attributes of use-wear polishes were obtained from the publications of L. Keeley (Keeley 1976, 1977; Keeley and Newcomer 1977) and from the initial twenty-six experiments.

Aside from the majority of the polish characteristics which were noted in writing, the experimental use-wear attributes were recorded by means of a data code (Vaughan 1981b:319–326). The resulting data (Vaughan 1981b:32–345) were submitted to sorting by the Statistical Analysis System on the IBM computer at the Uni-Coll Corporation, Philadelphia. The results of the computer-run correlations among use-wear attributes and test variables were summarized in tables (Tables 2.1–2.14), which are discussed in the following two chapters. The written descriptions of the microwear polishes were likewise compiled and summarized in a systematic fashion (Chapter 2).

Reliability Test

After most of the experimentation was completed, a 'blind test' was conducted to check my ability in detecting the location of intentional use-wear on stone tools, in separating out the results of nonuse wear, and in interpreting the use action and worked materials involved. From 24 flakes (8 of each of the 3 flint varieties), 12 edges were retouched by hammerstone or antler tine, and 9 edges—4 of which retouched—were used to scrape tanned hide, plane fresh hardwood, and groove soaked bone. The kinds of microwear patterns produced on the retouched and on the utilized flint edges are discussed in Chapter 2, particularly in the section on polishes caused by intentional use on bone, wood, and dry hide and by retouch with hammerstone and antler. After preparation of the retouched and the used pieces, the entire set of 24 flakes was then put through a series of tests designed to replicate certain basic ways in which stone tools are damaged by accident or through natural agencies, specifically, trampling, subsoil compaction, screening, bag storage, and handling. Procedures in the trampling-screening tests are outlined in the next chapter in the section on microchipping from nonuse factors, as are the wear traces induced by these nonuse tests.

The results of the microwear analysis were revealing. For the 24 flakes, there were five cases with discrepancies between the use-wear interpretation and the original notes on the actual location and manner of use. Of the five errors, three were found, upon reexamination, to be due to interference by soil or rock damage induced in the nonuse parts of the tests. Specifically: (a) two cases where poorly developed dry hide polish on flint was confused with grit polish from the soil, and (b) one flint edge where small smooth domes without grooves (resembling weakly developed wood polish) constituted a previously unknown aspect of soil damage. For the fourth case of error in interpretation, a very weak development of the diagnostic traces of hammerstone retouch caused some uncertainty and a change in the original interpretation, but the first designation was actually correct. And the fifth case was due to simple carelessness: the *entire* perimeter of a flint flake was not scanned, so the limited area with very clear traces of bone grooving was not detected.

The outcome of the reliability test does serve to point out an aspect of wear analysis which could not have resulted from other blind tests which have been published (Gendel and Pirnay 1982; Kajiwara and Akoshima 1981; Keeley and Newcomer 1977; Odell and Odell-Vereecken 1980). In those tests, the pieces were passed directly from experimenter to micro-analyst. While this does test the analyst's abilities, it is by no means an archaeologically realistic situation. The fundamental goal of use-wear analysis is to recognize and interpret the use of prehistoric stone tools which have passed through all sorts of damage mechanisms in prehistoric times, in the post-depositional cycle, and from post-excavation processing and handling. If microanalysts are to understand how much functional information has been lost to natural and accidental damage, systematic and well-designed experiments should be pursued along the lines of the above study.

2 / Experimental Use-Wear on Flint Tools

The results of the use-wear tests and nonuse experiments conducted with three types of flint are presented in this chapter by major categories of wear traces: microchipping, striations, rounding, micropolishes, and residues. Such an artificial division of otherwise unified constellations of wear traces is justified by the need for an orderly presentation of analytical criteria that are intended for application to archaeological material.

Where a data-code system of recoding was not possible (for polishes and residues), qualitative descriptions summarize the relevant test results. Otherwise, frequency tables express the outcome of correlating the attributes for the three categories of traces—microchipping, striations, and rounding—where some form of quantified data resulted from the use of a code. It must be stressed that the percentages expressed in the frequency tables are strictly relative, within the context of the manner in which the experiments were conducted. It is not expected that any prehistoric or ethnographic stone-tool assemblage would yield functional data which must correspond numerically. However, the *trends* and relative proportions brought forth by the tabulated data and percentages should be of direct relevance to prehistoric use-wear patterns.

Examples of microwear on archaeological flints are presented along with micrographs of the experimental wear traces, so that the reader may become aware of what microwear polishes and striations, in particular, look like on the 'real thing.' The problem of nonuse wear in the form of edge scarring and rounding, striations, and soil sheen on prehistoric flints is also discussed at length. The concluding section of the chapter summarizes the relative merits of each class of wear traces for the functional analysis of prehistoric stone tools and reviews the criteria which can be employed to interpret use action and contact substance.

Microchipping

Microchipping from Intentional Use

One of the more pressing needs of microwear research in the past few years has been the systematic presentation of the actual microscarring which results from a large organized program of tool-use experimentation. Such information has been forthcoming (Akoshima 1980, and n.d.; Keeley 1980:36−61) but was sparse at the beginning of this project (e.g., Keller 1966; Odell 1977:Fig. Appendix F4-12). The reported diversity of microchipping attributes and patterns discussed in Chapter 1 would logically lead one to question whether the proposed functional interpretive criteria that rely principally on edge chipping (e.g., Tringham et al. 1974; Odell and Odell-Vereecken 1980) are the results of an insufficient experimental sample (see Table 1.1). The flint microchipping data from this project (N=249 flint tests) would seem to support this interpretation.

While the microflaking results published by R. Tringham et al. (1974), by G. Odell (1977, 1981a; Odell and Odell-Vereecken 1980), and by K. Akoshima (1980, and n.d.) are discussed below in comparison to the microchipping obtained in the present experimental project, the edge-scarring data from L. Keeley's (1980) tool-use experiments cannot be directly compared, for the most part, to the results of the current study. In contrast to the present *attribute* analysis of microscars and their patterning (i.e., proximal and distal cross-sections, predominant surface of the edge, relative size, distribution along the edge, and edge-row microscarring), Keeley followed a fundamentally different analytical scheme in which "the smallest unit of analysis" was "the individual damage scar" (Keeley and Newcomer 1977:45). Keeley thus employed a *typology* of microscars (e.g., large deep scalar, small shallow scalar, large stepped, half-moon breakages, etc.) which was constructed from selected combinations of aspects of scar outline, depth, and size.

For each set of variable correlations in the present study, a chi-square test was performed to detect nonrandom variability among the microchipping patterns for each of the three flint types (Table 2.1). The null hypothesis being tested was that the observed differences in values among the three flint types in each microchipping correlation did not differ from randomness. Significant limits were set at the .05 level. Significance at the .001 level, for example, would indicate that a given p score could be expected by chance alone in 1 of every 1000 cases. By contrast, the .5 level implies that the p score could be the result of random factors in 5 of every 10 cases, or, 1 out of 2. Scores of p which were equal to or less than the .05 level in this study were taken to indicate that the null hypothesis could be rejected and that nonrandom variability existed in the microchipping patterns of the three flint types. In the majority of cases (17 out of 21), the factor of lithic raw material was not found to exert a significant influence in causing the differences noted among the scarring patterns on the three varieties of flint (Table 2.1).

Action. The distribution of microflake scars on the dorsal and ventral surfaces of a utilized flint edge is one of the criteria used by some researchers to distinguish the mode of action:

The *mode of action* is indicated by the distribution of the microflake scars on the two surfaces of the flake,

and along the flake's edge. This is the result of the fact that the amount, regularity, and direction of pressure, which varies with each action, will be directly reflected in the detachment of the microflakes (Tringham et al. 1974:187–188).

Specifically, in transverse actions such as scraping, planing, whittling, "microflakes are detached from one surface only, that is, the surface opposite the one which has direct contact with the worked material" (ibid.:188–189). Thus microchipping from transverse actions is "exclusively unifacial, or almost so" (Odell and Odell-Vereecken 1980:99). Longitudinal actions, on the other hand, produce scarring on both surfaces of an edge (Tringham et al., 1974:188; Odell and Odell-Vereecken 1980:98). It has been noted that "as the angle of the flake to the worked material is changed, the pressure, and therefore the scarring, will be that much greater on one surface than on the other" in longitudinal actions (Tringham et al., 1974:188).

Table 2.2, however, shows that the microchipping on tools of the three flint types does not entirely support the above generalities. Longitudinal motions did produce scarring that was primarily (65%) bifacial as expected, although a number of observations (17%) revealed only unifacial scarring, contrary to prediction. From the transversely used flint edges, a considerable proportion (46%) of observations were recorded where the scarring was (a) eminently *bifacial* (i.e., equal on both the dorsal and ventral surfaces), or (b) unique or predominant on the *wrong* surface from the one expected. Other researchers have also reported ethnographic or experimental evidence where edge scarring from transverse motions occurs on both surfaces of the working edge (e.g., Akoshima, n.d.: Fig. 4; Broadbent and Knutson 1975:119; Odell 1977: Fig. Appendix F4) or on the surface closest to, and not opposite from, the contact material (e.g., Fiedler 1979:69, 100; Gould et al., 1971:159; Keeley 1980: 36; White 1968b:515).

The distribution of scars along a used edge is also a criterion used to distinguish use motion (Tringham et al., 1974:188-189). Specifically, longitudinal actions produce discontinuous (uneven) scarring, and transverse actions result in continuous (dense) scarring. Table 2.3 shows that the longitudinal tests of this project conformed for the most part (66%) to the 'rule', whereas there were far more observations (52%) from the transverse actions which did *not* conform to expectations than observations which did (32%). For unexplained reasons, a significant difference (p=.035) was noted in the behavior of the three types of flint with regard to scarring distribution in the transverse-motion tests (Table 2.1). K. Akoshima (n.d.) has also reported a great diversity in the density of edge scars, based on an experimental series of 72 tests.

The scarring attribute of edge row—that is, small step or hinge scars within the proximal region of larger microchipping (Plate 1)—was expected to conform to the 'rule' of surface occurrence as a function of action, namely, unifacial edge-row scarring on the noncontact side of edges used in transverse actions and bifacial edge-row chipping from longitudinal actions (Tringham et al. 1977:188–189; Odell and Odell-Vereecken 1980:98–99). Table 2.4, however, indicates that such was not the case for edge-row chipping from either transverse or longitudinal actions in the current tool-use experiments with flints. For the transverse actions, 16% of the observations conformed to expectation and 11% did not, whereas 15% of the observations from the longitudinal did not conform and only 2% did (Table 2.4). However, the sample of flint edges which exhibited a scarring edge row was rather small: only 27% of the observations from transverse motions and 17% from longitudinal actions. The infrequency of the edge-row phenomenon may be due to the fact excessive amounts of pressure were not exerted during the tool-use tests. The opposite may have been true on occasion in aboriginal contexts, depending upon the strength, motions, or whim of a stone-tool user, which makes pressure a variable that can hardly be controlled.

Boring tests were limited (N=11 observations from 3 test pieces used on wood) but produced bifacial scarring. The chopping tests (two edges, also on wood) are also considered separately, since with this basically transverse motion the edge can be oriented perpendicularly to the wood and not necessarily predominantly to one surface as in other transverse actions. The scarring which resulted from the two chopping tests was bifacial and was not as small as the majority of scars on edges used transversely on wood (see Keeley 1980:38 for similar results).

Worked Material. The hardness of the contact material is a major consideration in scar analysis:

> The *nature of the worked material* is indicated by the morphological characteristics of the microflake scars. The experimental tests showed that variation in the hardness, friction, and resistance of the different worked materials is correlated with variation in size, shape and sharpness of the edge of the microflake scars (Tringham et al., 1974:188).

The vegetal and animal materials used in the experiments under consideration (pp. 13–15) have been divided into the following categories of hardness based on G. Odell's classifications (Odell 1980b; Odell and Odell-Vereecken 1980:101):

> hard: bone in any state, dry antler, dry woods, carcass;
> medium-hard: fresh and soaked almond wood, soaked antler;
> medium-soft: fresh and soaked cypress wood, reeds, barley and wild *Gramineae*, dried beef;
> soft: meat without bone, hides, green plant stems, cattail.

The distal termination of microscars (Fig. 2.1) is reportedly feathered in the case of edges used on soft and medium-soft materials (Odell and Odell-Vereecken 1980: 101), hinge-type for medium-hard materials (ibid.:101), and of the step variety for hard materials (ibid.:101; Tringham et al., 1974:188). The current experimental results did indicate a tendency for harder materials to produce hinge/step scars, [e.g., 63% of observations from edges used on hard materials involved predominantly hinge/step scars (Table 2.5)]. However, the proportion of observations in which predominantly feathered scars resulted from hard and medium-hard materials was by no means negligible (15%, 25% respectively); likewise, the occurrence of predominantly hinge/step scars from contact with soft and medium-soft substances (18%, 27%) was not insignificant (Table 2.5). Thus, the present data

Figure 2.1 Cross-sections of microscars.

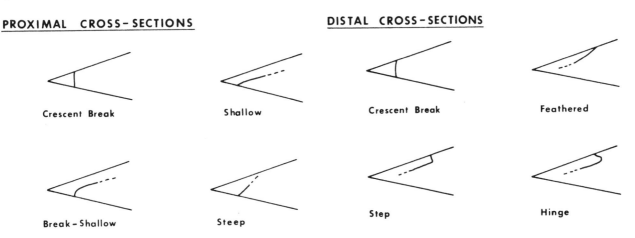

PROXIMAL CROSS-SECTIONS

Crescent Break

Shallow

Break-Shallow

Steep

DISTAL CROSS-SECTIONS

Crescent Break

Feathered

Step

Hinge

reveal only tendencies and not the clearcut patterns proposed by other researchers (Odell and Odell-Vereecken 1980:101; Tringham et al., 1974:188). Inexplicably, the three flints displayed highly significant nonrandom variability ($p=.001$) in distal cross-sections from medium-hard worked materials (Table 2.1). K. Akoshima (n.d.) has also reported a tendency for harder contact materials to produce a higher percentage of step scars, but these are also frequently the result of working soft and medium worked materials.

The proximal cross-section of the microscars (Fig. 2.1) is a more recently defined attribute (Cotterell and Kamminga 1979:105; Hayden 1979:133−135; Lawrence 1979:115−116) which seems to display as much variability as does the distal cross-section (Table 2.6). There was a tendency for harder worked materials in these tests to produce a greater proportion of shallow scars, for example, 69% of the scarring in observations from flints used on hard materials were shallow scars (Table 2.6). But at the same time, one-fourth of the observations from edges used on hard contact materials involved other types of proximal cross-sections of microscars; and there was great diversity in the predominant proximal cross-sections of scars displayed by edges used on medium-hard, medium-soft, and soft materials (Table 2.6). In a word, there was too much variability in the attributes of the proximal cross-section of use-related microchipping as correlated with worked material.

It has also been reported that microscars from contact with soft materials are "usually small," those from medium-soft substances "often fairly large (i.e., visible to the naked eye)," and those from medium-hard and hard materials are "medium-to-large in size" (Odell and Odell-Vereecken 1980:101). Table 2.7 shows that a greater proportion of observations from edges having worked harder materials exhibited larger-sized microchipping, as expected: 39% "very large" scars (i.e, easily discernible with the naked eye) and 24% "large" scars (visible with 10x hand lens) resulted from working hard materials. Similarly, a greater proportion of cases involving medium and soft contact materials displayed smaller-sized scarring— e.g., 17% "small" scars (visible at 84x magnification) and 8% "minute" scars (visible around 100x) from medium-soft substances, and 15% small-sized scars from soft contact materials. However, it is also obvious from Table 2.7 that there was generally a *very wide* spread of scar sizes that resulted from contact with *each* hardness category of worked material in the present tests. In other words, there was more variability than expected in scar size as correlated with contact material (see Akoshima, n.d., for similar results). The soft-worked materials resulted in highly significant

differences of scarring patterns ($p = .004$) among the three flint types (Table 2.1).

The microchipping edge row attribute (Plate 1), on the other hand, displayed a clearer pattern when correlated with worked-material hardness than was the case for scar cross-section and size (Table 2.8). Complete edge rows of microscars—that is, distributed along the entire used edge, or nearly so—were virtually only the product of contact with hard materials. Partial edge rows (i.e., along only parts of the used edge) resulted from working medium and hard materials. However, nearly half the observations of edges used on hard materials, and around 80% of those for edges contacting medium-hardness substances, did not exhibit microscarring edge rows at all. Thus, the frequency of microchipping edge rows on the experimental flint tools was too small to make the attribute a fundamental use-wear criterion to interpret worked substance.

Conclusions. The current experimental results either contradicted previously reported aspects of microflaking patterning (e.g., predominant surface of scarring and the distribution of scars along edges used in transverse actions) or revealed only general tendencies where others have proposed clearcut 'rules' (e.g., distal cross-sections and scar size; cf. Odell 1977: 597−610; Odell and Odell-Vereecken 1980; Tringham et al., 1974). The patterns of microflaking documented here are based on far more observations of experimental tests than have been reported by those who rely primarily on microflaking to perform functional analyses of stone tools (see Table 1.1): 249 experiments with flints in the current project as compared to 91 tests reported by R. Tringham et al., (1974) and 71 subsequent tests by G. Odell (1977, 1978, 1980b). It is entirely possible that the great variability in scarring results noted for the present set of experiments would not have stood out in individual smaller experimental samples, especially ones which involve certain unrealistic parameters such as maximum use duration of only 1000 strokes and working *un*soaked bone and antler (Odell 1977:647−649; Tringham et al., 1974:184).

The causes for substantial internal variability in edge microscarring patterns have been discussed by other researchers as noted in Chapter 1. A glance at Tables 2.2 and 2.5 will make it clear, for example, that lower (less than 65°) and higher (greater than 66°) edge angles of flints definitely behaved differently in the same contact situation during the tests. Specifically, thicker edges had a greater tendency to resist scarring when engaged in a transverse action (Table 2.2) and even when working medium and hard materials (Table 2.5). Some edges did not scar at all as a result of use:

16% of the observations from transverse actions and 18% from longitudinal motions (Tables 2.2–2.4), and from 39% of the observations involving soft materials to 6% of those with hard materials (Tables 2.5–2.7). Microwear polishes were found, however, in nearly all observations of used flint edges, including those cases where microchipping was lacking (Table 2.14). This stands in contrast to the claim that "scarring is the first to occur with utilization" (Odell 1975: 231). There are certainly cases where that is true (e.g., chopping motions), but it is not a valid general 'law'.

Since the purpose of use-wear experimentation is to arrive at interpretive criteria for the functional analysis of prehistoric stone tools, the reader is invited to reexamine Tables 2.2 through 2.8 using a hypothetical case. For example, what would the interpretation of use-motion and worked material be in the case of a flint edge which exhibits microchipping that is distributed discontinuously along both surfaces, is predominantly hinge/step at the distal termination and shallow in the proximal cross-section, is of medium size, and does not display a scarring edge row? This situation could result from any number of combinations of the tested actions and contacted materials—e.g., a longitudinal action on a soft material, a transverse motion on a medium-hard material, a longitudinal motion on a medium-soft substance, etc. Some combinations of action and worked material could eventually be called 'more likely' than others *if* one were to use probability statements based on a far greater number of experimental results than those reported here. It is, therefore, valid to conclude on present evidence that one cannot rely on microchipping *alone* to assess the modes of utilization (principally, action and worked material) of prehistoric flint tools because of the large degree of variability inherent in microscar attributes and patterning. In subsequent sections, it will be shown that a wider approach, encompassing striations, edge rounding, and microwear polishes in particular, can lead to more reliable results for functional lithic analyses.

Microchipping from Deliberate Retouch

Adapting a simple method mentioned long ago by A. Barnes (1932: 53), an experimental edge retouched by hammerstone percussion was coated with India ink and then used to scrape fresh wood and subsequently soaked bone. It was obvious even without examination under the microscope that the scars caused by the scraping actions were smaller than the majority of

the retouch scars (which still bore black ink). But on the parts of the edge where the smallest scars from the retouch were still present and coated black, it was not possible to distinguish them from the microscarring of wood and bone scraping, using scar attributes such as distal and proximal cross-sections, size, and distribution.

The same results are evident from the excellent series of micrographs presented by J. Brink (1978a) in which intentionally retouched edges are shown both before being used to work a substance and after the use. In each set of 'before-and-after' micrographs, one can detect that the microchipping along the edge is not the same—i.e., use of the retouched edge did provoke further microflaking. But if one were to remove the captions, it would be extremely difficult to identify properly the *unused* retouched edges as opposed to the *used* retouched edges on the basis of the microscarring alone. Other analysts have also experienced difficulty in distinguishing the smaller scarring caused by intentional retouch from the microchipping due to contact with a worked material (see p. 11).

Therefore, in the present experiments no systematic attempt was made to study the microchipping which occurred on retouched flint edges that were used in some task.

Microchipping from Nonuse Factors

A set of 24 flakes of the three types of flint was subjected to a series of tests designed to replicate certain natural and accidental damage mechanisms, as part of the reliability test. Twelve flake edges were retouched by hammerstone percussion or by pressure with an antler tine, and 9 edges (4 of which were retouched) were used to work hide, bone, and wood. Half of the flakes (N=12) were randomly chosen and placed on a ground surface which was a mixture of loamy soil and very small pebbles under one-half centimeter in size. They were then trampled upon for three minutes, with the experimenter wearing leather moccasins. The flakes quickly became buried in the loose soil. A new random sample of 12 flakes was chosen from the entire set of 24 flints, and these were buried from 10 to 12 cm in the ground, and then the area was stamped upon for three minutes. A total of 6 flakes underwent both the surface trampling and the subsoil compaction tests. All 24 pieces were then subjected to a couple of minutes of the usual dry-screening procedure, namely, moving around objects and soil with the fingers over a quarter-inch mesh metal screen. The pieces were then placed together in a plastic bag which was crushed by compressing it a number of times between the hands to simulate compaction in transport and storage. Finally, the pieces were poured onto a hard wooden surface about twenty times, to replicate an extremely common manner of removing archaeological samples from storage bags. The flints were then replaced in their separate plastic bags. They were examined for wear traces only after the entire series of nonuse tests was completed.

The microchipping which resulted was not analyzed quantitatively because the number of 'edges' on some of the more oddly shaped flakes or pieces of flint debris would have been a subjective assessment. Furthermore, two flints broke into several fragments as a result of the subsoil pressure tests. The scarring on most of the perimeters of the pieces was random with respect to surface, distribution, scar cross-section, and size. Acute edges on the whole bore more microchipping than obtuse edges. However, there were some edges, particularly among the flakes of fine-grained flint, where the scarring was as patterned as that produced by use on hard and medium-hard materials. Substantial portions of these edges exhibited continuous scarring that was bifacial but also unifacial in a couple of cases, and exhibited mainly hinge/step distal terminations and steep or shallow proximal cross-sections. One 90° edge even bore a "notch" which could not pass for deliberate retouch but could easily be the result of a crushing use motion against a hard material such as bone.

The design of these nonuse experiments was in some respects quite limited and not a realistic replication of nonuse wear mechanisms. S. Warren (1913, 1914) made it amply clear long ago that the elements of nature, for example, operate on a vastly extended time scale and in manners that are far less fortuitous than one would at first suspect. But greater efforts were not expended on the natural and accidental damage tests in this project for two reasons. First, there is a very large number of situations which would need to be carefully re-created, some of which can be operationalized rather easily and others which would involve very lengthy time periods. Second, numerous

references in archaeological literature already provide evidence to show that natural and accidental damage mechanisms *can* produce *patterned* edge chipping. Many of these studies deal with edge flaking on a macroscopic scale in connection with the now defunct eolith problem. But the difference of scale is inconsequential since the mechanics of *micro*chipping are basically the same as those which govern *macroscopic* flaking (Cotterell and Kamminga 1979; Lawn and Marshall 1979; Tsirk 1979, all with further references).

It would be most unfortunate if the lessons learned over the decades needed to be painstakingly rediscovered by microanalysts today. Of particular importance are the publications of S. Warren, who studied natural flaking of flints for over thirty years and succeeded in abstracting certain principles. For example:

> Under certain well-defined conditions governed by the form and quality of the flint operated upon, we find: *That forces acting from a wide range of angle upon either side of a flint tend to produce chipping in one direction only, rather than in the various directions corresponding to the incidence of the blows.*
> Such selective chipping in one direction, which is in reality the natural result of forces acting mechanically from all directions, not infrequently simulates the operation of intelligent design (Warren 1914:418).

In the 1970s, a study by J. Flenniken and J. Haggarty combined both macro- and microscopic observation of trampled obsidian flakes to arrive at essentially similar conclusions: "Our results indicate that trampling can cause substantial amounts of edge modification, and therefore can bias subsequent morphological and functional interpretation" (Flenniken and Haggarty 1979:208). Such information stands in contrast to the statement by Tringham et al. (1974:192) that "in analyzing the lithic material of prehistoric assemblage, there is no difficulty in distinguishing the damage resulting from deliberate usage from that which results from accidental or 'natural' agencies."

Thus, microanalysts must be aware of the fact that *patterned* as well as *random* edge chipping of various sizes and types result from nonuse damage mechanisms. (see pp. 11−12).

Striations

Striations from Intentional Use

Morphology. Three classes of striations resulted from the experiments: first, "deep striations" which exhibited depth in the form of a groove in the flint surface

(Plate 2); second, "superficial striation" which appeared to be spots of smooth-type grit polish that were linearly arranged over the surface but not sunk into the flint surface (Plates 3, 4); third, "directional indicators" which constituted features that were an integral part of the surface of micropolishes.

No attempt was made to distinguish further between the deep and the superficial striations as general categories because they seemed to be caused solely by grit or microchips which came between the tool surface and the worked substance (see Mansur 1982). As such, the deep and superficial striae were not found to be associated with any particular category of worked material. On the other hand, the directional indicators on the polish surfaces did exhibit some specificity in regard to contact material (e.g., bone, antler, wood, sickle gloss). Details of the directional indicators are presented in the discussions on the micropolishes later in the chapter.

Orientation. The striations detected in observations of edges used in transverse motions were all oriented perpendicularly or diagonally to the working edge (Table 2.9). Longitudinal actions, on the other hand, produced parallel and diagonal striations in nearly all instances. In four cases, longitudinal motions produced some perpendicular striae, but these were due to the special nature of the actions involved such as grooving. The fact that both longitudinal and transverse motions can leave only diagonal striations (9%, 14% of the respective observations) is a realistic reflection of the zone of overlap which exists between the two sets of actions (as in Semenov 964:16–21). The presence of only diagonal striae on a used edge does not, however, preclude an assessment of the use action of prehistoric pieces, as the use motion can also be inferred from other criteria such as the relative degree of polish development and the relative degree of edge rounding on the contact vs non-contact surfaces.

Surface. Transverse actions (74% of observations) usually resulted in the formation of striations solely or predominantly on the surface of the edge in contact with the worked material (Table 2.10). However, the opposite surface became more striated (6% of observations) in cases where a high or obtuse edge angle was held at a high angle of contact. Under such conditions, the 'noncontact surface' of the working edge is actually subject to more friction against the worked material than is the 'contact surface'.

Longitudinal actions did not always striate both surfaces of a used flint edge as one would expect (only 26% of the observations; Table 2.10). In 20% of the observations only one surface bore striations. In the case where only one surface is striated, the orientation of the striations or other criteria such as the relative degree of rounding or of polish development can be called upon for the proper interpretation of the use motion on archaeological flints (see "Rounding from Intentional Use" and "Distribution and Intensity of Polishes" below).

Finally, noteworthy is the fact that a high percentage of observations did *not* show striations on a used edge: 54% for the longitudinal actions and 20% from transverse motions (Tables 2.9, 2.10).

Striations from Nonuse Factors

A substantial amount of grit or soil is brought into dynamic contact with the surfaces of stone tools by means of various natural and accidental processes including soil movements, subsoil pressure and compaction, percolating water, trampling, screening, scrubbing, etc. In addition to rounding the edges and ridges of flints and producing a general sheen over the stone tools, the soil also causes striae which are sometimes heavily developed enough to be noticeable with the unaided eye (e.g., W. Clarke 1914; Bordes 1967: 54, Plate VIII; Sturge 1914).

The following tests were performed to replicate grit and soil contact: (1) four flints were dragged along a hardened ground surface consisting of loam and very small pebbles under 0.5 cm in diameter (Plates 120, 125); (2) mud made from the same soil was rubbed with a finger onto the surface of four other flints (Plate 138); (3) a plastic toothbrush was used to scrub off a dried mud coating which had been applied to five flakes (Plate 124); and (4) the nonuse damage tests described earlier. These experiments did not pretend to be accurate replications of the wide range of natural and accidental wear mechanisms which involve grit or soil. They simply tested certain basic contact situations between grit and flint surfaces that can occur in nature or by accident. The striae that resulted were again the deep and superficial types which were also seen on intentionally used edges where grit or microchips came between the tool surface and the worked material.

Deep and superficial striations are commonly found on portions of prehistoric flints which do not bear any more definite signs of intentional use. In addition, L. Keeley (1980:32) has noted the presence of what he termed "white striations" on flints from a context of soil movement. Short deep striations passing over the crests of ridges or the tops of elevated portions of a flint surface are especially common on prehistoric pieces (Plates 123, 125). The density of grit striations on archaeological flints is obviously a function of the degree of soil and rock contact experienced by the tools, just as variation in the morphology of deep striations (e.g., wide, narrow, U-shaped, V-shaped) can be caused by different sedimentological conditions. Similarly, the general orientation of nonuse striations will vary according to the mechanism which produced them, but generally they are random and intersecting. However, patterned striations can result from certain nonuse situations such as scrubbing mud off the flints. Whether random or patterned, however, striations caused by nonuse factors are easily distinguishable from deep and superficial striations caused by intentional use. The nonuse striae occur on surface and/or ridge areas which could not possibly be utilized, over far larger areas than are possible from intentional usage, and sometimes even over the entire surface of a prehistoric tool.

Rounding

Rounding from Intentional Use

Surface. The rounding of an edge as induced from a transverse action (e.g., Plates 38–41) was usually greater on the surface of the edge facing the worked material (63% of the observations; Table 2.11). However, where the contact angle was very high, the rounding became equal on both the dorsal and ventral sides of the edge (4%), or even greater on the noncontact surface (15%) of the working edge. Longitudinal motions, on the other hand, usually produced equal rounding on both surfaces of a used flint edge (62% of the observations; Table 2.11). But if an edge was held too far off a more or less perpendicular contact angle, then one of the two surfaces exhibited a greater degree of rounding than the other (11%). If the relative distribution of the greatest rounding is ambiguous on a prehistoric flint, then the orientation of the striations can give a further clue as to the use motion, as can the distribution of the greater degree of polish development.

Intensity. The longer a flint edge is used, the more it becomes rounded, except where intentional edge modification intervenes or where excessive microchipping continually removes portions of the rounded working edge. The relative degree of edge rounding should also depend on two contact factors besides the length of use: the lithic material and the worked substance. Although the current experimental project was not designed specifically to test these three variables on a systematic basis with regards to intensity of edge rounding in particular, the available data (Table 2.12) did exhibit the following general trends: (1) greater length of use produced more rounding; (2) a coarser-grained flint took longer to reach a given degree of rounding than a finer-grained flint used to perform the same task; and (3) harder worked materials induced a given degree of rounding much more quickly than softer contact materials. These patterns can be considered together with the relative degree of polish development to estimate in a *general* way the length of time that a prehistoric flint was used.

Grit Influence. A total of 11 tests were performed on wood, bone, and fresh and tanned hide where grit in the form of loamy soil was added to the working area. Where only minute amounts of grit were applied, edge rounding was not appreciably affected. But the addition of any obviously visible quantity of grit induced a greater degree of rounding than resulted under a control test without the presence of grit. J. Brink (1978a, b) and M. E. Mansur-Franchomme (1983a, b) have reported similar results from carefully controlled tests where measured amounts of soil were added to the working conditions. The result is not surprising since the very abrasive nature of quartz grains is actively exploited in construction and in industry (e.g., sand-blasting and sandpaper, to reshape surfaces in three dimensions).

Rounding from Nonuse Factors

It has long been recognized that extensive rounding of edges and ridges is exhibited by prehistoric flints which have been rolled by water action or by soil movements such as solifluxion (e.g., de Mortillet 1883:153–154; Bourgon 1957:50). It is not only the obviously rolled flints which bear natural rounding: *every* flint which has resided in a sedimentary or aqueous environment will show a greater or lesser degree of ridge and edge rounding upon microscopic examination (e.g., Plates 140, 141). Varying degrees of natural rounding within an assemblage or between assemblages can be a clue to differential exposure to erosion, displacement of flints from original context, etc., (Shackley 1974). However, any assessment of relative degrees of natural rounding on prehistoric flints must take into account differences in the granularity of the various kinds of flints present in the assemblage, and also in the sedimentology of the matrix which is responsible for the rounding. But naturally rounded edges and ridges on archaeological stone tools are very easily distinguished from edges or ridges which became rounded through intentional use, in that the latter exhibit only very localized rounding as opposed to the widespread if not ubiquitous distribution of naturally induced rounding.

Micropolishes

State of Unpolished Flint Surfaces

The three flint varieties used in the experiments and described earlier were distinguished by grain size on a relative basis only. On a macroscopic scale, the flints differed in their capacity to reflect light on a fresh break. The fine-grained flint was very shiny on a fresh break; the medium-fine grained type was somewhat light-reflective; and the medium-coarse grained flint was of matt or dull appearance. Under an optical microscope, it was seen that these differences were due to the average range of grain sizes present in the flint matrices. The surface of the fine-grained type appeared 'homogeneous' (at 280x) in that it did not usually display any individually discernible crystalline structures (Plate 5). The medium-fine grained flint displayed patches which were more reflective, and thus finer in granularity, than the surrounding matrix which appeared rougher and duller due to its coarser texture (Plates 6, 7). The medium-coarse flint exhibited a much rougher overall microtopography, indicating cleavage between larger-sized matrix components, and a greatly reduced proportion of reflective spots (Plate 8).

This association between light reflectivity and relative grain size has been well investigated in connection with the thermal alteration of silica materials (e.g., Flenniken and Garrison 1975; Olausson and Larsson 1982; Purdy 1974). The scanning electron microscope reveals far better than optical microscopy the structural nature of intra- and interflint variability in grain size, as demonstrated by P. Anderson-Gerfaud (1981: 36–37), R. Folk and C. Weaver (1952), M. Mandeville (1973), D. Olausson and L. Larsson (1982), and by R. Rottlaender (1975, 1976).

Anomalously large quartz crystals can occur in any flint but are easily distinguished from use-wear polishes by their more or less geometric appearance and highly reflective, glasslike surface (Plate 9). Quartz crystals become worn when subjected to intentional use (Plate 10) or to nonuse wear mechanisms (Plate 11). However, the wear patterns displayed by large quartz crystals within otherwise *crypto*crystalline silicates are not the same as those exhibited by the surrounding worn flint matrix. Rather, quartz crystals wear in the same manner as does obsidian, since obsidian is homogeneous silica as is the quartz within individual crystal structures (see Vaughan 1981b: 186–214).

It is advisable for the microanalyst to become familiar with the range of variability in the textures (grain sizes) of the various flints which comprise a collection of prehistoric tools under study. In this way, an unusual textural pattern which is actually natural will not be mistaken for generic weak polish or for a weakly developed or isolated patch of a developed use-wear polish.

Micropolishes from Intentional Use on Categories of Worked Substances

General Guidelines. The use-wear polishes induced by certain classes of worked materials may be distinguished in most instances by reference to various attributes: reflectivity (at 280x in this study), surface texture, volume, surface features, degree of linkage, and the extension of the polish into the interior away from the working edge. Isolated occurrences of polish spots should be suspect, since natural surface reflection patterns or aspects of nonuse damage could be mistaken for unlinked use-wear polishes. "Safety in linkage" is a good cautionary motto for ambiguous cases of isolated or small-sized polish areas.

A principal result of the current experimental program has been to document a striking regularity in the developmental processes and resultant microwear polishes across all three varieties of flints employed in the tests. It was consistently observed that tools of the three flint varieties subjected to exactly the same task developed micropolishes that differed for the greatest part not in quality (i.e., diagnostic characteristics) but only in quantity (i.e., degree of development, size of polish area). Specifically, tools of the fine-grained flint developed a given polish more quickly and to a more extensive degree than did the tools in flint of the medium-fine grain. In turn, medium-coarse flints were much slower in forming microwear polishes and exhibited overall weaker polish development than did the medium-fine flints. But the diagnostic features remained substantially constant throughout, except where the formation of such features was impaired by excessive microchipping or insufficient use time. The concept is illustrated in Plates 12 and 14, which show the results of subjecting each of the three experimental flint types to exactly the same task of scraping fresh cow bone for 9 minutes, at 1200 strokes. The resulting edge bevel of use-wear polish is most developed on the fine-grained flint (Plate 12), but comparatively poorly developed on the medium-coarse grained flint (Plate 14). A longer use time with coarser-grained flints is thus required for the formation of microwear polishes which are to appear as readily diagnostic as those polishes which form on finer-grained flints in a relatively shorter time.

Thus a sliding scale or continuum of patterns of distinctive microwear polishes has been established for a wide variety of flint types by testing only certain specific grain-size groups. This represents a great economy of research effort for other microanalysts, who will not be required to undertake extensive testing with every type of flint in a collection that is to undergo functional analysis. P. Anderson-Gerfaud (1981:37), C. Clayton and R. Bradley (n.d.), J. Gysels and D. Cahen (1982:223), L. Keeley (1978a:73), and M. E. Mansur-Franchomme (1983a:94−95) have also reported the same correlation between degree of polish development and flint texture from tests with various types of cryptocrystalline silicates.

Therefore, the polish descriptions which follow here should be applicable to flints from any area, as long as the factor of grain size or texture is taken into proper consideration. Specifically, the polishes on coarser-grained flints exhibit overall less linkage between polish components and thus more unpolished interstitial spaces, particularly on low surface microtopography, than do finer-grained flints. Areas which easily develop solid polish covers on finer flints (e.g, edge bevels from transverse actions on harder materials) will display less solid polish stretches on coarser flints. More extensive surface areas adjacent to the working edge become polished on finer flints, whereas coarser-grained flints usually exhibit polish areas more restricted in size. And individual polish components will be smaller on less-than-fine grained flints. These comparisons are predicated on *equal use time* with different flint types. Of course, when coarser flints are used for very long periods, it is possible for the resulting micropolishes to look as well developed as those on finer-grained flints employed for a shorter time. In the following pages, the various use-wear polishes are described after their well-developed manifestations on the fine-grained experimental flints. Extrapolations for polishes on coarser-grained flints are easily made by applying the above general guidelines.

The same used edge may exhibit differential formation stages of polish for various reasons. First, excessive microchipping eliminates well-developed polish areas and exposes fresh flint surfaces. Second, gross differences in macro- and microtopography of the flint surface may cause differences in the degree of polish development. For example, a surface protrusion on one side of a flint edge used in cutting may become far more polished than any part of the other surface of the same edge, but this anomaly is easily 'filtered out' when one judges relative degrees of polish development between surfaces so as to infer use motion. And third, intra-flint variability in lithic texture always induces differences in polish development. For example, the finer-grained natural bright spots on medium-fine and medium-coarse flints develop polishes more quickly and to a greater degree than does the surrounding duller (coarser) flint matrix. In any discussion of polish development, the above factors must be noted but eliminated from the final interpretation since they represent understandable yet ultimately insignificant departures from the general patterns of polish development.

Stages of Polish Development. The initial result of contact with worked materials on edges of fine and medium-fine grained experimental flints was a "generic weak polish" that is a dull and flat with a surface texture which can be described as stucco-rough or lightly terraced in comparison with the unused flint surface (Plates 15−17). Generic weak polish occurred with very limited contact. For example, on the fine-grained flints it occurred at 100 strokes of cutting cattail, 50 strokes in working wood and soaked antler, and at only 10 strokes from working bone. The phenomenon was not noticed on medium-coarse grained flints, perhaps because there is a certain threshold of textural coarseness beyond which generic weak polish cannot form. This micropolish should not be confused with 'weakly developed polishes' which are not very progressed examples of further stages of polish development. Generic weak polish had not been isolated or discussed by previous researchers, but L. Keeley (1980:53−54) seems to be describing it in his discussion of the surface texture of meat polish, whose formation is slow enough to make it a prime candidate for a generic weak polish which would not pass into subsequent stages of polish development. However, M. E. Mansur-Franchomme (1983a:94−99) has described what she experimentally found to be the first stage of use-polish development from all contact materials (*micropoli indifférencié*), which can be equated with the generic weak polish.

The second common stage noticed on all flints used on all worked materials was the presence of a polish whose overall pitted aspect in conjunction with smooth-surfaced polish components earns the title of "smooth-pitted polish" (e.g., Plates 18−21). The smooth aspect of this polish consists of the individual polish components with smooth surfaces, even though these components may be quite small. The pitted aspect is caused by micropits and pit-depressions in the surfaces of the linkage between polish components, and by incomplete joining up of polish components which leaves dark interstitial spaces. Usually the smooth-pitted stage did not last very long at all on the experimental flint edges, as more prolonged contact increased polish development into the third and final stage. Although L. Keeley (1980) discussed use-wear polishes such as from working bone and sawing antler that are essentially smooth-pitted polishes, he did not generalize from them nor isolate this second common stage in the development of use-wear polishes on flints. M. E. Mansur-Franchomme (1983a:98) has defined a second level of polish development—the beginning of the formation of the characteristic traits found in the well-developed polishes—which would correspond to the third stage of polish formation defined below.

It was repeatedly noticed that a sawing action on solid materials such as bone, antler, wood, and reeds did not seem to push the resulting polishes past the smooth-pitted stage. Therefore, sawing bone, antler, wood, and reeds often left virtually indistinguishable polishes. Some potential ways of distinguishing between the smooth-pitted polishes left by the sawing of solid materials is presented in Table 2.13. For example, bone-sawing edges displayed a number of troughs and grooves that run through the polish components, whereas such linear indicators were not present on wood-sawing edges. The causes for very similar polishes from sawing solid materials may reside in the fact that substances such as antler, bone, wood, and reed are anisotropic, that is, they have very different structural properties in different directions (Anderson-Gerfaud 1981:61–62; J. Speth, personal communication). Alternatively, it may be caused by the dispersal of contact forces over a wider area in a sawing action than is the case with transverse motions and grooving, where a small part of the edge is submitted to more intense, sustained contact than the rest of the used area. It is also possible that both material anisotropism and low intensity of contact act together to keep flint edges that saw solid materials from reaching a higher stage of polish development.

In the third and final stage, further linkage of polish components and the formation of diagnostic surface features on the polish surface occurred in the areas of greatest contact on the flint edges. Such areas were primarily the immediate edge area and surface elevations, but also the interior area away from the crest of the edge if contact was quite prolonged or intense. It was at this third stage that the polishes became most characteristic and served to distinguish among the worked materials, as is discussed at length in each case below. On the fine-grained flint tools, a diagnostic polish was very quick to form from the harder contact substances (e.g., a couple of minutes from bone scraping) but much slower from softer worked materials (e.g., a half-hour or more from cutting soft plants). L. Keeley had previously described and illustrated the diagnostic use-wear polishes of various categories of worked substances, and the following descriptions of the use-wear polishes which resulted from the present research essentially concur with those published by L. Keeley (1980); Keeley and Newcomer (1977); P. Anderson-Gerfaud (1981); E. Moss (1983a), and by M. E. Mansur-Franchomme (1983a).

The mechanical and/or chemical processes which underlie the three stages of polish development remain to be investigated in detail with the scanning electron microscope. The various mechanisms of polish formation in general have already been discussed: abrasion, frictional-fusion, and amorphous silica gel models. The above typology of polish developmental stages is only an empirical construct pieced together from hundreds of observations with an optical microscope. In the actual analysis of prehistoric flints, generic weak polish and smooth-pitted polishes due to intentional use are not seen as often (e.g., Plates 20, 71) as the well-developed polishes. However, it is necessary for the microanalyst to be aware that 'undiagnostic' or 'insufficiently developed' use-wear polishes can occur since they are an inherent part of the overall sequence of polish development.

Area of Polish Formation. The progression of polish formation over the stone surface follows a general scheme. First, the polish begins to form on the perpendicular edge, that is, the very crest of the working edge. Then the higher topography in the immediate edge area (up to 0.1 mm in from the working edge), and perhaps the surface ridges and elevations near the edge, become polished. Next, the lower microtopography of the regular flint surface in the immediate edge area is affected. Finally, more and more of the high and then the low microtopography of the interior edge regions progressively become polished. This sequence is more easily detected when working softer materials such as plants because of the slower rate of polish formation from softer materials.

Classification of Polish Types. The various micropolishes which resulted from numerous tests on each of the worked materials are arranged below according to the category of contact substance, as well as to the general first- and second-stage polishes (generic weak polish and smooth-pitted polish). Classifying polishes by the worked material is the method used by L. Keeley and most other microanalysts. An alternative approach was initiated by the members of the Tohoku

University Microwear Research Team (Kajiwara and Akoshima 1981; Serizawa et al., 1982), who employed attribute analysis to class the polishes as independent types, and to which they then assigned the categories of contact substances which produced each polish type. This method of polish classification has the advantage of underscoring the fact that there is no simplistic one-to-one correlation between contact substance and micropolish, which is the erroneous oversimplification at the basis of G. Holley and T. Del Bene's (1981) critique of Keeley's microwear approach.

In the polish descriptions presented below there are indeed various possible polish types for most contact substances, usually based on the length of use and whether the material has been sawed/cut or scraped/planed. In fact, just the scraping of harder materials such as bone, antler, and reed results in different polishes on the contact surface as opposed to the noncontact surface of the flint edge. That is, the surface of the stone edge which is held close to the worked substance polishes differently from the surface which is facing away from the worked object. It is therefore necessary to view both surfaces of the edges of prehistoric stone tools and to take into consideration all the polish types present before arriving at a functional interpretation. Hopefully, reliable techniques for *quantifying* polish attributes will be further refined, to allow for more objectivity in the analysis and reporting of use-wear polishes (e.g., Dumont 1982; Grace et al., n.d.).

Generic Weak Polish

Description. Generic weak polish is a dull polish which is, nonetheless, somewhat brighter than the natural reflective background of the flint, yet definitely less reflective than a well-developed polish on the same surface (Plates 15–17). The surface texture can be described as stuccolike or lightly terraced, and it may contain some pit-depressions, so that it is rougher than most developed polishes. But at the same time, the surface of generic weak polish looks smoother than an unpolished flint surface. Generic weak polish is usually flat but sometimes exhibits very slight volume. It forms in small patches mainly within the immediate edge area and on surface elevations (Plates 15, 16), but it may extend inwards from the working edge (Plate 17), depending upon the action, angle of contact, and the suppleness of the worked substance. Generic weak polish is often very difficult to distinguish from individual natural bright spots in the background of the medium-fine grained flints (e.g., Plate 7). Candidates

for generic weak polish areas on such flints are more credible when they occur in association with slight edge rounding and a thin line of polish on the crest of the working edge. Generic weak polish has not been noticed on the medium-coarse experimental flints, and so it would probably not form on even coarser textured flints.

Major Characteristics: dull, stuccolike or lightly terraced surface, more or less flat, difficult to distinguish from natural bright spots on flint surface and from soil sheen.

Soil Sheen. As explained earlier, generic weak polish seems to be the first stage of polish development from all contact materials. Since use-wear polishes such as those from hide, plants, and meat are slower-forming than those from harder materials, there is more of a chance that generic weak polish detected on a prehistoric flint edge will be from working softer materials. However, a major inconvenience in distinguishing use-related generic weak polish on archaeological flints is that the first stage of grit polish or soil sheen is also the generic weak polish (Plates 134, 135). Since soil sheen usually covers archaeological flints in their entirety, great care must be taken to substantiate the identification of generic weak polish due to intentional use on a prehistoric flint tool (e.g., by limited distribution, association with use-related striations).

Smooth-Pitted Polish

Description. Individual small polish components, with more or less smooth surfaces, form on the higher points of the microtopography of the generic weak polish in the contact area (Plate 18). Since the components are incompletely linked, numerous darker interstitial spaces are left between the polish components (Plates 19, 20). In addition, what linkage has formed between polish components is replete with micropits and pit-depressions, which together with the interstitial spaces impart an overall roughish aspect to this stage of polish development (Plate 21). Thus the pitting is the result of incomplete linkage of the polish area. But since the surfaces of the small polish components themselves are more or less smooth, the term "smooth-pitted" is a concise description of the polish. Of course, varying degrees of linkage and pitting can occur depending upon precise contact situations, especially the length of use and the worked material. Likewise, the size and volume of the individual polish components vary according to the amount of contact. The resemblances between the smooth-pitted polishes left by sawing solid materials such as antler, bone, wood, and reeds have been discussed earlier (Table 2.13).

Major characteristics: small smooth polish components separated by pitted linkage polish and darker interstitial spaces; may appear with areas of generic weak polish in lesser affected portions of the flint edge.

Bone Polish

Description. Working fresh or soaked bone of cow and rabbit produced a bright polish whose characteristic surface texture is best revealed once the bone residue has been removed with hydrochloric acid. As other researchers have noted (Anderson-Gerfaud 1981: 58−60; Keeley 1890;42−43), bone polish typically presents a rather pitted appearance (Plate 21), particularly as a result of longitudinal actions. The polish components which form on the higher microtopography of the flint surface do not link up to any great degree and thus form a lattice riddled with micropits, pit-depressions, and interstitial spaces, all of which play a role in imparting a pitted appearance to bone polish. Moreover, the removal of bone residue from the polish area by hydrochloric acid has the effect of making the pitted aspect more pronounced. Bone polish does not usually cover an extensive surface area on the tool since even soaked bone is a very hard substance to penetrate. In particular, the noncontact surface of a bone-scraping edge typically bears limited polish development in the form of small polish areas localized within the vicinity of the working edge, but the exact contact angle of the edge on the bone could alter this. Longitudinally used edges (i.e., sawing, grooving bone) exhibit numerous troughs and grooves running through the larger polish components, indicating the relative direction of the use motion (Table 2.13).

Rough bone polish is, in effect, a very pitted version of the second general stage of polish development, the smooth-pitted polishes. It forms on surfaces adjacent to the working edge which are not subjected to very intense, sustained contact, namely, on the noncontact surface of bone-scraping edges and on either surface of bone-sawing edges. In regard to the problem of resemblances between smooth-pitted polishes produced by sawing solid materials, the bone polish from a sawing motion was indistinguishable from antler-sawing polish in particular (see Keeley 1980:56 for similar results). Table 2.13 offers some potential distinctions between the two polishes. For example, sawing bone produced a smooth-pitted polish with a large number of troughs and grooves running through the individual smooth polish components, whereas such linear indicators were few or absent in antler-sawing polish. Less frequently, bone-sawing polish

looks very much like wood-sawing polish (Anderson-Gerfaud 1981:61), again because a sawing motion on a solid material produces a basically smooth-pitted polish.

Extremely prolonged sawing of bone (or antler) produces not only areas of smooth-pitted polish but also patches of intensive polish which are limited to the higher portions of the stone microtopography such as elevations, edge crest, ridges of scars, etc. Smooth, raised polish spots containing vague parallel troughs can appear very localized at the edge (Plate 22); but if they are spread over wider areas of the interior away from the working edge itself, the polish can resemble plant polish at its incompletely linked stage (see Plate 73). Even more intensive sawing contact leads to a bright polish with a very flat surface (Plate 23), which can become undulating, however, if the polish development is heavily affected by flint microchips or other sources of grit, which make it resemble completely linked plant polish. But stone edges used in lengthy sawing of bone (or antler) are readily distinguishable from plant-cutting edges for two reasons. First, the bone/antler-sawing edges lack the developed polish and the pronounced rounding on the cutting edge itself which are typical of plant wear (Plates 75, 78, 80), since sawing in hard materials provokes major edge chipping which 'chews up' the crest of the edge. Secondly, intensive bone/antler polishes are distributed in a band roughly parallel to the sawing edge, unlike the generally triangular or at least asymmetrical distribution of plant polishes.

The edge areas of the most intense and sustained contact with bone occurred on the contact surface of transversely used edges and on the ventral and dorsal surfaces of trihedral edges used for grooving bone. These areas bore a very heavily linked polish which is quite different from the pitted bone polish, yet is far more diagnostic of bone working. Although this aspect of bone polish had not been reported previously, it was found on every flint edge used to scrape and to groove fresh or soaked cow and rabbit bone. On scraping edges, the contact surface became beveled at the very edge and presented an extremely bright, wide, flat, solid polish bevel (Plates 12, 13, 24−26) which characteristically bore numerous directional indicators which could be termed "comet-tails," after an analogous phenomenon in sickle gloss that J. Witthoft (1967: 384) called "comet-shaped pits." The heads of these diagnostic features are unabraded grains which face the direction of the on-coming motion (Plate 24). The tails behind seemed to be ridges (i.e., elevated portions of polish) because the polish surface of the bevel between them appeared to be at a lower level.

Bone-grooving edges (Plate 27) developed an identical very bright polish band with comet-tails, except that the polish band is not beveled off at an angle as on bone-scraping edges. These bevels or bands were not slow to develop: around 50 strokes on the finer flints, 150 strokes on the medium-coarse flint. They presented a more fragmented appearance on coarser flints (Plate 14).

On some experimental and archaeological bone-scraping edges, the noncontact surface of the edge presented some very localized patches of highly linked, very smooth, very bright polish in addition to the smooth-pitted bone polish described above. These polish spots (Plate 28) could at first glance be mistaken for antler polish with diffuse depressions (Plates 33, 34). But upon close inspection, the surfaces of the special bone polish on the noncontact surface of scraping edges are definitely *flat* and do not imitate the undulating or depressed antler polish topography.

Major Characteristics: (a) from sawing action: bright, smooth-pitted lattice of polish, possibly scored with grooves and troughs; (b) from transverse and grooving motions: very bright, flat polish bevel or band with numerous comet-tails in the polish surface.

Dry Bone. A cow tibia which had been boiled and then stored indoors for five months was worked with a scraping motion. The only difference noted in the resulting polish (Plate 29) was that the contact surface bevel contained far fewer comet-tails than resulted from working fresh and soaked bone (cf. Plates 12, 13, 24–27). This caused the bevel from dry bone to resemble somewhat the bevel produced by scraping soaked antler (Plate 39). Evidently, a still different polish results from scraping old but not dried-out bone, giving a polish which is highly scored with thin black striations (Plate 30; see Keeley 1980: 75 and Plate 64). However, working hardened bone with flint edges is an unproductive task in terms of the amount of bone removed, and it is also extremely damaging to the edge which crushes and dulls very quickly. One would think that hunter-gatherers would have a sufficient supply of fresh bone to work, but repairs to already fabricated bone tools might have necessitated working old or dried bone.

Antler Polish

Description. L. Keeley (1980:56) noted that different polishes result from sawing water-soaked antler ("rough antler polish") and from the scraping, planing, or grooving of soaked antler ("smooth antler polish"). This is essentially the same situation as already described for bone polishes and is, again, due to differ-

ences in the degree of intense, sustained contact with the various zones of a used edge. Another contributing factor may be anisotropic structure of antler, which implies that sawing edges cut "across the grain" and thus contact more irregular structures than is the case when working "with the grain" in scraping, planing, and grooving (Anderson-Gerfaud 1981:61–62).

The rough antler polish produced on both surfaces of an edge used in sawing soaked antler is another example of the basic smooth-pitted stage of polish formation (Plate 31). As noted above in the discussion of bone polishes, antler-sawing polish can look very similar to bone-sawing polish; but sometimes the two can be distinguished, particularly if there are small patches of very linked polish with diffuse depressions in the immediate edge areas of the surfaces of antler-sawing edges (Table 2.13). Very prolonged sawing of soaked antler results in the same types of intensive polishes notes above for bone.

When *not* well developed, the smooth antler polish produced by transverse actions and by a grooving motion can often resemble wood polish produced by the same actions (Keeley 1980:56). The points of resemblance are: (a) raised polish domes in various stages of linkage, and (b) a developed band of polish, instead of a true bevel, at the contact edge which is nothing more than a highly linked row of polish domes that follows the contours of the edge relief. However, when *well* developed, smooth antler polish is quite different from wood polish. The most diagnostic aspect of developed smooth antler polish from transverse and grooving actions (Plates 32–36) is the localized, highly linked polish areas whose smooth surfaces bear diffuse depressions which impart a gently undulating look, or the appearance of a "melting snowbank" in L. Keeley's words (Keeley 1980: 56). These diagnostic areas are a result of the continued linkage between separate polish domes and the extension of polish over previously unaffected interstitial spaces. Depending upon the degree of linkage in the polish area, some interstitial spaces can remain along with the diffuse depressions (Plate 33), giving "an evenly pockmarked appearance" (Keeley 1980: 56). It must be stressed that smooth-type antler polish is usually of localized distribution in limited patches (and on the noncontact surface of the edges), although this would also depend on the angle of contact of the working edge to the antler surface during scraping/ planing or grooving actions.

The same undulating aspect was also found on the bevel produced on the contact edge of flints used to scrape and plane soaked antler (Plates 37–41). In cross-section, the antler polish bevel is curved or rounded—as opposed to the truncated surface presented by the bone polish edge bevel—and has a gently undulating flow along the edge, in contrast to the flat nature of the bone bevel. Vague perpendicular troughs may run through the otherwise smooth antler bevels (Plate 41). A few comet-tails were seen, though very rarely, on experimental antler bevels (Plate 39). But the characteristic forms of the bone and antler polish bevels are quite distinct. Nevertheless, it is possible for archaeological flints to display not very well developed polish features, and an interpretation of "bone *or* antler" may be necessary.

Major Characteristics: (a) from sawing action: bright smooth-pitted polish, possibly with small areas of diffuse depressions near the working edge; (b) from transverse and grooving motions: very bright, localized heavy linkage, diffuse depressions in polish surface, undulating smooth rounded bevels with some vague directional troughs.

Dry Antler. Like dried bone, antler in the hard state is almost impossible to work in any productive efficient manner and furthermore is highly damaging to the flint edges. Nevertheless, a couple of flints were used to scrape four-year-old red deer antler in the hard state. The resulting edge bevels were not solid but rather fragmented stretches of polish exhibiting a bumpy-rough surface that was very scored with perpendicular troughs and grooves (Plate 42). A particular type of deep-narrow striation occurred through the polish on the contact edge and seemed diagnostic of dry antler, although it was not always present (Plate 42). The localized polish areas of heavy linkage occurred as from scraping soaked antler, but the diagnostic diffuse depressions which resulted with soaked antler were rare or lacking from scraping the dry antler.

Wood Polish

Description. The experimental polishes produced by working fresh and resoaked seasoned woods are essentially the same as previously reported wood polishes (Anderson-Gerfaud 1981:47−49; Keeley 1980:35). And as other researchers have already noted (e.g., Anderson-Gerfaud 1981:48−49; Hayden and Kamminga 1973a:4; Kamminga 1977:207), the softwoods (pine, in this instance) leave noticeably more polish than the hardwoods (almond) after the same working time. However, the characteristics of these polishes are the same, at least under optical microscopy.

Since wood polish is not very fast forming, as compared to bone polish at least, it is important to understand the continuum of polish development

which can be seen on both experimental and archaeological wood-working flint edges. From a generic weak polish base, individual domed polish components of slight volume and basically smooth surface texture (with possibly a few micropits) begin to form on the higher points of the microtopography (Plate 17) and develop with more contact into full polish domes (Plates 43−49), then into bulging and sagging domes (Plates 50), and next into an undulating polish cover (Plates 51, 52), and ultimately with very extended contact into a smooth polish blanket. Concomitant with the increasing linkage in this polish formation is the inverse process of the elimination of pit-depressions and the interstitials from the polish linkage between polish domes. When the individual wood polish domes constitute only a very lightly linked lattice pattern (Plates 18, 44−46), the overall polished area has a definite smooth-pitted aspect. As the polish domes expand in size and volume and link up with each other, the pitting features decrease (Plates 43−52) until with extended contact all wood polish surfaces are more or less smooth. The polish lattices or covers from wood contact are generally not localized in clumps near the edge (as from bone and antler) but are more extensive, more evenly widespread, and more continuously distributed along the edge area and into the interior away from the working edge (e.g., Plates 46, 50−52). This is due to the fact that fresh wood is softer than bone or antler, and the stone edge penetrates farther. Very vague directional indicators run like "valleys" between individual wood polish domes in the direction of the use motion (Plate 52), just as domes in the sagging state also indicate the direction of polish formation. Various stages of this continuum can be seen on the same wood-working edge, particularly from transverse actions, depending on the proximity of the polished area to the working edge itself. But at whatever stage of linkage, wood polish is always very bright.

Sawing wood does not seem to induce much polish development past the basic smooth-pitted polish, although certain criteria—such as a solid band of polish on the crest of the working edge—can be used to distinguish wood-sawing edges from other smooth-pitted sawing polishes, if these characteristics are present (Table 2.13). Scraping, planing, whittling, and grooving wood can all produce well-developed and very easily distinguishable wood polish (Plates 46−52). A true bevel is not found on edges used to work wood transversely, apparently because wood is not hard enough to truncate the flint. Instead, a developed edge band of polish results on the contact edge (e.g., Plates 43, 51). It is a highly linked string of polish domes, with vague interdome "valleys" running in a perpendicular sense (Plate 50). Unlike antler and particularly bone polish bevels which alter and flatten the contours along the contact edge, the polish band on wood-scraping/whittling/planing contact edges follows the sinuous contours of the topography of the working edge of any microscar ridges at the edge.

Wood boring left variously developed stages of wood polish on the lateral edges and dorsal ridges of the borer. Such a distribution can only result from a penetrating action such as boring. Chopping wood produced more limited areas of wood polish and less interdome linkage than resulted from other transverse actions, most likely because a greater amount of edge chipping was continually removing already polished parts of the flint edge and exposing fresh flint surfaces. Furthermore, chopping results in less sustained contact with the wood, unless the edges are used for a very extended period of time.

Major Characteristics: (a) from sawing action: bright, smooth-pitted polish; (b) from transverse and grooving motions: very bright, smooth polish domes in various stages of linkage, vague interdome "valleys" indicating use direction, more widespread coverage of the stone surface than from bone or antler but less than from plants.

Seasoned Wood. Cypress and almond branches that had been seasoned indoors for eight months were harder to work with flint edges than was fresh or soaked, seasoned wood, and the resulting polishes were slower to form than those from fresh wood. Otherwise, the polish resulting from planing seasoned wood was generally the same as that resulting from fresh woods. The only consistent difference noted in polish characteristics is that seasoned cypress wood left pronounced troughs in the polish band along the contact edge of transversely used flint edges. These troughs are somewhat reminiscent of those on soaked-antler scraping edges, but well-developed antler bevels are quite different from wood polish bevels at the contact edge. Furthermore, the polish on the noncontact side of such edges is quite different in either case, particularly with the diffuse depressions in the antler polish.

Reed Polishes

Description. Although micropolishes from reeds had not been studied previously, expectations at the start of the present experimentation were that reeds would give a polish identical to that of wood. The solid fibrous nature of reeds makes them appear more simi-lar to new green tree branches than to soft nonwoody plant stems, despite the fact that reeds are classified in the *Poacoideae* subfamily of the *Gramineae* family as are domesticated cereals and other grasses (Fernald 1950). The results of the present use-wear experiments with two varieties of reeds [*Phragmites communis* Trin. and *Pseudosasa japonica* (Sieb. & Zucc.) Makino] indicate that certain aspects of reed polish do resemble wood polish, other aspects are unique, but still other features of reed polish can be mistaken for smooth antler polish.

Cutting both types of reeds into sections by a sawing action produced yet another example of the basic smooth-pitted polish (Plate 53), which in its early stages of development looks more like the smooth-pitted polish from wood-sawing than the smooth-pitted polishes from bone- or antler-sawing (see Table 2.13). However, with prolonged sawing of the solid parts of the reeds the polish became very developed and was quite different from wood-sawing micropolish. The edge area and the high microtopography of the flint surface became covered with large domed polish agglomerates which kept a certain number of interstitials and pit-depressions even in highly linked areas (Plate 54). Thus the polish domes were not as glistening smooth as very developed wood polish domes and undulating wood polish covers which form from transverse actions. Also, the undulating, domed aspect of very developed reed-sawing polish distinguishes it from the flatter plant-cutting polish known as sickle gloss (Plates 54, 80). Sawing reeds for an extended period can result in a macroscopically visible, faintly lustrous shine on the flint edge, if fine-grained.

Transverse actions, such as planing on reeds, act to smooth the reed surfaces for such uses as arrow shafts, tools, furniture, etc. However, two distinct, yet overlapping, sets of polishes resulted from transverse actions on the reeds. Relative intensity or duration of contact seemed to be the critical factor, since both varieties of reeds that were worked (*Phragmites* and *Pseudosasa*) produced at least the first type of reed polish from transverse actions.

For the first type of transverse reed polish, the *noncontact* surface of the flint edge consistently bore a unique micropolish which seemed to be a highly developed version of the generic weak polish in that its overall appearance was very terraced (Plates 55–58). Most of the individual polish components (which may be smooth-surfaced or lightly rough) are not domes but rather quite small and variously shaped, and of differing volumes. This, together with pit-depressions and small interstitial spaces, imparts the characteristic rough "terraced-bumpy" look to the reed polish on the noncontact surface of transversely used flint edges. Also diagnostic is the fact the this polish forms a widespread, solid cover across the noncontact edge area, that is, continuously linked over both high and low microtopography and also into the interior of microscars. It can also extend into the interior of the noncontact side away from the working edge, depending on the angle of contact of the flint to the reed. The small components, the terraced-bumpy aspect, and the continuous coverage across the noncontact surface of the flint edge make reed polish from transverse actions quite unmistakable on experimental and archaeological pieces (Plates 55–58).

But the polishes produced on the *contact side* of the same transversely used edges resembled either the polish formed on the contact surface of antler-scraping edges (i.e., smooth, lightly undulating bevel with some perpendicular troughs; Plates 59, 60) or, in lesser developed cases, the polish on the contact surface of wood-scraping edges (i.e., large, smooth polish domes in the edge area, and at the very edge a continuous polish band of highly linked polish domes between which were some vague perpendicular "valleys"; Plates 61–63).

The second type of transverse-motion reed polish resulted from *Phragmites* reeds planed until the flint edges dulled. The *contact* surface of these edges developed a solid, very flat, very bright bevel whose truncated aspect in cross-section rivaled even the best bone polish bevels (Plates 64, 65). However, the reed polish bevel was perfectly smooth. The *noncontact* surface of the same edges bore areas of the unique terraced-bumpy polish described above (Plate 66, left), but along the most used section of the edges there developed a gently undulating polish cover replete with diffuse depressions (Plates 66, right, and 67). At first sight, this latter polish was indistinguishable from the smooth antler polish which also bears diffuse depressions. However, the version formed by working reeds covered a much more extensive, continuous area across the noncontact surface than was usually the case on antler-scraping edges. (Moreover, the unique, terraced-bumpy variety of reed polish was always found on some lesser used portion of the edges.) The close similarities now documented between smooth antler polish and one kind of reed polish can give rise to ambiguities in the analysis of micropolishes on archaeological flints. But dubious cases can simply be reported as "reed *or* antler," just as "bone or antler" interpretations are sometimes necessary.

Major Characteristics: (a) from sawing motion: a bright smooth-pitted polish; or if well developed, a well-linked pattern of domed polish agglomerates and interstitials, highly reflective; (b) from transverse motions: either (1) woodlike or antlerlike polishes on the contact edge, and a continuous terraced-bumpy polish alone on the noncontact surface, or (2) a very flat, smooth, highly reflective polish bevel on the contact surface of the edge, with the noncontact side bearing areas of the above terraced-bumpy polish and, along the more developed sections, an extensive cover of smooth, very bright, gently undulating polish with diffuse depressions in the polish surface.

Seasoned Reeds. The *Phragmites* reeds from Greece were worked with a planing motion after having been stored indoors for six months. The result was a very flat, wide, and very bright bevel on the contact surface of the edge (Plate 68). The polish bevel was not perfectly smooth as from planing fresh *Phragmites* reed, but rather contains some vague perpendicular troughs. Scarcely any polish spots were found on either side of the bevel. This is most likely a reflection of the very hard nature of dry reeds and corresponds to an observation made while planing them. In effect, very few shavings were removed from the dry reeds in the planing process, and the task seemed very inefficient compared to working fresh reeds. However, the isolated polish bevel which resulted from planing seasoned reeds is very similar to some archaeological use-wear polishes which could be attributed to "unspecified harder materials" because there is not really enough evidence, aside from the polish bevel, to make a more specific, yet still highly probable, determination (see later section, "Micropolishes From Contact With Soil and Grit"). In other words, in the cases of both the seasoned reeds and the unspecified harder materials, the used flint edge bears only a bevel and no other polish spots on either the contact or the noncontact surfaces of the edge.

Plant Polish

Description. Four genera of plants, belonging to three different families, were cut or sliced: (a) *Gramineae* family (domesticated barley, *Hordeum;* wild *Gramineae*); (b) *Typhaceae* family (cattail, *Typha*); and (c) *Compositae* family (marsh-elder, *Iva xanthifolia*). Despite the phylogenic diversity of the plants used in the tests, basically the same types of polish were formed on the experimental flint edges. More precisely, there was the same continuum of polish formation in each case. At the most developed stage, plant polish is the well-known "sickle gloss" (Keeley 1980:60–61; Witthoft 1967). It formed much more quickly and far more extensively from cutting the grasses (barley, wild

Gramineae) than from the other plants. For example, after four hours of cutting fresh cattail, the polish was well developed only in the area of the immediate cutting edge and on microscar ridges at the edge, whereas after just three hours of harvesting both barley and wild *Gramineae* (with separate edges) a sickle gloss in the classic sense formed and extended considerably farther into the interior of the piece (a few mm) and was just visible along the edge with the unaided eye. Cattail dried for six months indoors left the same polish as the fresh cattail, just in a lesser quantity.

Plant polish is very slow-forming compared to the micropolishes already discussed. So as with wood polish, a flint edge used to slice plant stems exhibits various stages of polish development depending on the use duration and on the distance from the working edge. From a base of generic weak polish, there develops a bright smooth-pitted polish composed of very small, smooth individual polish components (Plates 69–72) which expand and become progressively linked together but still retain varying amounts of micropits, pit-depressions, and interstitial spaces (Plate 73). In fact, until the ultimate stage of complete linkage into a solid, flat, smooth polish blanket (sickle gloss), the pockmarked aspect of plant polish remains very characteristic (Plates 74–78). As the individual polish components grow in size and volume with more extended contact, it becomes increasingly evident that the polish topography is definitely raised above the unaffected flint surface since the interstitial spaces between polish components appear 'sunken' in comparison to the top of the plant polish surface (Plates 73, 77, 78).

As linkage attains the maximum stage—which occurs soonest in areas closest to the working edge—the plant polish become a highly reflective, solid, level expanse (not undulating) and the individual polish components are no longer distinguishable—in other words, what is usually referred to as sickle gloss (Plates 79, 80). The direction of use is betrayed by striations superimposed upon the gloss (some of which look 'filled-in' or partially eroded; Plate 79) and by the diagnostic "comet-shaped pits" (Witthoft 1967:384) whose circular heads face the oncoming motion (Plates 81, 82). The comet-shaped pits are caused when "pits in the flint have had their edges rounded and wiped away, with their leeward sides hollowed out" (ibid).

Plant polishes at any stage of development are characteristically distributed in a very widespread, continuous, and invasive fashion over the flint edge as compared to the polishes left even by materials of medium-hardness such as wood and reeds. Even when weakly developed, plant polishes extend a couple of millimeters into the interior of the flint away from the crest of the edge and cover even the insides of microflaking along the edge. And it is not uncommon to find prehistoric flints with sickle gloss extending more than a centimeter or two into the interior of the edge, with the gloss forming a solid, highly reflective cover over the entire surface including the inside of retouch scars. Thus the nature and the distribution of plant polishes are quite diagnostic.

Major Characteristics: bright to extremely bright, pockmarked aspect until completely linked in a solid level mass; elevated above the flint surface; very widespread and invasive coverage of the edge; and filled-in striations or comet-shaped pits within the polish surface.

Archaeological Examples. Flint edges which bear very well developed sickle gloss that is even discernible with the unaided eye are most probably the result of cutting members of the *Gramineae* family or other silica-rich herbaceaus plants such as sedges (*Cyperaceae* family) or true rushes *(Juncus),* since silica-poor plants such as cattail *(Typha)* or other nongrass weeds take much longer to develop the degree of sickle gloss which can be attained after only a few hours of cutting *Gramineae, Cyperaceae,* or *Juncus* (see Anderson-Gerfaud 1983). In addition to the silica content of plants, their relative water content at the time of cutting seems to greatly influence polish formation. Plants cut in a green state produce more polish than when they are cut dried (Anderson-Gerfaud 1983; Unger Hamilton 1983). Analysis by scanning electron microscopy of phytolith bodies fused within the plant polish is the most certain way to narrow down an identification of plant polish to the family or subfamily of the plant that was cut by a prehistoric stone tool.

Prehistoric flint edges which bear plant polish in its initial stages of development as a generic weak polish (Plated 69–70) require special care in interpretation, since the soil sheen which covers archaeological flints can also manifest itself as a ubiquitous generic weak polish (Plate 135). If the weak plant polish, however, shows a distribution limited to a utilizable edge (but still invasive into the interior of the used edge, as is characteristic of plant-cutting edges) and if the weak plant polish contrasts with the soil sheen over the rest of the tool, then a reasonably certain determination of plant cutting can be made. Once prehistoric plant polishes manifest large smooth polish components (Plate 72), it is easier to distinguish them from soil sheen.

Gloss on an Iron Sickle Blade. In connection with polishes a microscopic study was attempted on an old crescent-shaped iron sickle with a wooden handle, which had served to harvest cereal crops in southern

Greece from ca. 1870 to 1930. It was apparent that the iron blade had received substantial use, since the denticulate teeth, which are cast on one side of the cutting edge of this kind of iron sickle, had been worn down completely by resharpening the blade with a metal file. A shiny band could be seen with the unaided eye all along the cutting edge, extending about 3 to 5 mm into the interior of the iron blade. Under the microscope, this glossy area proved to be a very thin layer of highly reflective, very smooth-surfaced, glasslike material which was cracking and exfoliating from the rusting iron surface underneath (Plates 83, 84). The layer could not be dissolved or removed with medicinal alcohol or acetone. Although the glossy layer was damaged and scratched, in well-preserved sections it appeared to consist of a vitreous substance which had rapidly hardened upon contact with the iron blade, since in some areas the layer was ripply or of the nature of deflated bubbles (Plate 83) but perfectly flat in other areas (Plate 84). At the outer limit of the glossy band, there was a definite zone in which minute, barely formed patches of the gloss could be discerned (Plate 85). Portions of the same iron blade (and of other antique iron sickles) not displaying a shiny surface bore no such vitreous, glossy layer when examined under the microscope but instead showed patches of striations within the iron surface (Plate 86).

The glossy deposit on the iron sickle blade would seem to represent a phenomenon similar to that which P. Anderson-Gerfaud has proposed for sickle gloss found on flint, bone, and ceramic tools, namely, a layer of hardened amorphous silica gel (Anderson 1980a; Anderson 1983a, b; Anderson-Gerfaud et al., n.d.). The dissolution of plant silica during the cutting of silica-rich cereal stalks would have led to the smearing of a plant silica gel onto the iron cutting edge, where it would quickly harden. But the mechanism which loosely bonds the plant silica gel to the iron surface needs to be investigated, since on flint edges the plant silica becomes part of a general dissolution and reformation of the flint surface itself. This theory will be tested by inspecting portions of the gloss on the iron sickle under the scanning electron microscope for diagnostic *Gramineae* phytoliths. Similar investigations could establish whether plant silica is also present on the "smoothed, rounded, and highly polished" edges of mountain-sheep horn which are known from ethnographic records to have been used by Utah and Colorado Indian groups as sickles for cutting grass (Heizer 1951:249).

Tanned or Dry Hide Polish

Description. Scraping tanned hide and leather produced the same distinctive results regardless of the animal skin involved (deer, cow, rabbit in these tests). Furthermore, the polish was identical to that described by L. Keeley (1980:49–50) and by P. Anderson-Gerfaud (1981:55) for flint edges which worked hides that were simply dried but not tanned. After passing briefly through the generic weak polish stage and the smooth-pitted polish stage, dry hide polish becomes dull and takes on a rugose look due to the extremely pitted nature of the polish surface (Plate 87). Dry hide polish develops along the edge in a very widespread and continuous fashion due to the suppleness of the material. It may affect the noncontact surface of hide-scraping edges as much as the contact surface, depending on the angle of contact of the flint edge to the hide and the degree of suppleness of the hide or leather (e.g., hard leather vs. suede). The extensive rounding of the working edge and of all microscar ridges and surface elevations in the immediate edge area is as diagnostic of working dry hide as is the dull, highly pitted polish (Plate 87). Adding grit to the surface of the hide only acts to intensify both the edge and ridge rounding and the pitted aspect of the dry hide polish (Plates 88–92), while also introducing numerous perpendicular and diagonal grooves through the polish plus the "microcraters" which usually betray the presence of grit on a worked material.

Working dry hide in a slightly dampened state reduces the build-up of frictional heat on the working edge, and ultimately in the interior, of flint hide-scrapers. In the present tests, scraping remoistened tanned hides attenuated somewhat the surface pitting of the polish and maintained a more bright smooth-pitted component to the hide polish, particularly on the contact surface of the scraping edge (Plates 93, 94). But the working edge and the scar ridges along the used edge still underwent substantial rounding (Plate 93; see Mansur-Franchomme 1983b). The addition of a natural lubricant (lard, in this instance) to a tanned hide considerably slowed the process of polish development and edge rounding, and also tended to maintain a certain smooth-pitted aspect to the hide polish as opposed to the highly pitted polish which resulted from working plain tanned hide.

Major Characteristics: dull, highly pitted rugose surface to the polish; widespread coverage over the used edge; extensive rounding of the working edge and surface ridges or elevations; numerous striations when grit is added in the process of hide preparation.

Archaeological. Flints which have become fairly rolled in the ground or in streams may exhibit edges which on first inspection differ little from heavily used dry-hide scraping edges (compare Plate 87 with 141, and Plate 90 with 138). This is due to the fact that the developed stage of naturally induced grit polish or soil sheen is also a dull, pitted polish which is accompanied by heavy edge and ridge rounding (e.g., Plates 137, 138). The two phenomena can be distinguished, however, as soil sheen usually affects *all* the edges, ridges, and surfaces of a flint and the accompanying striations or directional indicators in the soil sheen are generally randomly oriented if not intersecting (e.g., Plate 139).

Polish From Fresh Hide and Meat

Description. It is not surprising that working fresh animal hides by skinning, defleshing, or dehairing produced the same polish as did cutting meat, fat, and tendons (but *without* bone contact), regardless of the animal involved (cow and rabbit in these tests). The polish is very slow-forming and dull, and does not contrast very much with the surrounding flint surface, as others have noted (Anderson-Gerfaud 1981:54; Keeley 1980:53). Unlike other microanalysts, however, I did not systematically notice a "pronounced greasy luster" to meat and fresh hide polish (Keeley 1980:53). Be that as it may, polish from meat and fresh hide is, in effect, the generic weak polish, which is distributed in uneven patches usually very close to the working edge (Plates 95–97). With prolonged contact, the crest of the working edges used on meat and fresh hide developed a bright, thin, smooth polish band. Between this polish band on the edge crest and the generic weak polish in the immediate edge area small patches of a bright smooth-pitted polish were sometimes found (Plate 96). E. Moss found that cutting meat leaves a band of polish farther *away* from the cutting edge, whereas working fresh hide leaves a polish more limited to the crest of the edge (Moss 1983a:147, 158; Moss and Newcomer 1982:Fig. 1).

The traces produced by defleshing fresh hides were distributed more or less equally on both surfaces of the used flint edge, because removal of the fleshy tissues from the inside of a fresh animal skin is most efficiently accomplished by a slicing or shaving motion (i.e., longitudinal action) rather than a scraping action. Dehairing the outside of an animal skin also necessitates the same motion, unless the hairs are just pushed off easily with a bone or antler implement once the skin has been treated (e.g., Mason 1891; Pfeiffer 1910; Witthoft 1958).

No polish resulted from cutting dried beef, but a characteristic residue was left on the flint edges.

Major Characteristics: patches of dull generic weak polish; crest of working edge with polish band; difficult to distinguish.

Archaeological. The general problem of soil sheen introduced by natural and accidental agencies is of great import for detecting meat/fresh hide polish on prehistoric flints. Even the weakest form of soil sheen can potentially disguise meat and fresh hide polishes, because it means adding a general cover of generic weak polish to a piece that once bore use-related generic polish along only the edge(s) used on meat or fresh hide (compare Plates 95–97 with 135). A more substantial degree of grit polish (e.g., Plates 137, 138) will completely replace a use-related generic weak polish, whereas it may only damage well-developed use polishes as from bone, antler, wood, reeds, etc., (e.g., Plate 65). The polish band on the crest of the working edge, and patches of smooth-pitted polish near the working edge of flints used on meat or fresh hide (Plate 96) would be of great importance in distinguishing ambiguous archaeological examples of meat cutting or fresh hide working.

Polish from Butchering

Depending on the relative amounts of bone vs. meat and skin contact during the butchering tasks on cow, rabbit, and fish in these tests, the experimental flint edges presented the following characteristics: (a) smooth thin polish band on the crest of the working edge; (b) generic weak polish within parts of the immediate edge area; (c) small patches of smooth-pitted polish (Plate 98), possibly with parallel troughs running through (Plate 99); and (d) areas of bone residue, often in linear arrangement (Plates 100, 101). The polished areas resulting from butchering were not extensive, since microchipping due to bone contact continually removed precisely the portions of the edge where butchering traces in the form of polishes developed. If such polishes are not well developed on archaeological flints, there may be difficulties in distinguishing them from aspects of soil sheen.

Influence of Grit on Polish Characteristics

Grit added to contact situations with other worked materials leaves some of its own characteristics to varying degrees, depending on the amount of grit that is added (see also Brink 1978a, b; Mansur-Franchomme 1983b). A substantial number of grit particles will act to replace existing polishes with grit polish, or it will completely dominate the polish formation to leave only its own characteristics, basically heavy pitting and extreme edge rounding.

Even a little grit within the working area induces some deep and superficial striations on the flint surface, or grooves and troughs on polish surfaces (Plates 88–90, 102, 103). Grit also acts to roughen other use-wear polishes in formation by making them more pitted (Plate 104), just as it also generally flattens use-polish accumulations. Most diagnostic of grit influence is the presence of what could be termed "microcraters": variously sized, roundish depressions in polished areas, which display well-defined sides and whose bottom surface exhibits an unusual multi-colored glittering aspect (Plates 103, 104). Sometimes the microcrater contains what appears to be a silica grain (Plate 105), which perhaps indicates that these microcraters are formed by grit particles that physically tear out part of the flint surface. Equally as diagnostic of the presence of grit is a heavy degree of edge rounding and often a 'chewed-up' look to the crest of the edge, that is, where the polished area is composed of small broken spots of rough polish separated by interstitial spaces. The above features occurred to different extents on flint edges which were used to work wood, bone, and fresh and tanned hides onto which varying amounts of loamy soil were added.

Subsequent 'pure' contact situations not influenced by grit particles, however, resulted in the grit polish or the grit-influenced micropolish being more or less changed to the polish normally induced by the worked material. But heavy edge rounding and, to some degree, the 'chewed-up' aspect of edges or ridges cannot be altered by subsequent working of the material without the presence of grit.

Polishes from Finger Prehension and Hafting

Traces left by finger prehension against flint edges or surfaces were quite rare on the experimental pieces, most likely due to the lack of grit and dirt on the fingers. Some patterned deep striations did occur on one experimental flint which was gripped with purposefully dirtied fingers (Plate 106). The dorsal ridges of archaeological flints used extensively in working dry hide with added grit have been seen to bear very developed traces of prehension with gritty fingers: pronounced rounding, a dull, rough grit polish, and striations parallel or diagonal to the ridge which indicate slight movement of the tool under the fingers (Plates 107, 108). The prehended areas of the experimental flints used for three hours in barley and wild *Gramineae* fields bore occasional deep striations and sometimes areas of generic weak polish or very poorly developed smooth-pitted polish in the edge areas gripped by the fingers. On other rare experimental pieces, a generic weak polish was detected on a ridge which served as a finger rest (Plate 109).

The current experimental project did not include any hafting tests. G. Odell (1977, 1978) and E. Moss and M. Newcomer (1982) have published the results of hafting experiments conducted for the purpose of wear

analysis. Although Odell viewed the hafting traces at lower magnifications, he has reported very localized rounding and polish spots on lateral edges or on dorsal ridges of the hafted flints, in addition to striations and microchipping. This is, in fact, what one would expect in the way of polish formation on hafted flints, because the haft and binding materials would contact only limited zones of the tool and notably the lateral edges and the most elevated portions of the interior of the flints. Moss and Newcomer described their experimental hafting traces as follows:

> During the course of experimentation, we observed that either (a) the tool does not and is not intended to move in the haft during work, and, therefore, few wear traces should form, or (b) the tool is intended to move against the haft and prominent wear traces should occur, as happens with flint bits hafted loosely in a bow drill spindle. Microwear analysis showed that hafting by means of pine resin and beeswax or sinew frequently left no wear traces and when they were present they took the form of minuscule bits of un-identifiable polish on one or two of the ridges or other high points of the microtopography; this is not surprising as the tool did not move in the haft. Edge damage was so minimal it could not, archaeologically, be attributed to hafting (Moss and Newcomer 1982:292).

L. Keeley has expressed a very practical approach to the study of hafting traces on prehistoric stone tools:

> In answer to [the] query about hafting traces, there is no simple discrete wear pattern that can be called "haft wear." Such traces are simply wear on tools which makes little sense as traces of utilization but does conform to what is known or expected of wear from minor movements of a tool against its haft (Keeley in Cahen, Keeley, Van Noten 1979:681).

Similarly, P. Anderson-Gerfaud (1981:41) interpreted certain wear patterns on Mousterian flint tools as being due to hafting because the traces were localized on parts of the tools other than the utilized sections and because the wear patterns did not look like traces caused by natural agencies or by intentional usage.

Specifically, P. Anderson-Gerfaud (1981:41−44) has listed the following microwear traces in connection with hafting wear on Mousterian stone tools from southwestern France: (1) traces of "linear abrasion" accompanied by a plant polish on the ventral surface of the flint, along with a rounding of parts of the tool's lateral edges, dorsal retouch scars, or dorsal ridges—a pattern which would be caused by vegetal bindings wrapped around the flint; (2) two clearly different and well-localized patterns of surface wear on a flint; (e.g., one area is "fresher looking," less affected by soil sheen than the rest of the tool) perhaps indicative of the presence of a haft whose gradual decomposition in the ground over the millennia would be responsible for the differential surface alterations of the once hafted flint tool; (3) highly localized spots of wood polish produced by wooden hafts rubbing against the edges, ridges, and surfaces of hafted flint tools (see also Plisson 1982b: 285); (4) a smoothing of the bulb of percussion or striking platform of a tool because of friction against the haft (see also Jensen 1982:325); (5) traces of abrasion and parallel striations on a hafted flint's lateral edges or its proximal end, and these traces not accompanied by other use-wear marks; and (6) certain morphological characteristics of flint tools due perhaps to intentional modifications designed to facilitate hafting procedures (e.g., thinning retouch on the proximal end; notches on both lateral edges; also, Keeley 1982) or the result of accidents while using a hafted tool (e.g., torsion breaks toward the proximal end, as also discussed by Keeley 1978a:77–78).

Superposition of Micropolishes

When a previously used portion of a flint edge is reused but on a different contact material, the second micropolish becomes superimposed over the first. If the first polish is widespread and well developed, but the second polish is of limited extent, then both polishes can be detected—for example, scraping dry hide with a former sickle flint (Plates 110, 111). But if the first polish was of limited extent or weakly developed, and the subsequent polish was widespread and well developed, then all traces of the first would most likely be replaced by the formation of the second use-wear polish. For example, a thin flint edge used to skin an animal and then to harvest cereals would be interpreted only as a sickle flint, unless the meat/fresh hide polish survived on a portion of the edge which did not contact the cereal stalks subsequently.

Distribution and Intensity of Polishes
Due to Intentional Use Actions

Surface Distribution. Flint edges used in transverse actions usually displayed the greatest degree of polish formation on the contact side of the working edge (Table 2.14). However, the polish development was equal on both surfaces of the used edge, or even greater on the noncontact side of the edge, in the cases where a very high contact angle of flint edge to worked material was involved. Longitudinal actions usually produced a more or less even degree of polish development on both sides of the used flint edge, although edges held substantially off a perpendicular contact angle did polish to a greater degree on one side of the edge (Table 2.14). As with the wear attributes of

edge rounding, the above exceptions to the general patterns of surface of greatest polish development reflect realistic human motor habits. The orientation of striations on the flint surface, or that of directional indicators in the polish topography, can give clues to the use motion in cases where the distribution of greatest polish development is ambiguous.

The areas of greatest polish development are often distributed along a used flint edge in a way that is indicative of certain use motions. Only transverse actions can produce a polish bevel, and only on one surface of the used edge (e.g., Plates 12, 13, 38–41). Cutting, slicing, and grooving result in an overall triangular pattern of polish development on the used flint edge, at least in the case of hand-held tools. The cutting or slicing motion involves an initial shallow entry into the substance by part of the edge closest to the worker, while at the end of the cutting/slicing stroke the opposite end of the edge (away from the worker) is embedded more deeply into the contact material. The triangular pattern of resulting wear trades (polish, striations, rounding and smoothing) thus involved the working edge and the adjacent edge where the stroke ended. Grooving harder materials produces a triangular distribution of traces far more restricted in size than the pattern left by cutting or slicing soft substances. However, hafting arrangements on a flint tool could alter any such distributional patterns.

The relative trajectory of a working edge can be discerned by "polish shadows," this is, differential polish formation with regard to some surface feature on or near the used edge. One side of a microscar or one slope of a surface elevation becomes more polished than the other when a one-way longitudinal motion such as cutting or slicing is employed (e.g., Plates 74–76). A two-way or reciprocal longitudinal action such as sawing causes both sides of microscars or surface elevations to become more or less equally polished.

Intensity. It was not possible to measure the intensity of polish development as was done in a relative fashion for edge rounding (Table 2.12). According to the general scheme of polish development outlined earlier, a solid cover of a well-developed, diagnostic microwear polish on a used flint edge is the highest degree of polish formation (e.g., Plate 80). The less linkage exhibited by a polished surface (i.e., the more interstitial spaces between polish components), the lower the degree of polish development (e.g., Plate 73). However, it is not possible to state categorically that x worked material will produce a completely linked polish cover on flint edges in y amount of time. The basic variables which come into play in each instance of tool use are: the relative grain size and hardness of the worked material; the presence of grit in the working area; the duration of contact; and the use motion, or more precisely the direction of the working edge in relation to the internal structure of the contact material. After a certain amount of experimentation, a microanalyst can begin to discern general patterns of the relative degree of polish development given specific contact situations. It is beyond the scope of this book to provide photographic documentation of even a limited portion of the possible situations.

In conjunction with the intensity of polish development, one can employ the better defined criterion of degree of edge rounding (Table 2.12) to arrive at an idea of what can be called the "effective use duration" of a prehistoric flint (Hayden 1979a:17). Polish development and edge rounding are basically covarying phenomena. The greater the degree of polish formation on a working edge, the more that edge is rounded. Excessive microchipping, intentional edge modification, or the presence of grit on a working surface may all act to disguise such covariation on a particular flint edge. But with a certain amount of experience, a microanalyst can attempt reasonable estimates of use duration (e.g., a couple of minutes; a few minutes to twenty minutes or so; up to one hour, etc.).

Micropolishes from Knapping and Retouching Flints

Hammerstone (Plates 112–116). Retouch by percussion with a limestone pebble produced very diagnostic polish patterns on experimental flint edges. On the side of the edge actually struck with the hammerstone, there resulted a slight beveling of the edge consisting of a thin band of bright polish which is characteristically bumpy or uneven because it contains concentrations of well-formed, short, deep, wide grooves which are oriented perpendicularly or diagonally to the edge crest depending on the trajectory of the hammerstone (Plate 112). Just beneath the bevel, on the surface contacted by the hammerstone blow, were found patches of the hammerstone residue which is described in the section on residues. On the more prominent ridges of the retouch scars near the edge on the noncontact side, flattened areas often resulted from the hammerstone blows (Plate 113). These flattened, retouch ridge areas bore dense patches of perpendicularly oriented, deep grooves that are an integral part of a dull-bright polish which exhibits varying amounts of volume but is generally on the flat side, and which is of

very uneven surface texture because of the numerous grooves which score it. Obviously, the more times a flint edge is struck with a hammerstone, the more developed these various traces will become. However, pressure retouch with a pointed stone implement rarely left any of the above traces. A hammerstone-retouched edge that is subsequently used to work some substance will continue to exhibit the above dull-bright, grooved polish until the use-wear polish formed by the contact material completely covers or obliterates the hammerstone traces.

The striking platform of flakes detached by hammerstone percussion usually bore patches of the same dull-bright, flat polish of uneven surface texture and scored with grooves as found on the retouch ridges flattened by hammerstone percussion (Plates 114–116).

Bone and Antler (Plates 117, 118). Percussion blows with bone and antler hammers produced less striking wear traces. The immediate edge area of the struck flint surfaces bore variously sized patches of lightly linked, bright, smooth-pitted polish, through whose smooth parts occurred some short grooves indicating the direction of the blow by the softhammer. Superficial and deep striations sometimes occurred on the unpolished flint surface near the edge that was struck. The extension of the smooth-pitted polish and of the surface striations into the interior of the flint away from the retouched edge depended on the angle at which the percussion blow was delivered onto the edge. Pressure retouch with an antler tine and a bone point, however, left hardly any smooth-pitted polish on the contact surface of the flint edges, since the pressure technique of retouching tends to remove exactly the portion of the edge which is contacted by the pressure flaker.

Wood. Retouch by pressure or percussion with a hardwood point or baton left only patches of the generic weak polish near the contacted flint edges, and some very small wood polish domes on the crest of the retouched edge itself.

Archaeological. The experimental wear traces left by softhammer retouch with antler, bone, and wood could not really be expected to be archaeologically visible given the problems of soil sheen or grit polish on prehistoric flints. However, even the more striking hammerstone effects documented on experimental flints are very rarely observed on percussion platforms or on obviously retouched but unused edges of prehistoric flints. Weak remnants of the diagnostic hammerstone traces have been observed in a few instances only (e.g., Plate 116; see Bosinski et al., 1982:305). Either hammerstone percussion was not the technique being employed, or the wear patterns from hammerstone retouch were removed. The latter is probably more likely not only in view of the general problem of nonuse wear, but also because it was noticed on experimental hammerstone-retouched flint edges that the dull-bright, very grooved hammerstone polish wore away with continued handling of the flints. It was also partially removed with hydrochloric acid, leaving a polish of the same basic characteristics, only less pronounced. This constitutes the only example from the present experimentation where a microwear polish (if it is indeed that) seems to be at least partially removable after its formation. Otherwise, all use-wear polishes produced in the tests were found to withstand cleaning with acid and solvents and to remain after continued handling of the used flints.

Micropolishes from Contact with Soil and Grit

The four sets of nonuse tests undertaken to replicate certain basic contact situations with grit and soil produced distinctive results as far as polishes are concerned. In effect, there seem to be two facies to the microwear polish caused by contact with grit and soil. The first could be termed the *smooth-type grit polish:* very bright polish spots in the shape of raised domes with a surface that is smooth but for a groove which sometimes passes through the center (Plates 119–123). These polish components are usually separate or only lightly linked together, and may be linearly arranged to form superficial striations on the flint surface (Plates 124–126). Smooth-type grit polish forms especially on elevated portions of a flint such as the edges, ridges, and surface projections, and also on the higher microtopography of surface areas (Plates 121–129). Caution must often be exercised to avoid mistaking smooth-type grit polish, especially when the diagnostic grooves are rare or absent, for (a) weakly developed or poorly linked wood polish (Plates 127–131), or (b) weakly linked smooth-pitted polishes (Plate 119). If such precautions are not taken during the use-wear analysis of prehistoric flints, then 90% of the tool edges would seem to have been utilized in 'very light woodworking'! Moreover, when smooth-type grit polish with the surface groove in it occurs along a utilizable edge, it can easily be mistaken for an isolated patch of bone polish bevel produced by the transverse working of bone (Plates 132, 133; compare with Plates 12, 13, 24–27). A preliminary survey of an assemblage of prehistoric flints under study will reveal the ubiquitous nature of smooth-type grit polish on most edges, unus-

able surface ridges, surface projections, etc. This fact should thus be taken into consideration in making functional interpretations from existing microwear on the tools.

The second facies is a *rough-type grit or soil polish* which is well known in its very developed state as the brilliant sheen which entirely covers flints that have been obviously rolled in streams or solifluicted layers, for example. Using soil and moisture as agents of surface alteration, natural mechanisms have imparted a uniform cover of dull-bright (at 280x), very pitted, flat, or gently undulating polish or soil sheen, which has previously been referred to as "glossy patina" by other researchers (Keeley 1980:29; Stapert 1976:12; but cf. Sturge 1914:151). Flints which are covered with a heavy degree of this soil sheen and the concomitant heavy edge and ridge rounding are useless for use-wear analysis, as the extensive nature of these surface alterations usually precludes the survival of original prehistoric use-wear polishes or striations. However, the same general soil sheen is present in *lesser degrees* on every archaeological flint that has resided in a sedimentary or aqueous matrix. This fact is easily ascertained by locating a post-excavation microscar on the edge of a prehistoric flint: the interior of the scar reveals an unaltered surface of the flint whereas the outside surface around the scar exhibits a soil sheen of one degree or another (Plates 134, 135).

At the lowest stage of development, rough-type grit polish or soil sheen is simply the generic weak polish (Plate 136). More extensive soil contact produces a dull polish with an overall rough and pitted look that is due to the differences in volume of the polish components (flat to full-volumed) and to the varying numbers of micropits, pit-depressions, and interstitial spaces within the polish (Plates 136–139). Short grooves or troughs can run through individual polish spots (Plate 123), just as longer, deep, and superficial striations can run through the affected area of the flint surface (Plates 139, 140). Associated features are the microcraters indicative of grit contact (Plates 136–139) and a certain degree of edge and ridge rounding (Plates 137, 138, 140, 141). Rough-type soil sheen is usually not limited solely to edges and projections on the flints, since surface areas and lower microtopography (but not recessed or sunken areas) also become very much affected by rough-type soil sheen. The degree to which the grit polish is linked depends on the extent of the alteration. Aside from the rough-pitted texture of the polish and the grooves, troughs, striations, and microcraters associated with it, a very diagnostic feature is that rough-type grit polish is very widespread over large parts of a flint (e.g., from scrubbing flints to remove soil or concretions), if it is not completely covering a flint in its entirely as is usually the case (e.g., from natural causes).

The extensive coverage assumed by soil sheen on prehistoric flints is the most important criterion in distinguishing it from any intentional use-wear polish which it might resemble under certain circumstances. In particular, dry hide polish and grit-influenced hide polish can look like well-developed soil sheen (cf. Plate 87 with 141, and Plate 90 with 138). Meat and fresh hide polish can be identical to the lesser developed end of soil sheen (cf. Plates 95–97 with Plate 135), just as the polish resulting from very limited plant cutting can resemble the generic weak polish of lesser developed soil sheen (cf. Plates 69–71 with Plate 135). Of course, the generic weak polish resulting from *any* intentional use can become disguised in a general cover of weak soil sheen on archaeological flints.

Yet grit polish and soil sheen go further than just resembling or disguising certain intentional use polishes. Their formation is a potential source of damage to otherwise very distinctive, well-developed microwear polishes resulting from intentional usage in prehistoric times. Use-wear polishes on archaeological flints can vary from pristine or looking almost like experimentally produced use polishes (e.g., Plates 28, 30, 36) to cases where post-use edge chipping has removed some of the evidence (e.g., Plates 25, 26, 35, 46) to badly abraded use-polish areas which present only a few remnants of the original micropolish (e.g. Plates 65, 144, 145). Aside from general reports that soil damage can render specimens completely unfit for microwear analysis (e.g. Keeley 1980:19, 84–87, 120–128), the implications of nonuse grit and soil damage for the identification of prehistoric use-related micropolishes has been neglected until recently (cf. Anderson-Gerfaud 1981; Jensen 1982; Mansur-Franchomme 1983a; Plisson 1982). Of particular importance is a new line of experimentation initiated by H. Plisson and M. Mauger (1984; Plisson 1983a), who have demonstrated in preliminary tests that under certain sedimentological conditions, such as strongly alkaline soils, chemical processes can severely alter, if not eradicate, well-developed use-wear polishes.

It is not simply a case of whether the archaeological flints are or are not in 'suitable condition' for yielding prehistoric use-wear polishes created by intentional utilization. It is, rather, a question of what *degree* of damage has been inflicted upon the prehistoric use polishes by natural and accidental wear mechanisms and by the formation of soil sheen in particular. In this regard, P. Anderson-Gerfaud (1981: vol 2, 69) employs a point system to reflect the degree

of certitude in the determination of the worked material from prehistoric microwear polishes:

1 = faint evidence for interpreting wear traces which are weakly developed or are obliterated;
2 = probable interpretation of traces which are sufficiently developed or preserved;
3 = most probable interpretation of traces which are well developed and well preserved.

The system of polish identification which resulted from the Cassegros analysis (Part II) likewise reflects the degree of certitude with which one can identify a prehistoric use-wear polish, given the fact that all archaeological stone tools recovered from a soil or aqueous matrix have undergone some degree of nonuse damage which may have altered the traces left by intentional utilization in prehistoric times. In the optimal case, the use-wear polish on an archaeological flint is very well preserved and is identical, or nearly so, to some experimentally produced polish. These determinations are "definite" or at least "very highly probable," and the worked material or materials are stated without qualification (e.g., "bone," "wood," "bone or antler," etc.). Next are the "most likely" determinations (e.g. "most likely bone"), where not quite completed polish development or a certain amount of nonuse damage has given rise to minor ambiguities in the presence or nature of diagnostic features needed to interpret the polish. Third is the level of polishes interpreted as from "unspecified harder materials" (e.g., Plates 142–145). This basically consists, at least according to the present experimental evidence, of remnant stretches of polish bevels which can only have been produced by transverse actions on a solid substance such as bone, antler, reeds, and perhaps some woods. In these cases, the absence of polish on either side of the bevel (i.e., on the contact and noncontact surfaces of the working edge which bears the bevel remnants) hinders application of the usual use-polish interpretive criteria, and the bevel remnants alone do not present enough characteristic features even to allow a "most likely" determination, let alone a "definite" one. And finally, there are the cases of use-wear polishes which are "too abraded": there are only a few remnants of what seems to have been a polish caused by intentional use, but on the whole the evidence is insufficient to make inference beyond the fact that the edge or area was used.

As .completely separate categories which deal only with the degree of polish development, there are the cases of (a) prehistoric use-wear polishes which are simply undiagnostic because they are "insufficiently developed" (e.g., a smooth-pitted polish), or (b) "unfamiliar" polishes which are not known from previous experimental work or other publications but nevertheless seem to be the result of intentional use because of their limited or localized distribution on prehistoric flint.

The microanalyst may ascertain at the end of a study that the proportion of determinations other than "definite" is small enough for some of the fine distinctions of interpretation to be dropped during higher levels of data analysis. On the other hand, a sufficient

degree of nonuse damage, particularly in the form of soil sheen and edge crushing, may have caused a large number of uncertain interpretations of use-wear polishes. In either event, at one point or another in the presentation of his data the analyst should report the degrees of certitude behind the functional determinations (e.g., Table 4.1; see also Anderson-Gerfaud 1981: Tableaux VIII—X). In this way, other researchers can judge for themselves what condition the flints were in and what the overall certitude of use-wear interpretation is.

Residues

Residues from Intentional Use on Bone/Antler, Dried Beef, Hammerstone

The term "residue" is employed here in a very restricted sense, that is, only those surface deposits visible with an optical microscope which do not wash away with soap and water, alcohol, or acetone but are removable with hydrochloric acid. Thus the residues described here are of a completely different nature from those which electron microscopy has shown to be permanently attached to a flint surface by their inclusion in a fused silica gel (Anderson 1980a; Anderson-Gerfaud 1981, 1982; Mansur-Franchomme 1983a).

Working nonwoody vegetal substances leaves a quick-forming, very covering film over the surfaces of the flint cutting edge. A similar build-up of glossy plant-juice substance, called "lignin," also occurs just behind the cutting edges of the steel cutting elements in modern harvesting machines (personal communication, R. Throckmorton, International Harvester Company, Chicago). On flint, this deposit also appears somewhat lustrous to the unaided eye, but it is dull under inspection with optical microscopy. However, since the plant-juice substance is easily washed off with water from both flint and steel, it would certainly not survive on prehistoric stone tools, unless the circumstances were exceptional. It is, therefore, not counted among the residues described here.

Residues as defined above were regularly detected on edges which contacted bone and antler, dried beef, and a limestone pebble used as a hammerstone. The residues are reported as empirical phenomena, and no attempt is made to explain the mechanism of deposition. The fact that they all wash off with hydrochloric acid (HCl), but not with medici-

nal alcohol or acetone, would seem to imply that they are constituted from calcium or phosphorus, at least in part. For example, L. Keeley 1980:43) has suggested that bone apatite, which is destroyed by HCl, would be a candidate in the case of bone residue. It has been demonstrated that the inorganic constituent of bone (hydroxyapatite) is composed of calcium and phosphorus (references in Anderson-Gerfaud 1981:121). The extent to which any of the residues described below would be detected on prehistoric flints depends upon the relative acidity of the sediments in which the tools were deposited.

Bone/Antler. An identical residue resulted from working bone and antler in any state, although water-soaked bone and antler left far more residue than did dry bone or antler. With the unaided eye, the residues could sometimes be seen as a diffuse luster along the used flint edges, if they had been deposited in a generous manner. But under higher magnification (280x in this study) bone and antler residue is dull-bright, as compared to microwear polishes from bone and antler. The entire residue cover on the used flint edge was either more or less uniform (flat yet stucco-rough) or, more usually, it had a rough or bumpy aspect due to the great differences in volume of its constituent parts (e.g., Plates 100, 146—148). Individual components of this residue layer have a lightly rough surface, best described as stucco-rough. These components are of no consistent shape, but sometimes near the working edge they can be found in linear arrangements which reflect the use motion (Plates 100, 147, 148). This deposit is very quick-forming, a matter of a few strokes on any variety of flint tested. It accurately reflected the depth of penetration of a flint edge into the bone or antler, or into the shavings produced by the work. Therefore, the residue can be invasive into the interior of the edge. Experimental butchering edges characteristically bore small patches of residue, with parallel-oriented components sometimes, in the immediate edge area (Plates 100, 101). These were caused, of course, by intermittent bone contact.

Dried Beef. Commercially available beef jerky left patches of a dull residue whose surface texture varied from lightly rough (again like stucco) to irregular and very rough. The residue also varied in thickness from thin (Plate 149) to substantial blobs at the working edge. The residue also varied in extent of area covered. Completely diagnostic of this residue alone was the fact that an acetone or alcohol wash caused a multicoloration effect, especially purples and blues, under the microscope. Furthermore, acetone and alcohol made the beef jerky residue swell in volume and caused it to be partially removed (Plate 150). These effects may be related to the anti-lipid nature of acetone and alcohol, since dried beef contains an abundance of complex animal fats.

It would be of interest to find such deposits on prehistoric flints so as to infer the process of meat preservation by drying, which is well known ethnographically and in the American West.

Hammerstone. Retouching flint edges by percussion or pressure techniques with a limestone pebble also left an obvious residue in the area near the edge surface which was struck. It is a dull-bright residue of rough bumpy overall texture (due to difference in volume) and sometimes scored with short deep grooves (Plates 151, 152). It was characteristically very localized in small patches at the very edge. Although I have viewed numerous retouched but unused edges on prehistoric flints, the hammerstone residue has not been detected, since it was most likely washed off by (acidic?) ground water passing through the sedimentary matrix.

Soil Residue

Cleaning archaeological flints with hydrochloric acid improves the "visibility" of a flint surface or micropolish, even in cases where there are no obvious concretionary or calcite deposits along the edge (see Keeley 1980:11). Perhaps it is percolating ground waters which leave a kind of calcium-based precipitation as a thin film over the flints, especially in regions of limestone formations. However, this residue does not appear systematically on all flints from a single site, at least in my experience.

The advantage of removing the film is that weakly developed or fragmented polish spots stand out more clearly. No differences were noted in the visibility of well-developed prehistoric micropolishes before and after HCl treatment of the flint edge. However, there are drawbacks to the systematic HCl treatment of archaeological flints before viewing them under a microscope. First, the use-related residues discussed above will be destroyed before they can be detected (if indeed they survived the post-depositional and post-excavation rigors). Second, flints containing even minute quantities of limestone impurities will partially dissolve in the HCl, and their surfaces and any micropolishes and striations on them will be badly damaged and perhaps made useless for wear analysis.

Microwear Interpretation in Perspective

The results of the present use-wear experiments with flint tools have revealed that microchipping by itself is a far less reliable indicator of use action and worked material than are patterns of microwear polishes, striations, and rounding.

While certain patterns were detectable among the microscarring attributes as correlated with motion and contact substance, they were only general tendencies and not diagnostic features, or they stood in contradiction to expected or previously reported aspects of microflaking patterning. In effect, it seems that microchipping exhibits far too much variability in regard to use action and contacted material. In other words, other variables such as edge angle, contact angle, pressure, and intentional retouch also play a major part in determining the ways in which flint edges scar during use. Furthermore, it has long been known that patterned edge chipping can often occur when flints are subjected to natural and/or accidental damage mechanisms. Thus for the expressed purpose of reconstructing prehistoric use motions and worked materials, microchipping alone is of very limited reliability.

Striations and relative edge rounding are especially helpful in determining the kinematics of tool utilization. But it must be remembered that 'expected' patterns of edge rounding and striating do not always result from use motions which accurately reflect true human hand movements, as opposed to rigidly precise mechanical motions. Microwear polishes, on the other hand, can be diagnostic of the worked substance because their formation is dependent primarily on the contact material, while the length of use and the texture of the flint also exert a certain influence. It was consistently observed in the experiments that the same worked material contacted by flints of different grain sizes produced wear polishes which differed for the most part in quantity (i.e., degree of development) and not in quality (i.e., characteristic features). If a polished area has passed through the first two stages of development which seem to result from all contact materials (namely, generic weak polish and smooth-pitted polish), then the developed use-wear polish is *usually* diagnostic of the category of material worked by the flint edge (e.g., bone, antler, hide, etc.). The "usually" is stressed because there are certain zones of overlap between various use-wear polishes which can result in certain ambiguities. The Venn diagrams in Figure 2.2 illustrate the distinctive and overlapping aspects of use-wear polishes in their *developed* forms. Surface alterations such as soil sheen due to nonuse damage may also render prehistoric use-related polishes less than diagnostic. The microanalyst should assess the damaged polishes to the greatest extent that the evidence allows and then make the interpretation of worked material based on a scale of degrees of certitude.

If a flint assemblage is found to be in adequate condition for a high-powered microwear analysis given the problems of non-use-induced wear to prehistoric flints, the following criteria may be employed to interpret use action and worked material of the utilized flints:

(a) Worked Material: nature and distribution of microwear polishes
special features (e.g., residues)
elimination of polishes, striations, and edge chipping due to nonuse factors

(b) Action: orientation of surface striations and of directional indicators in the polish surfaces relative to the working edge
distribution and relative degree of edge rounding and polish development with respect to ventral and dorsal surfaces of a used edge
particular areas of greatest polish development (e.g., edge bevel, triangular distribution of polish)
"shadows" in the polish topography for relative tool trajectory

Figure 2.2 Distinctiveness and overlap of micropolishes in their developed forms. NB: Sizes of the overlap zones as drawn are arbitrary and do not reflect exact degrees of resemblance between contiguous circles. Generic weak polish and smooth-pitted polish are excluded since they represent the common initial stages that are antecedent to the developed forms of the use-polishes.

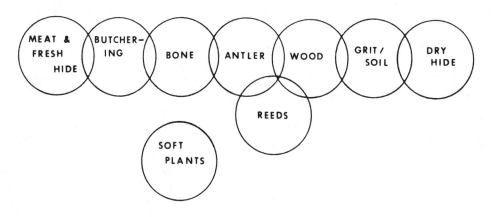

Part II

Functional Determination
of the Magdalenian "0" Flints

3 / The Site of Cassegros

Location, Description, and Excavations

Situated near the top of a high, densely forested limestone butte, its entrance 140 m above the lower alluvial plain of the Lot River, the cave of Cassegros ("large oak" in local dialect) affords a commanding view of the extraordinarily verdant northeast section of the administrative department of Lot-et-Garonne in southwest France (Fig. 3.1). Located 120 km southeast of Bordeaux, near the town of Trentels, Cassegros is one of the few Paleolithic sites situated in the Tertiary limestone region of the department of Lot-et-Garonne. Just to the north of the cave, the Gavaudun-Sauveterre area, the density of paleolithic sites is far greater. Also to the north of Cassegros lies the renown Périgord area of the department of Dordogne with its rich concentration of Paleolithic rock shelters, caves, and open-air sites (Bordes 1968, 1972; Laville et al. 1980; de Sonneville-Bordes 1967). Although long known by local speleologists, the cave of Cassegros was not brought to the attention of archaeological authorities until the site fell victim to clandestine diggings in 1972. In the following year, the Department of Prehistoric Antiquities entrusted the salvage excavations to J-M. Le Tensorer. The promising nature of the site's deposits led to a regular program of excavation and study.

The mouth of the cave (Plate 153) opens directly south, onto the steep slope of the limestone butte, about 10 m from a natural spring that is now dry. The plan of the cave (Fig. 3.2) consists of: (a) the *first chamber*: around 10 m deep and 5 m wide on the average; oriented north-south; lighted by daylight; the area of greatest artifact density; at its discovery, almost completely filled with roof collapse and habitation sediments; (b) a *gallery*: about 15 m long, running northwest from the first chamber; (c) and (d) *two long chambers*, separated by large stalagmitic formations. In the gallery and back chamber three monochrome black or red wall paintings have been found, along with several wall sections which exhibit a confused mass of engravings or animal-claw marks.

Excavations at Cassegros began during the summer of 1973 and continued for an average of six weeks per summer on a yearly basis. During the 1973–1979 seasons the work was concentrated principally in the first chamber and on the terrace in front of the cave, but soundings were also made in four meter squares within the gallery (Figs. 3.2 and 3.3). Out of a total of approximately 50 m² within the enclosed area of the first chamber, 16 meter squares, or nearly one-third of the

All information concerning the site of Cassegros has been summarized from Le Tensorer 1981. The reader may refer to Bordes 1968 and 1979, and to Laville et al., 1980, for explanations of the standard geological periods, the typological and sedimontological terminologies, and the methods of paleoclimatic reconstruction.

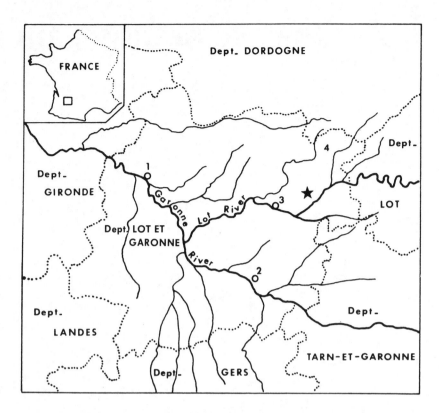

Figure 3.1 Location of Cassegros (Lot-et-Garonne, France). Star: site of Cassegros. 1: Marmande. 2: Agen. 3: Villeneuve-sur-Lot. 4: Gavaudun-Fumel area (after Le Tensorer 1981: Figure 122).

enclosed area, were excavated to varying depths (Fig. 3.3: squares F25-27, G25-30, H25-29, I27-28). Eleven more meter squares were opened up on the terrace area in front of the cave entrance (Fig. 3.3: squares G31-35 and H30-35). Thus, a total of 31 meter squares on the terrace, inside the first chamber, and inside the gallery were opened for excavation between 1973 and 1979.

As will be explained in the following section, the stratigraphy of the cave has been divided basically into the levels formed during Würm IV and afterwards (levels 1–10) and those levels laid down prior to Würm IV (numbers 11–25). Level 10, whose Magdalenian "0" (zero) assemblage of flint tools was submitted to use-wear analysis, was exposed and excavated in 7 meter squares on the terrace in front of the cave, and also in 7 meter squares within the cave or 14% of the enclosed area of the first chamber (Fig. 3.3). Level 10 has been divided into sublevels a, b, and c on the basis of fine sedimentological differences. Up to 1979, sublevels 10a, 10b, and 10c were all completely excavated only in the 7 squares on the terrace. In the 7 excavated squares of level 10 within the first chamber

of the cave, where the finds are densest for the level, only sublevel 10a was taken down in its entirety by 1979, although sublevels 10b and 10c were exposed over some squares. Level 10 was not found in place within five meter squares just at the cave entrance (Fig. 3.3: squares G29-30 and H29-31) due to disturbances by neolithic or protohistoric burial pits and by recent clandestine diggings.

The maintenance of the grid system of meter squares for the excavation is assured by a suspended metal framework that is permanently attached to the cave ceiling (Plates 153, 154). Each meter square is slowly excavated over its entire area within the context of a minutely controlled sedimentological stratigraphy (Plate 155). By using small paint brushes, the earth is gently moved to expose artifacts, faunal remains, rocks, etc. The three-dimensional coordinates of all bones and artifacts larger than one centimeter are recorded; and a series of plans showing artifacts, bones, ash, rocks, etc, is drawn for each quarter-square as the work progresses (Plate 156). Flints, bone fragments, and other artifacts larger than one centimeter are individually wrapped in aluminum foil and numbered.

Objects smaller than one centimeter are removed, noted and bagged by quarter-square. Once all visible objects within a quarter-square have been recorded, marked on a plan, removed, wrapped, and numbered, the sedimentary matrix which remains is usually dry-sieved (or occasionaly water-sieved) in 1.5 mm mesh screens. These careful excavation methods ensure a high degree of precision in subsequent spatial reconstructions of archaeological, paleoethnological, and paleoenvironmental information.

Since the excavations at Cassegros were still in progress at the time this book was written, the study reflects only preliminary analyses of artifactual, faunal, and sedimentological remains.

Stratigraphy, Paleoclimate, and Dating

The history of the first chamber of the cave of Cassegros can be divided into two major segments: prior to Würm IV, and Würm IV and postglacial times. During the earlier segment, karstic activity played a major role in forming the cave, as is common in such limestone regions. Information on the pre-Würm IV levels is sketchy because the levels have only been tested by limited sondage in parts of 4 meter squares on the terrace (Fig. 3.3: squares G31-32 and H31-32). It is certain that the cave was frequented during the earlier Würm glacial periods by carnivores, particularly hyenas, and by people who left behind typical Levallois flakes. The presence of Acheulean remains in the cave cannot be excluded, as bedrock has not yet been reached in the deepest soundings. In any event, at the end of Würm III, during a cold and relatively wet climate, there was a general collapse of the cave ceiling within the first chamber. This formed a layer of debris consisting of large blocks (level 11, 0.15–0.50 m thick), created a wider opening to the cave, and enlarged the terrace area in front of the cave. During the Würm III–Würm IV interstadial period, the onset of a milder and wetter climate caused both chemical activity in the form of corrosion and concretions on the ceiling debris and the formation of stalagmites and stalactites within the fist chamber.

The first phase of Würm IV (level 10, 0.05–0.25 m thick) brought a return of a generally colder climate: a

Figure 3.2 Schematic ground plan of the Cave of Cassegros. a: first chamber. b: gallery. c,d: long chambers (after Le Tensorer 1981: Figure 123).

Figure 3.3 Excavations at Cassegros (1973–1979) (after Le Tensorer 1981: Figure 124).

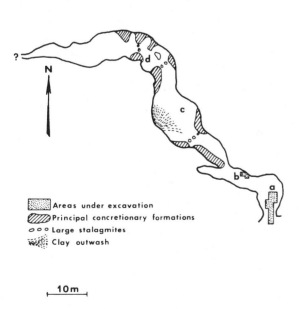

? N

Areas under excavation
Principal concretionary formations
∘∘∘ Large stalagmites
Clay outwash

10 m

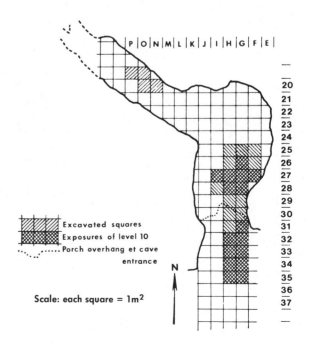

Excavated squares
Exposures of level 10
Porch overhang et cave entrance

N

Scale: each square = 1m²

sudden intense cold with moderate wetness (sublevel 10c), then a short, wet, but only moderately cold subphase (sublevel 10b), and then a very cold and drier climate (sublevel 10a; see Table 3.1). The intense cold of the first phase of Würm IV not only caused substantial cryoclastic activity within the first chamber in the form of frost fracturing and deposition of ceiling fragments and frost slabs, but it also split the large blocks of level 11 along with the stalagmites and concretions which had formed on them during the Würm III–Würm IV interstadial. Humans with a lithic industry termed Magdalenian "0" occupied the first chamber and the terrace area throughout this first cold phase of Würm IV (level 10). Even at the start, their occupation was mainly inside the cave entrance, within the first chamber, but with a few hearths on the terrace in front. As the weather became colder, the group moved farther back into the first chamber under the protection of the ceiling. It was thus a sheltered habitat with little trace of activity outside the cave. About 90% of the cultural remains have come from the excavated squares inside the first chamber (Fig. 3.3: squares F27, G26-28, H27-28, I27).

The distribution of remains in the area of greatest artifact density within the first chamber of the cave was still being studied in the mid-1980s, but the following points could be noted for level 10a at least: a small hearth (Fig. 3.3: square H28), swept-out hearth debris (G28), a concentration of red ocher (H28), a decreased concentration of remains towards the east and north in the first chamber, and everywhere an abundance of cryoclastic limestone rocks and bone fragments from cold-climate herbivores, particularly reindeer, ibex, and bison. The bone fragments are rarely larger than 10 cm. Level 10 as a whole is as distinct a sedimentological entity as an excavator could hope for: its earth is an unmistakable red to brown-red due to the large quantities of red ocher which the Magdalenian "0" inhabitants brought into the cave and onto the terrace.

Subsequently, there followed a milder, wetter period (level 9, 0.05–0.15 m thick), during which there was a substantial occupation which left clearly defined artifact concentrations, but no ocher staining of the sediments. Thus the stratigraphic division between levels 10 and 9 is very clear: ocher-stained sediments in level 10 vs. brown sediments in level 9. The lithic industry of level 9 is that of Lower Magdalenian with raclettes, also known as Magdalenian I. The distribution of cultural materials in level 9 follows the same general pattern as that of level 10, namely, most (90%) of the remains are located within the enclosed portion of the first chamber. The faunal remains are as fragmented as those in level 10 but represent a wider range of herbivores, in the following order of relative importance: reindeer, cow or bison, horse, and red deer. The presence of the red deer, which is a forest animal, is indicative of a climate that is less intensely cold than that of the period of level 10 (Table 3.1).

With a renewal of very cold and rather dry conditions (level 8, 0–0.20 m thick), there was only discontinuous occupation towards the back of the first chamber of the cave. Only slightly greater human presence is attested during the following return to a significantly milder climate (level 7, 0–0.10 m thick). The retouched tools recovered from levels 7 and 8 (up to 1979) are too few to characterize the industries beyond "Lower Magdalenian." A very intensely cold and dry climate (level 6, 0.10–0.30 m thick) brought only sporadic occupation of the cave, during Lower or Middle Magdalenian times. Finally, there is a series of postglacial levels (numbers 1–5) which reflect increasingly milder and wetter climatic conditions. These top levels contain occasional traces of human passage from the Neolithic to the Middle Ages.

Absolute dating of the principal Lower Magdalenian levels at Cassegros is possible only by analogy with a carbon-14 date from the Magdalenian "0" levels at Laugerie-Haute-Est (Les Ezyes, Dordogne). A composite sample of bone fragments from levels 18–20 at Laugerie-Haute-Est gave a date of 16,310 ± 360 B.C. (Ly-972; Laville et al. 1980:307, 310–11). Thus, if the Magdalenian "0" levels at Cassegros and at Laugerie-Haute-Est are at least roughly contemporaneous, level 10 of Cassegros can be dated to the seventeeth millennium B.C.

Flint Industry of the Magdalenian "0" (Level 10)

The flint nodules that were available to the Cassegros inhabitants in Upper Paleolithic times were generally small, judging from the fact that in level 10 blades or flakes larger than 5 cm are few and those longer than 10 cm are very rare (e.g., Fig. 4.1:10). A great variety of flints was used for manufacturing stone tools, but the three major types of flints recovered from level 10 are: (a) the lighter-colored, slightly grainy-textured Tertiary flints from limestone layers in the immediate area of the cave; (b) the darker-colored, very fine-grained Senonian flints from the Gavaudun-Fumel area 15 km to the north of the cave; and (c) a fine-grained white- or brown-spotted yellow jaspoid flint that is found 80 km to the northeast in the Martel-Gramat area (Dordogne), but it is also found in the alluvial deposits of the Lot River adjacent to the site, having been transported by the river from more distant sources upstream to the east.

Table 3.2 presents the general characteristics of the débitage patterns of the flints excavated from level 10 during the 1973–1978 seasons. ("Débitage" is used here in the French sense of the term, "that which is knapped," as opposed to the common American usage that implies "waste material"; cf. Crabtree 1972:58.) The most notable characteristics of the débitage from the Lower Magdalenian of level 10 are:

(1) The unusually small percentage of blades for an Upper Paleolithic assemblage. Unretouched blades and bladelets make up just 3.63% (N = 31) of the totality of the flint débitage; and only 20.35% (N = 35) of the retouched tools are on blades (Table3.2). In general, the blades of level 10 are short and of poor quality (e.g., Fig. 4.1:1, 2, 3, 4), but there are rare exceptions (e.g., Fig. 4.1:10).

(2) The flakes are generally thin and not very large (i.e., 90% under 5 cm), and are very irregular in shape.

(3) Cores are rare (0.9%, N = 8), very small (usually under 5 cm in length), and were knapped to the fullest. Forms include 3 spherical, 4 shapeless, and one more or less pyramidal-shaped core.

(4) Burin spalls were relatively numerous (3.27%, N = 28) compared to the small quantity of burins recovered. Some of the burin spalls are of good quality considering the mediocre nature of the dihedral burin tools. The spalls include 13 first removals, 14 secondary spalls, and one transversal burin spall.

Although the excavation of level 10 had not been completed, it is apparent given the present sample that for a Magdalenian assemblage, level 10 is very poor in flint débitage. The same is also true of the assemblages from levels 7, 8, and 9: "A Cassegros, dans tous les niveaux, nous avons l'impression que le silex était rare et a été utilisé jusqu'au bout" (The impression obtained from all the levels at Cassegros is that flint was rare and was used to the last bit) (Le Tensorer 1981: 309). However, it is clear that the débitage and the retouched tools of level 10 were manufactured at the site because of the high proportion (46%) of flints in level 10 which bear cortex (see Chapter 4, Table 4.32) and because of the minute retouch flakes which have been recovered in sieving of the excavated sediments from squares within the first chamber.

The retouched tools recovered in the 1973–1978 excavations are numerous enough (N = 172) to allow the lithic industry of level 10 to be classified as Lower Magdalenian, specifically Magdalenian "0." The classification was carried out by the excavator, J-M. Le Tensorer, following the Upper Paleolithic type list developed by D. de Sonneville-Bordes and J. Perrot (1953–1956). Table 3.3 presents the excavator's type list for material studied up to 1978. The stone tool industry from level 10 exhibits several unusual characteristics:

(1) There are about as many end-scrapers (N = 20; Table 3.3: #1, 3, 5, 8, 11, 12) as there are burins (N = 21; Table 3.3: #27, 29, 30, 37, 38, 39, 41, 43). The end-scrapers and burins combined, plus the composite end-scraper/burin tools (N = 3; Table 3.3: #17), make up only 25.85% or one-quarter of the industry (N = 172).

(2) The becs (N = 24; #24) are more numerous than either the end-scrapers or the burins.

(3) Notched pieces (N = 28; #74), denticulated flints (N = 7; #75), splintered pieces (N = 18; #76), and side-scrapers (N = 18; #77) make up an uncommonly high proportion (41.28%) for a Late Upper Paleolithic industry. Notched pieces (N = 28) are the single most abundant tool type in level 10. The side-scrapers give a peculiar characteristic to the industry in that they are very typical Mousterian types such as straight, convex, concave, double concave-convex, convergent biconvex, etc., (e.g., Fig. 4.5:1–8). There is even one side-scraper with Quina-type retouch and another with semi-Quina retouch.

(4) Aurignacian-like qualities are exhibited by the retouch of the carinated end-scrapers (e.g., Fig. 4.1: 9) and of one side-retouched blade. The equal proportions of end-scapers and burins is also a further Aurignacian characteristic of the level 10 industry.

Similar Magdalenian "0" industries are known only from two other sites: the Abri Fritsch (Indre, 300 km north; Allain 1983; Allain and Fritsch 1967) and particularly from Laugerie-Haute-Est (Dordogne, 50 km north; Bordes 1958). At Laugerie-Haute-Est, the Magdalenian "0" levels are stratified under other Lower Magdalenian levels (specifically, Magdalenian I, II, and III) but above the Final Solutreal levels (Bordes 1958:207−210; Laville et al., 1980:307).

4 / Use-Wear Analysis of the Magdalenian "0" Stone-Tool Assemblage

Choice of Site and Assemblage: Goals of the Study

The site of Cassegros was chosen for microwear analysis because of the careful excavation procedures employed and the restricted size of the site itself and of its lithic assemblages. Since a serious lithic use-wear study is a time-consuming proposition, far more contributions can be made to the holistic functional interpretation of a site if the stone tools' spatial and temporal distributions are well established. This can be accomplished only by meticulous excavation recording, as practiced in the excavations at Cassegros. But equally as important is the nature of the analyzed sample of stone tools recovered from the site. Optimally, the sample of pieces to be studied is chosen to be representative of such things as the excavated areas of the site, of the total number of stone tools recovered, of the technological and typological variations exhibited by the lithic assemblage, and of the raw materials from which the tools were manufactured. The usual practical alternatives are sampling from a large collection or conducting a complete study on a smaller series of lithics.

Cassegros offered the opportunity to analyze all the flints which had been recovered in seven seasons of excavation (1973–1979), since both the Magdalenian "0" and the Magdalenian I stone-tool assemblages of levels 10 and 9, respectively, did not contain excessive numbers of chipped stone tools (e.g., Table 3.2). The assemblage of level 10 was singled out for study first because the level constitutes a clearly demarcated stratigraphical entity due to heavy ocher

staining of its sediments as pointed out in the last chapter. Also, the excavator had already noted striking differences in flint distributions and patterns of raw-material exploitation. Therefore, the sample of flints analyzed from level 10 at Cassegros comes from a single, well-defined stratigraphical unit and is representative of the excavated portions of the site (see Fig. 3.3).

The Magdalenian "0" chipped stone tools were analyzed by microwear methods which relied basically on interpreting use-wear polishes, striations, and edge rounding which had previously been produced in experimentation (Part I). The goals of the analysis were twofold: first, to document patterns of tool usage with reference to two basic functional units, the individual, used edge (termed the "independent use zone") and the entire tool as a typological and technological entity; second, to locate activity areas within the excavated portions of level 10 by plotting the functional aspects of the flints according to the horizontal coordinates of the pieces. Schematized line-drawings of the flints which exhibited microwear traces assignable to intentional use relate graphically the tools' utilized portions with the shapes of the artifacts (Fig. 4.1–4.13). Micrographs showing examples of the various use-wear polishes found on the Cassegros flints have already been presented in conjunction with the discussion of experimentally produced microwear polishes, but they are referred to again in the appropriate sections of the discussion of use-wear on the archaeological flints. The data on the microwear attributes collected in the study have been presented in coded form elsewhere (Vaughan 1981b:353–360).

The final section of the chapter discusses other applications of the micropolish method of functional lithic analysis. General trends visible in the results of these studies are outlined, and implications are drawn from them for future research.

Methodology

Procedures. The microwear methods employed in the study of the Cassegros lithic material were basically the same as those outlined earlier for the experimental tool-use study. The flint edges or surfaces to be viewed were cleaned with medicinal alcohol and/or acetone, and in many cases with dilute (15%) hydrochloric acid if a filmy soil residue or concretions were detected on first inspection. The normal viewing magnification was 280x on a WILD-M50 metallurgical microscope. Higher and lower magnifications were used as needed (minimum 34x, maximum 560x). A flint was viewed systematically on both its ventral and dorsal surfaces from proximal, to left, to distal, to right edges and then on its dorsal ridge(s). The interior of the ventral and dorsal surfaces and the center of the striking platform were not viewed unless wear traces detected along the edges or ridges seemed to extend into the interior of the piece.

Of the wear traces found, preference was given to assessing micropolishes, striations, and edge rounding (see Chapter 2), whereas edge damage in the form of microscarring was taken into account only to a limited extent, primarily as an indicator of nonuse damage. Functional interpretations were made from patterns of microwear traces which from my own experimental work, or from similar published studies (e.g., Keeley 1980), could be assigned to specific intentional utilization in prehistoric times. Limited assessments and/or written notes were also made for use-wear patterns which were unfamiliar but which appeared systematically. The exact extent of each portion of a flint with intentional use-wear traces was indicated on the tool with pencil marks, a few mm *away from* the edge. Micrographs were taken to document typical and unusual examples of the range of patterns of use and nonuse wear traces (e.g., Plates 25, 26, 28, 30).

Variables and Definitions. The bulk of the data-recording during the microwear study of Cassegros lithics was carried out with a data code (Vaughan 1981b:346–352) which was designed after that used by G. Odell (1977, 1979), to speed field recording and subsequent data analysis. But supplementary notes were made for any out-of-the-ordinary observations. The data code consists of three groups of variables:

(1) *Technological and typological aspects of the tool*: square and piece number, typology, flint type, technological class, presence of cortex and/or patina, and the horizontal coordinates of the piece within the square;

(2) *Functional variables concerning the piece as a whole*: total number of independent use zones on the entire piece, use actions on the entire tool, materials worked by the tool as a whole, and the greatest relative use duration on the piece;

(3) *Functional variables concerning each independent use zone (IUZ) on a tool*: position of the use-wear traces, sequential number of the IUZ, type of IUZ, modification-reuse cycle, maximum and minimum edge angle groups within the IUZ, state of the majority of the edge in the IUZ, condition of the use-wear polish at its two extents and mid-section, use action of the IUZ, and relative use duration.

All of the above 25 variables were recorded for pieces which bore microwear that was assignable to a specific intentional use in prehistoric times. For pieces which did not exhibit such intentional use-wear, only the first seven variables (technological and typological aspects) were recorded.

"Utilization" was defined simply by the presence of microwear patterns which have been demonstrated by systematic use-wear experimentation to be the consistent result of intentional usage of flint tools. If a tool was used too briefly in prehistoric times for interpretable microwear traces to form, or if use-wear traces have been entirely removed or completely obscured by subsequent nonuse damage, then the implement could only be counted among the "unused" flints.

Each portion of a flint with interpretable use-wear was counted as an "independent use zone" (IUZ). An IUZ is basically a left, right, proximal, or distal edge or a dorsal ridge that was used to accomplish a certain task or function. The term "task" and "function" are both operationally defined as the combination of an action, a contact angle of working edge to the work surface, and a worked substance. If another task involving a different motion, contact angle, or worked material took place in a portion of the tool contiguous to, or slightly overlapping with, that used in a prior task, then two IUZ were distinguished. Similarly, if exactly the same portion of a tool was used for more than one function (that is, with different actions, contact angles, or worked materials), then it was again a case of two IUZ. However, caution was exercised not to count as distinct entities the different portions of a single IUZ which were merely separated by subsequent retouch or by nonuse microscarring damage.

The concept of the independent use zone is basically similar to that proposed by others: the "employable unit" of R. Knudson (1979:270) and G. Odell (1980a:417), the "altered edge" of J. White (1969: 23), and in a general way the "use" unit of M. Schiffer (1979:19). In each case, though, these terms seemed inadequately defined or implemented. Specifically, R. Knudson's "employable unit" and J. White's "altered edge" were identified by the presence of macro- and microscopic edge chipping, which systematic tool-use experimentation has found not to be a reliable indicator of intentional use (Chapter 2). G. Odell's version of the "employable unit" allowed for more than one task per unit: "an 'employable unit' (EU) will be considered as an edge (or part thereof) or a projection assessed to have been used prehistorically for one or more purposes" (Odell 1980a:417). M. Schiffer's "use" unit was defined as "the minimal instance of behavior directed toward completion of a task" (Schiffer 1979:19). As such, the "use" unit can be employed in higher-level behavioral studies, but it is not operational for the initial gathering of use-wear data. Nevertheless, the rationale behind the independent use zone (IUZ) of the present study is the same as that behind "employable unit" and "use" unit, namely, to isolate separate or 'independent' incidents of edge/ridge utilization and thus view the implements and the assemblages in terms of their *basic functional parts*. But at the same time, the present study also employs the complementary approach to viewing function in relation to the whole tool as a technological and morpho-typological entity.

Sampling. Although the aim of the study was to view all the excavated flints from Cassegros, level 10, there was one practical restriction. It was impossible to include the truly minute retouch and debris chips which were no more than a few millimeters in size and could not be handled effectively in the viewing process on the microscope. Therefore, the number of flints available for study was 532, in contrast to the 855 pieces of flint débitage which had been recorded from the 1973–1978 excavations (Table 3.2). Furthermore, flints from the 1979 excavation were also included in the use-wear study, if they were not too small to handle.

An initial sample of 222 pieces from the available 532 flints of level 10 was viewed on the microscope so as to become familiar with the basic range of microwear patterns and nonuse damage traces in the collection, and to survey the varieties of flint types. The sample consisted of all the retouched tools available from level 10 and a portion of the unretouched flints. The sample was not chosen randomly since the lithic material was already sorted and stored in boxes according to typological or technological considerations. During the first viewing of this sample, the data code was not used. Notes were simply made to separate used from unused pieces. Only on the second viewing of the sample did the recording procedure commence with the data code.

As a further check on consistency and reliability in the analyses, 30 pieces consisting of 10 used and 20 unused flints were reexamined at the end of the study. Only in one case was a discrepancy found between the original and the test results. On one used flint (Fig. 4.13:27) the right edge was found to bear use-wear polish from *light* dry-hide cutting, in addition to the left edge whose use had been detected originally.

Data Analysis. The Statistical Analysis System on the IBM computer of the Uni-Coll Corporation, Philadelphia, was used to process the data recorded on the 532 analyzed flints, according to various correlations of variables. The results are summarized in Tables 4.1 to 4.41 and are discussed in the following sections. While the text is concerned with the 283 IUZ on the 158 flints which bore interpretable use-wear traces, a discussion is merited on a series of special observations concerning two unusual kinds of micropolishes which reoccurred consistently on the Cassegros flints.

Basically, they appeared as very smooth-surfaced polish spots which presented either a completely flat or a ripply topography. These special polish spots were found anywhere and everywhere on 100 of the 532 analyzed flints: near edges and ridges, within microscars, in the middle of ventral and dorsal tool surfaces. By comparing the nature and the surface distribution of these polishes to the aspect and positioning of experimental use-wear polishes and of the other micropolishes observed on the Cassegros flints, it was concluded that the special polish spots were the results of as yet uncertain nonuse mechanisms which caused a dissolution of the flint surface and a subsequent precipitation of a silica layer, but only in very restricted areas. Since these factors do not reflect patterns of intentional tool utilization, detailed discussion of the phenomenon is presented in Appendix B.

Analysis of the 532 Flints by Function

Functions of the Independent Use Zones

The functions of the independent use zones (IUZ) are discussed by considering the worked materials, actions, edge angles, use duration, overlapping IUZ, edge state, tool types, curation, and nonuse wear.

Worked Materials. By far the principal microwear polish of a material worked by the analyzed flints from Cassegros, level 10, was that of dried or tanned hide, principally with added grit (Table 4.1:Plates 89–91, 94, 102). Nearly 60% of the total 283 IUZ were involved in dry-hide working, with a slightly lower proportion of hide scraping or softening (43% transverse actions) than of hide cutting (54% longitudinal actions). Second in numerical importance was wood microwear (Plates 48, 49) at 13% of the IUZ (Table 4.1). Wood was primarily scraped, planed, or whittled (92% transverse actions). Although bone polish and antler polish were clearly distinguishable on some IUZ (Table 4.1), bone and antler are considered together here because their respective proportions are small and because it is sometimes difficult to distinguish between the two polishes (e.g., Plate 20). Together bone and antler polishes (Plates 25, 26, 28, 30, 35, 38) made up 11% of the IUZ. Bone and antler were worked primarily by transverse actions (84%). Unspecified harder materials (e.g., bone, antler, and reeds; Plates 142, 143, 145) accounted for 9% of the IUZ, virtually all from transverse actions as by definition of this special category of worked material. Thus the majority of the tasks involving the analyzed IUZ were performed on dry hide, principally with added grit, and about equal but small proportions on wood, bone, and antler, and unspecified harder materials. The importance of hide-working in producing clothes and coverings is well known ethnographically (Gallagher 1977; Mason 1891; Steinbring 1966) and the addition of grit seems to absorb fat and moisture during hide preparation (Audouin and Plisson 1982; Brink 1978a).

Use-wear polishes from other categories of worked materials accounted for less than 2% each of the IUZ: fresh hide or meat, plants, and grit. The fresh hide or meat and the grit examples involved edges and dorsal ridges (e.g., Figs. 4.1:1,7; 4.11:6; 4.13:5) used as grip areas in finger prehension, an action which is further discussed below. It is surprising that there were no certain cases of polishes from working fresh hide or meat, nor from butchering. This could be a reflection

of: (a) actual patterns of stone-tool use at the site (no such tasks were performed with stone tools, or for an insufficient length of time for the polishes to develop); (b) subsequent soil damage, masking the traces; or (c) misinterpretation of the use-wear traces.

Plant micropolishes were also very rare, with only one example of probable plant cutting (Fig. 4.12:18; Plate 71). The other cases involved what could only be interpreted as hafting traces left by vegetal fibers on the corner edges of a large flake (Fig. 4.7). The polish was bright, very smooth-surfaced, and distributed bifacially only along three short stretches of the right edge of the tool. Moreover, the same polish also occurred on two stretches of the dorsal ridge near the distal tip, corresponding to the distribution one would expect from vegetal-fiber bindings that were wrapped around the distal end of the piece to secure part of a haft (as in Keeley 1982:Fig. 2-D). The same large flake also bore unfamiliar, small, bright polish spots aligned intermittently near the ventral edge of the proximal break surface. The best interpretation of these polish spots is a special wood polish left on higher points of the proximal flint surface by a piece of wood used in hafting the tool. A probable reconstruction of the hafting, based on the position and nature of the vegetal and wood (?) polishes, is presented in Fig. 4.8. Such hafting would fit well with the fact that the right edge of the flake was involved in a transverse action, such as planing or chopping on wood.

Finally, there were a few IUZ which bore micropolishes that could not be interpreted with much certainty (Table 4.1). In two cases, there were "insufficiently developed" use-wear polishes in the form of undiagnostic smooth-pitted polishes. Five IUZ bore use-wear polishes which had been "too abraded" by subsequent nonuse damage for any interpretation beyond the fact that the edge had been utilized. And lastly, six IUZ presented micropolishes which were simply "unfamiliar" within the context of prior use-wear experimentation.

Actions. From the motions involved in the tasks represented by the IUZ (Table 4.2), nearly 60% were transverse actions, that is, motions perpendicular to the working edge such as scraping, planing, whittling. Such actions were performed primarily on dry hide (44%) and wood (22%), and to a lesser extent on bone and antler (16%) and on unspecified harder materials (15%). Longitudinal actions such as cutting, slicing, and sawing accounted for only 35% of the motions in general, with dry-hide cutting taking the lion's share (92%).

Only two flint corners were used in grooving, and just on bone and antler (Figs. 4.1:5 and 4.12:11). Boring was as poorly represented, with only two cases (Figs. 4.3:9 and 4.11:4). Surprisingly, the only "bored" material was dry hide, which would make the motion more like a rotative piercing action for making or enlarging holes in the dried or tanned skins. Although counted among the transverse actions, two edges seemed to have been used to chop wood, judging from the heavy, irregular, bifacial microchipping which accompanied intermittent stretches of wood polish. The right edge of the previously discussed hafted flint (Fig. 4.7) was one case. A more certain example was the proximal-right edge of Figure 4.11:5, which is off-set obliquely in just the right manner for chopping when the tool is held in the right hand.

Seven IUZ bore well-developed traces of what must be gritty finger prehension, to extrapolate from evidence on prehended edges on experimental pieces. Furthermore, the traces occurred in areas which would be contacted by the fingers given the presence of use-wear polishes on other edges of the same tools. Where the prehension traces occurred on lateral edges (Figs. 4.1:1; 4.11:6; 4.13:5, 14), the crest of the prehended edge consistently displayed a light degree of rounding. The immediate edge areas on either side of the edges bore (a) short deep striations which were oriented mainly parallel to the edge but also diagonally and perpendicularly in some cases, and (b) small patches of generic weak polish and/or smooth-pitted polish. The dorsal ridges of three flints (Figs. 4.1:7; 4.2:13; 4.3:10) bore definite, well-developed grit polish (dull, very pitted, and rough) with principally parallel striations (Plates 107, 108). Both the grit polish and the striations were limited to the area immediately adjacent to the crest of the ridges. Each of the above pieces with prehension traces on lateral edges or dorsal ridges bore at least one IUZ which had been used on dry hide with added grit. This helps to explain the gritty nature of the traces from finger prehension. The only other case of prehension traces involved a long blade (Fig. 4.1:10) whose 120° dorsal ridge bore the typical polish from dry hide with grit, along with striations running parallel to the ridge. Since a ridge of such an obtuse angle could not have served to cut or to incise dry hide, the traces were interpreted to be the result of manual prehension of the tool with a leather hand pad.

Hafting traces were seen on only three IUZ, all pertaining to the large "axe" flake discussed above (Figs. 4.7 and 4.8). It is possible that some of the

observations involving "uncertain" actions (N = 7 IUZ; Table 4.2) or "unfamiliar" micropolishes (N = 6 IUZ; Table 4.1) could be related to hafting, since no hafting experiments were conducted in the tool-use tests.

Contact Surface and Angle. Since such a large proportion of IUZ were involved in transverse actions (60%; Table 4.2), it would be of interest to establish preferences for any of the possible combinations of contact surface (ventral or dorsal) and relative contact angles of the flint to the worked-material surface (low-medium or high contact angle). The overwhelming majority (73%) of the IUZ used in transverse motions was performed with the ventral surface down, that is, facing the object being worked (Table 4.3). In the case of bone and antler, dry hide, and unspecified harder materials, low-medium contact angles (0–75°) and high contact angles (76°–90°) were of about equal frequency. Even the retouched proximal and distal ends of end-scrapers showed no preference for low-medium contact angles (N = 6) or for high contact angles (n = 7) in scraping or softening dry hides. However, low-medium contact angles were definitely preferred for transverse wood-working with the ventral surface down (74%). Of the minority of cases (27%) where the dorsal surface of the flint edge was facing the worked material (Table 4.3), bone and antler showed some preference for high contact angles, but wood, dry hide, and unspecified harder materials for low-medium contact angles.

Edge Angles. There also appear to have been preferences in the edge angles used for certain kinds of tasks, a point which has been well documented in ethnoarchaeological studies of stone-tool use (Gould 1978, 1980; Hayden 1977, 1979a; Strathern 1969; White 1969; White and Thomas 1972; White et al., 1977). For the Cassegros flints, a maximum and a minimum edge angle reading were taken for each IUZ, since not every part of a used edge always has the same thickness. Measurements were made with a simple plastic goniometer and were registered by 10° groups (e.g., 20 ± 5°, 30 ± 5°, etc.).

Tables 4.4 and 4.5 present the data from the Cassegros, level 10, flints with respect to edge angles, use motion, and worked materials. For the edges used transversely (Table 4.4), the patterns from both the maximum and the minimum edge angles were virtually identical in the cases of bone/antler and unspecified harder materials. For these hard substances, the higher edge angles were usually chosen, most likely because they are more solid edges. Specifically, 85% of the edges which worked bone and antler transversely measured 85° or greater, 70% to 75% of the edges used transversely on unspecified harder materials measured more than 75°. Wood and dry hide, however, were worked transversely with a wide range of angles, namely, from 35° to 95° in 89% of the wood-working edges and from 35° to greater than 95° in 96% of the dry-hide working edges. Thus, there seems to have been for the most part a deliberate choice of the more solid edges for working the hardest substances in transverse motions, whereas less hard materials such as wood and dry hide were worked transversely with a wide range of edge angles.

Data on longitudinally used edges were numerous enough for edge-angle comparisons only in the case of dry hide (Table 4.5). The maximum edge-angle measurements on dry-hide cutting edges usually (69%) measured between 35° and 75°, whereas the range for the minimum edge angle was usually (78%) between 25° and 65°. These data demonstrate that while the higher and obtuse edge angles (greater than 75°) were not very often used to perform longitudinal motions, they were sometimes enlisted in cutting actions (average 25% of the IUZ used in such motions). The data also reveal that thin edges measuring less than 35° were not preferred for cutting dry hide, perhaps because they would snap or chip too easily due to the resistance provided by dry hide. Thus, working hide longitudinally seems to have required an edge which had a certain degree of solidity but which was usually not too thick.

In addition to demonstrating that there were certain preferred ranges of edge angles for various tasks during the Magdalenian "0" at Cassegros, the above data also show that assessing a specific edge function on the basis of the edge angle alone is an unsound procedure (cf. Beckhoff 1970; Cantwell 1979; Hester et al., 1973; Wilmsen 1968a, b, 1970; Wilmsen and Roberts 1978). For example, edges measuring within the 46−55° range on Cassegros flints were used for scraping wood and for scraping and cutting dry hide; and obtuse angles (90° or greater) were used transversely on bone, antler, wood, dry hide, and unspecified harder materials and even longitudinally on dry hide on occasion (Tables 4.4 and 4.5).

Use Duration. The relative lengths of time for which the IUZ were used also displayed certain trends (Table 4.6). The word "relative" should be stressed, since the assessment of use duration is based on the author's use-wear experience that involved certain motions and certain kinds of flint. Kinematics, the tool raw material, and the worked substance are completely interrelated factors which determine the degree of polish development and the amount of edge rounding produced in a give use time. Nonetheless, assessments of use duration as based on polish de-

velopment and edge rounding, were attempted in a very general way (Table 4.6). The most prevalent use durations (80% of the IUZ) were the "moderate" (from a few minutes to around twenty) and "long" (up to one and one-half hours) use periods. "Very extended" use (more than one and one-half hours) was rare and seen only on edges used to scrape or soften dry hide with added grit. These "very extended" use cases are perhaps questionable, since grit is an agent which can substantially increase edge rounding and alter polish development.

Bone and antler, and the unspecified harder materials, were mainly worked for "short" and "moderate" lengths of time (a couple of minutes to twenty, more or less), whereas wood and dry hide were worked primarily for "moderate" and "long" periods (from a few minutes to one and one-half hours). Thus, the harder objects tended to be worked for a shorter length of time.

Overlapping IUZ. Most IUZ (84%) were isolated on the tools' perimeter (Table 4.7), that is, they did not overlap or coincide with another IUZ (e.g., Figs. 4.1:2; 4.2:2, 5, 17). A small percentage (10%) of the IUZ overlapped slightly or connected with each other (e.g., Figs. 4.1:1, 3; 4.2:11; 4.12:14). They involved hide-working in virtually all cases. There were also 10 cases on 9 flints where two IUZ coincided completely with one another, that is the same portion of an edge was used for two tasks (Figs. 4.1:3, 7, 10; 4.2:6; 4.3:5, 7; 4.11:2; 4.12:17; 4.13:28). Again, most of the IUZ (80%) in these 10 cases involved hide-working, usually in a combination of cutting and scraping dry hide.

Such overlapping and coinciding IUZ, which together accounted for 16% of the IUZ (Table 4.7), can be seen as evidence for some degree of intensive utilization of available flint tools. The excavated portion of level 10 at Cassegros has revealed that there are far fewer flints than is normally the case for a Magdalenian stone-tool assemblage. Perhaps the paucity of flint at the site necessitated reusing pieces. At least in a situation of abundant lithic resources near a site, one would expect that an individual stone tool would rarely be reused unless it worked particularly well or unless it bore special cultural or personal significance. Comparative evidence from functional analyses of other site assemblages both rich and poor in stone tools is needed to determine whether the 16% overlapping and coinciding IUZ from level 10 at Cassegros is a significant figure indicating a degree of intensive utilization of available flint resources.

Edge State. To ascertain whether certain kinds of edges were used for certain tasks, the edge state of the IUZ was correlated with actions and worked substance

(Table 4.8). Possible edge states included unretouched edges, retouched edges, scarred edges (referred to as "utilized or lightly retouched" by the excavator; Table 3.2), break edges, sides of burin facets, and retroflexed edges.

When considered in general, the states of the used edges showed a wide spread: 40% unretouched eges, 25% retouched, 17% scarred, 13% break edges, and 5% sides of burin facets (Table 4.8A). Transversely used edges also showed a wide spread: 33% unretouched edges, 26% retouched, 19% break edges, 15% scarred, and 7% sides of burin facets. But longitudinally used edges were nearly 50% unretouched, with the other half composed mainly of equal proportions of scarred edges (22%) and retouched edges (22%). The longitudinal data thus support the common adage that no edge is sharper for cutting than an unretouched edge.

The sides of burin facets and break edges were used primarily (85%) in transverse actions, which is understandable given their generally solid, obtuse angles. A majority (60%) of the retouched edges was also used in transverse actions, of which 70% was on dry hide. Unretouched and scarred edges were about evenly divided between transverse and longitudinal actions.

Turning to the edge states and worked materials (Table 4.8B), bone and antler were worked mainly with unretouched edges (42%) and with break edges (32%), but only with very few retouched edges (10%). Similarly, polishes from unspecified harder materials appeared mainly on unretouched edges (40%) and on break edges (32%), but on only a few retouched edges (12%). Thus, retouched edges were not often employed to work the hard contact substance. Furthermore, no scarred edges exhibited bone or antler micropolishes and only rarely (N = 2) did scarred edges bear polishes from unspecified harder materials, even though heavily scarred edges have been proposed as an interpretive criterion for contact with hard materials (Tringham et al., 1974:189, 191; Odell and Odell-Vereecken 1980:101). This is perhaps due to the fact that at Cassegros bone, antler, and unspecified harder materials were worked primarily with edge angles greater than 75° (Table 4.4). The use of such edges would skew the microchipping patterns because thicker angles scar less easily than acute edges. Furthermore, water soaking can considerably alter the hardness of bone (Pfeiffer 1912:194, 1920:21) and particularly of antler (Clark and Thompsen 1953:149; Odell and Odell-Vereecken 1980:101), which would also have an effect of lessening the degree of edge scarring.

Wood-working edges, on the other hand, showed a wide range of edge states, but to the exclusion of sides of burin facets. Dry hide was worked with all classes of edge states but mainly with unretouched (39%), retouched (30%), and scarred edges (19%). The presence of *macroscopically* visible edge scarring on flints used on a soft pliable material such as dry hide calls into question the identification of "soft" substances by microscopic edge scars (cf. Tringham et al., 1974:189; Odell and Odell-Vereecken 1980:101).

As noted above, retouched edges and scarred edges did not often bear use-wear polishes from hard materials, or even from wood, but rather were employed mainly on dry hide (70% of retouched edges and 65% of scarred edges). In contrast, about half of the break edges (47%) and of the sides of burin facets (54%) were used on hard substances. The data on the use of the sides of burin facets substantiate experimental and ethnographic evidence on the usefulness of burin sides for working bone and antler and will be discussed further in the following section. Finally, unretouched edges were used on *all* categories of contact materials, but most particularly on dry hide (60%).

The analyzed flints from level 10 at Cassegros provided clear examples of two of the functions often attributed to secondary retouch, namely, facilitating prehension and rejuvenating ("resharpening") edges rendered ineffective by use-wear. Figure 4.1:1 shows an end-scraper with a retouched proximal area which bears definite traces of gritty finger prehension. Other retouched tools, particularly the side-scrapers, exhibited a used area *opposite* a retouched edge (e.g., Figs. 4.2:13; 4.5:1−6, 8). In such a configuration, the retouched edge could very well have served as a finger rest even though no certain traces of finger prehension were found. As examples of rejuvenating edges by intentional retouch, some edges (particularly the rounded ends of end-scrapers) were obviously retouched as part of the use process because the line of retouch was irregular and the degree of polish development along the IUZ varied accordingly, which implies episodes of use-retouch-use-etc. (e.g., Figs. 4.1:6−9, 11; 4.3:5; 4.5:3).

Tool Types. What traditional, typologically defined classes of tools were chosen to perform the various tasks represented by the IUZ? The retouched tool types present in level 10 at Cassegros (Table 3.3) have been combined into the following tool classes: end-scrapers, becs, burins, side-retouched blades, notches/denticulates, splintered pieces, side-scrapers, and diverse retouched tools (which include backed blades, truncated blades, raclettes, and miscellaneous retouched types). The unretouched flints have been divided into three groups: pieces with a retouched dorsal ridge (i.e., burin spalls taken off of retouched edges), scarred flints (described by the excavator as "utilized or lightly retouched" pieces; Table 3.2), and ordinary unretouched flints.

Table 4.9 shows that bone and antler were worked with most type groups of retouched and unretouched tools, particularly with ordinary unretouched flints and burin tools (each 24% of bone/antler IUZ), but to the exclusion of splintered pieces and the notches/denticulates. Wood was also worked with most groups of tool types (except side-scrapers and retouched-ridge pieces) but particularly with ordinary unretouched flints (32% of wood IUZ) and with scarred pieces (29%). Dry hide was worked with all type groups (except the becs) but especially with ordinary unretouched pieces (22% of dry hide IUZ), end-scrapers (20%), and scarred flints (14%). Finally, the unspecified harder materials were also found on most type groups, particularly the ordinary unretouched flints (31%), but not on retouched-ridge pieces.

Thus there is striking evidence from Cassegros, level 10, that each class of contact material was worked with a variety of typologically distinct flint tools, but with some preferences for certain tool types. Specifically, bone and antler, wood, dry hide, and unspecified harder materials were often worked with ordinary unretouched flints. In addition, bone and antler were often worked with burin tools, wood with scarred flints, and dry hide with end-scrapers and scarred flints. In the following section, correlations between function and typology will be considered in further detail.

Curation. Some IUZ reflected various forms of 'curation', that is, reuse and/or modification over a period of time (L. Binford 1977:34; Hayden 1975). Six percent (N = 17) of the IUZ were on edges that had been broken after a use which involved working dry hide in all cases (e.g., Figs. 4.1:6; 4.2:11, 12). There were rare examples (N = 3) of burins having been struck from part of an edge previously used in dry-hide working (Figs. 4.2:10 and 4.10:8). More numerous (N = 20, or 7% of the IUZ) were the use zones on the dorsal ridges of burin spalls, which attest to tasks—mostly (70%) working dry hide—which had been performed before the spall was removed from a larger implement (Figs. 4.10:5–18; 4.11:1). In 16% of the IUZ (N = 44), the use-polishes terminated abruptly, or were interrupted in their mid-section, by retouch that was performed subsequent to a utilization of the edge, that was again principally (90%) dry-hide working (e.g., Figs. 4.1:6, 9; 4.3:9; 4.4:5, 10). Finally, 13% (N = 36) of the IUZ were involved in what could be termed cycles of modification-reuse. That is, subsequent to an initial use on any kind of edge, the IUZ

was modified by intentional retouch, breakage, or a burin removal, and the modified edge was then reutilized. Not surprisingly, most (80%) of the IUZ involved in modification-reuse cycles were used in working dry hides (e.g., Figs. 4.1:8, 11, 12; 4.3:5; 4.11:2).

Thus, there was a fair number of IUZ (N = 84, or 30%) which showed that utilized flint edges were often purposefully modified after use, and sometimes (N = 36, or 13%) used yet again after the edge modification. Working dry hide was the principal task involved in edges which displayed curatorial activities.

Degree of Nonuse Wear. The condition of the use-wear polishes on the IUZ can be taken as a reflection of the degree of nonuse damage by abrasion, chipping, and such, that was inflicted after the edges of the flints were utilized. Even though all the flints studied from level 10 at Cassegros exhibited at least a modicum of ubiquitous soil sheen (Plates 127–132, 138, 139) and usually a few post-excavation microscars (Plates 134–135), in *no instance* was it necessary to eliminate a flint from consideration altogether because of heavy soil sheen or substantial post-depositional or post-excavation edge scarring. Some flints bearing an intense white patination posed problems of excessive light refraction in the microscope, but this was partially resolved by the use of polarizing filters.

Most (80%) of the use-wear polishes on the Cassegros flints were sufficiently well preserved to allow a "definite" determination of the worked substance (Table 4.10). Only 7% (N = 20) of the IUZ exhibited use polishes with the slight ambiguities which necessitated a "most likely" determination of the worked material involved. Polishes that could be determined only as "unspecified harder materials" were found on just 9% (N = 25) of the IUZ. And use polishes abraded beyond more specific recognition than as being due to intentional utilization comprised only 2% (N = 5) of the IUZ. Thus, only 18% of the IUZ (N = 50) bore micropolishes which had been sufficiently damaged by nonuse wear to affect the degree of certitude in interpreting the use-wear polish.

Another factor reflecting nonuse damage to the flints is the number of IUZ whose interpretable use-wear polishes were abruptly terminated or disrupted by microchipping (N = 50, or 18%) or by abrasion (N = 15, or 5%). Thus on the whole, the wear traces from intentional use of flint tools in prehistoric times in level 10 at Cassegros were in good shape.

Summary. The major task performed with the 283 independent use zones (IUZ) located on the 532 flints analyzed from Cassegros, level 10, was working dry hide (58% of the IUZ), mostly with added grit (88% of dry hide IUZ). Judging from the extant microwear patterns on the tools recovered in excavation during the 1973–1979 season, the working of wood, bone and antler, and unspecified harder materials played relatively minor roles (13%, 11% and 9%, respectively). Transverse actions such as scraping, planing, and whittling predominated (60%) over the longitudinal motions such as cutting, slicing, and incising (35%) among the IUZ. Other actions including boring and grooving were very infrequent.

Longitudinal motions were performed primarily (92%) on dry hide and usually (74%) with flint edges measuring between 25° and 75°. Transverse actions on hard substances such as bone/antler and unspecified harder materials were usually (85%, 75%) executed with solid flint edges of angles greater than 85° or 75°, respectively. By contrast, transverse motions on wood and dry hide were accomplished with a wide range of edge angles, namely, from 35° to 95° or greater. But regardless of the material being worked by a flint edge moving transversely across it, the majority (73%) of transverse actions were performed with the ventral surface of the working edge facing (i.e., in contact with) the worked material. A low-medium contact angle (0–75°) of the ventral face to the worked surface was preferred (74%) in transverse motions on wood, whereas low-medium and high (greater than 75°) contact angles were of about equal frequency in the transverse working of bone and antler, dry hide, and unspecified harder materials. Substances were generally worked for "moderate" or "long" durations, that is, from a few minutes to around an hour and a half, to extrapolate from experimental evidence. Hard substances such as bone, antler, and unspecified harder materials tended to be worked for a shorter length of time than less hard materials such as wood and dry hide.

The same section of an edge was sometimes used for two different tasks, one of which was usually working dry hide. This resulted in a not insignificant proportion (16%) of overlapping or completely coinciding IUZ. In general, a variety of tasks was performed on each kind of edge such as unretouched edges, retouched edges, scarred edges, and break edges. Nevertheless, certain kinds of edge states were preferred for certain tasks. For example, use-wear polishes from hard materials (bone, antler, unspecified harder materials) were usually (71%) found on either unretouched edges or break edges, whereas retouched edges and scarred edges usually (70%, 65%) bore polishes from dry hide. Similarly, every class of contact substance was worked with a variety of typologically

distinct tools. But there were some preferences for accomplishing tasks with certain tool types, too. For instance, bone and antler were often (48% of their IUZ) worked with ordinary unretouched flints or with burin tools; wood was usually (61% of its IUZ) worked with scarred flints or ordinary unretouched pieces; and dry hide was usually (56%) worked with end-scrapers, scarred pieces, or ordinary unretouched flints. Finally, a fair number of edges (N = 84, or 30% of the IUZ) were purposefully modified after use, and even reused following the modification (N = 36, or 13%). Dry-hide working was always the principal task involved in the edges which underwent curatorial activities.

Patterns of edge utilization on the analyzed flints from the Magdalenian "0" at Cassegros can be characterized most succinctly by summarizing various aspects of the *principal tasks* displayed by the independent use zones (Table 4.11). The principal tasks represented by 87% (N = 247) of the IUZ were: longitudinal actions on dry hide (32%), and transverse actions on dry hide (25%), wood (12%), bone and antler (9%), and unspecified harder materials (9%). Table 4.11 presents the major patterns exhibited by these principal tasks with respect to the variable of contact surface and contact angle, edge angle, edge states, tool types, IUZ overlapping (edge reuse), and curation.

For the variable of contact surface and angle, it is clear that in transverse actions among the principal tasks, the ventral surface was the preferred contact surface; only in wood-working was there a preference for holding the edge at a certain angle to the working surface (in the low-medium range, 0–75°). Hard substances such as bone, antler, and unspecified harder materials were worked transversely mainly with solid edges greater than 75°, whereas wood and dry hide were scraped with both lower and higher edge angles. All the principal tasks were accomplished with a certain number of unretouched edges. In addition, dry-hide working was frequent on retouched and scarred edges; transverse actions on wood were frequent on scarred, retouched, and break edges; and scraping bone, antler, and unspecified harder materials was often accomplished on break edges. Each principal task was executed with edges located on a variety of typologically distinct tools. However, hide-working was done mainly on ordinary unretouched pieces, end-scrapers, and scarred flints; transverse actions on wood were especially common on ordinary unretouched pieces and scarred flints; bone and antler were scraped mainly with ordinary unretouched flints, burin tools, and becs; and unspecified harder materials were worked transversely primarily with ordinary unretouched flints, scarred pieces, becs, and burin tools. Finally, intensive utilization of flint edges, as reflected by overlapping or coinciding IUZ and by curated edges, was exhibited for the greatest part by hide-working edges.

Function of the Tool Type Groups

The retouched and the unretouched tools present in the Magdalenian "0" flint assemblage from Cassegros (Tables 3.2 and 3.3) have been combined into the following groups:

(1) *Retouched tools*: end-scrapers (Table 3.3: #1–17), becs (#24), burins (#17, 27–43), side-retouched blades (#65–66), notches/denticulates (#74–75), splintered pieces (#76), side-scrapers (#77), and diverse retouched tools consisting of backed blades (#58), truncated blades (#60–63), raclettes (#78), and miscellaneous retouched flints (#93).
(2) *Unretouched pieces*: flints with a retouched dorsal ridge (i.e., burin spalls struck off a retouched edge), macroscopically scarred pieces, and the ordinary unretouched pieces.

Since the use-wear analysis of the level 10 flints included pieces from the 1979 excavations at Cassegros, the number of retouched tools and unretouched flints reported in the following sections is slightly different from the counts provided earlier in the typological discussion of the level 10 industry as known from the 1973–1978 excavation seasons (Table 3.3). Furthermore, the three composite tools (all end-scrapers/burins) were included in both the end-scraper counts as well as the burin counts.

In this section, the functions of the tool type groups are discussed with respect to the degree of tool use, actions, worked materials, use durations, and curation. In addition, there is a discussion of the problems raised by the patterns of use that were discerned on the burin tools and on the splintered pieces. Finally, patterns of tool utilization are succinctly summarized for each individual tool type group (Table 4.12).

Degree of Tool Use. Of the 532 flints analyzed, 158 or 30% bore microwear polishes which could be attributed to specific intentional utilizations (Table 4.22). It is more instructive, however, to delineate the degree of tool use along the lines of retouched vs. unretouched flints.

The retouched tools totaled 36% (N = 189) of the analyzed pieces. An average of 41% (N = 78) of the

retouched tools bore microwear polishes from intentional use. Side-retouched blades showed the highest proportion of used pieces (70%) among the retouched tool groups. End- and side-scraper groups both displayed about a 60% use factor. About half the burin tools (46%) and splintered pieces (54%) exhibited use-wear polishes. From the diverse group of retouched pieces, 43% of the analyzed tools showed use. Only a low 18% of the becs and of the notches/denticulates bore use-wear polishes. Among the used retouched pieces in general there was a steady inverse ratio between the number of used tools and the number of IUZs per piece, that is, only a few tools displayed a large number of IUZs. For example, among the burin tools there were 7 pieces with one IUZ, 3 pieces with two IUZs, and only 1 piece with three IUZs.

About half (49%) of the used retouched tools in general displayed use-wear on only one edge or ridge (Table 4.13). Conversely, 51% of the used retouched pieces in general bore two or more IUZ, 27% of them had three or more IUZ, and 14% had four or more IUZ. The one retouched type group which exhibited significantly different trends from this average was the end-scraper group, of which two-thirds had three or more IUZ (Table 4.12; e.g., Figs. 4.1:3, 7, 10, 11). Thus, the end-scrapers constituted the most intensively used group among the retouched tools. Only 8% (N = 6) of the used retouched tools bore IUZs whose positions on the tool coincided completely: 3 end-scrapers (Figs. 4.1:3, 7, 10), 1 burin (Fig. 4.2:6), and 2 side-retouched blades (Figs. 4.3:5, 7).

Unretouched flints made up 63% (N = 343) of the analyzed pieces, but a comparatively small proportion (24%, N = 82) of the unretouched flints showed micropolishes from intentional use (Table 4.12). However, the various type groups of the unretouched flints displayed quite contrasting proportions: 79% of the retouched-ridge pieces showed intentional use-wear, 43% of the scarred flints were used, but there was only 17% used from the ordinary unretouched pieces, which was the lowest use ratio of any individual typological tool class. It is not surprising that the retouched-ridge flints displayed a high use ratio, since the used part is the retouched or burined ridge which at one time was part of an edge on a retouched tool. The purpose for removing these pieces by the burin technique would thus seem to be the rejuvenation of a use-worn edge, at least in the majority of cases.

The high proportion (57%) of scarred flints which did not bear micropolishes due to intentional use is another cautionary note for the interpretation of edge chipping on prehistoric flints. The macroscopic edge

KEY TO TOOL DRAWINGS IN FIGURES 4.1–4.13

Markings around the perimeter of each tool indicate:

(1) the LOCATION OF WEAR TRACES due to intentional utilization

(2) the USE ACTION involved:

———————————————————— longitudinal motion (eg, cut, slice, saw)

—.—.—.—.—.—.—.— transverse motion (eg, scrape, plane, whittle)

_ _ _ _ _ _ _ _ _ _ _ _ rotative motion (eg, bore, pierce)

+   very small area bearing traces of any kind of action, including uncertain actions

. . . . uncertain action

xxxxxxxxxx.xxxxxxxxxxxxxxxxxxxxx finger prehension

————————————┤ bars at ends indicate abrupt termination to use-wear polishes because of intentional modification or accidental damage to the edge after utilization

├—.—.—.—.—

A BRIEF SYNOPSIS accompanies each Figure, giving the major aspects of the discernible function of each tool. The following abbreviations are used:

    D = dorsal surface
    dist. = distal edge
    longit. = longitudinal action
    ml = most likely
    prox. = proximal edge
    trans. = transverse action
    UHM = unspecified harder material (eg, bone, antler, reeds, hardened woods)
    V = ventral surface
    w/ = with

#	Piece Number	Typology	Independent Use Zones	Action	Worked Material
1	G26-321	end-scraper on end of blade	proximal	grip	finger
			left	longit.	gritty dry hide
			distal	transv.	gritty dry hide
			right	longit.	gritty dry hide
2	H27-313	end-scraper on end of blade	prox.-right	transv.	gritty dry hide
			prox.-left	transv.	gritty dry hide
			distal	transv.	gritty dry hide
3	G27-354	end-scraper on end of blade	proximal	transv.	gritty dry hide
			left-prox.	longit.	gritty dry hide
			left-dist.	transv.	ml wood
			right	longit.	gritty dry hide
			right-center	transv.	ml wood
4	H28-348	end-scraper on end of blade	left	longit.	gritty dry hide
			distal	transv.	gritty dry hide
5	G28-273	end-scraper on end of blade	left	uncertain	grit (?)
			distal	groove	bone or antler
6	G27-254	atypical end-scraper	left	transv.	gritty dry hide
			distal	transv.	gritty dry hide
			right	transv.	gritty dry hide
7	I27-222	double end-scraper	proximal	transv.	gritty dry hide
			left	transv.	gritty dry hide
			left	longit.	gritty dry hide
			distal	transv.	gritty dry hide
			distal	longit.	gritty dry hide
			dorsal ridge	grip	gritty fingers
8	H27-328	end-scraper on a flake	proximal	transv.	dry hide
			distal	transv.	gritty dry hide
			right	transv.	gritty dry hide
9	G27-215	carinated end-scraper	distal	transv.	gritty dry hide
10	H27-311	end-scraper on retouched blade	proximal-V	transv.	gritty dry hide
			proximal-D	transv.	gritty dry hide
			left	transv.	gritty dry hide
			distal	transv.	gritty dry hide
			right-dist.	transv.	gritty dry hide
			right-prox.	longit.	gritty dry hide
			dorsal ridge	grip	gritty hide pad
11	H28-359	end-scraper/burin	left	longit.	gritty dry hide
			distal	transv.	gritty dry hide
			right-dist.	longit.	bone or antler
			right-prox.	transv.	bone
			dorsal ridge	transv.	gritty dry hide
12	I27-220	end-scraper/burin	distal	transv.	dry hide
			right	transv.	UHM
13	G28-165	bec	right	transv.	UHM

FIGURE 4.1

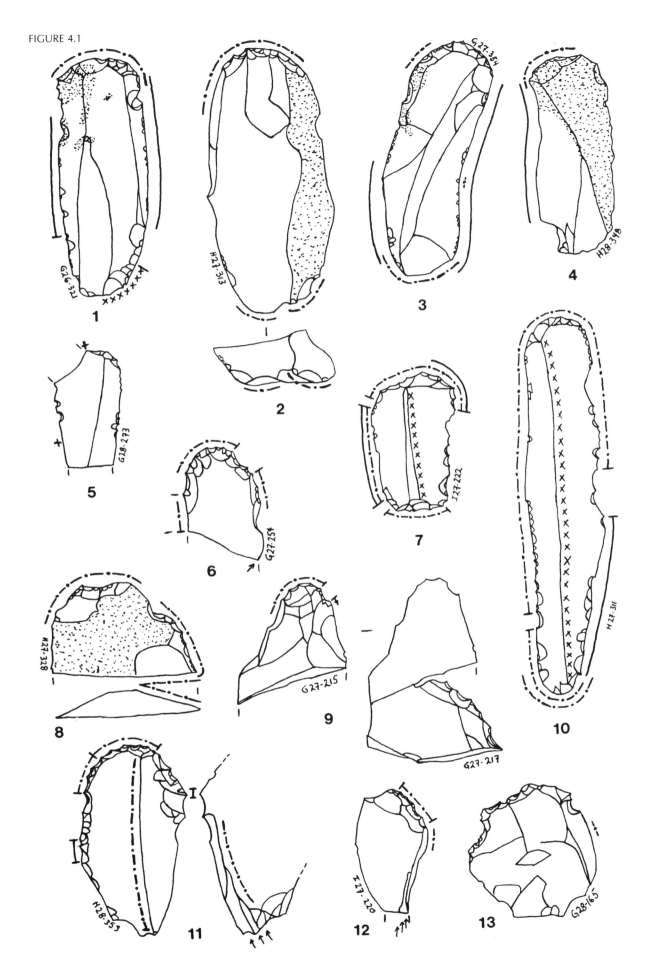

#	Piece Number	Typology	Independent Use Zones	Action	Worked Material
1	G31-47	bec	left	uncertain	UHM
2	G27-292	bec	left	transv.	ml bone
			right	transv.	ml bone
3	G26-324	straight dihedral burin	proximal	transv.	dry antler
4	H27-366	bec	right	transv.	UHM
5	H27-552	bec	proximal	transv.	bone
			left	transv.	wood
			distal	transv.	bone
6	H33-90	straight dihedral burin	left	longit.	gritty dry hide
			dorsal ridge	transv.	bone
			dorsal ridge	transv.	antler
7	H28-308	straight dihedral burin	distal	transv.	UHM
8	G27-459	straight dihedral burin	left	transv.	gritty dry hide
9	G33-87	angled dihedral burin	proximal	transv.	antler
10	G27-256	angled burin on a break	distal	transv.	gritty dry hide
			right	transv.	gritty dry hide
11	I27-339	angled burin on a break	proximal	transv.	gritty dry hide
			left	transv.	gritty dry hide
			right	transv.	gritty dry hide
12	G27-272	transversal burin on a notch	left	longit.	gritty dry hide
13	G28-210	transversal burin on a notch	distal	transv.	UHM
			right	transv.	gritty dry hide
			dorsal ridge	grip	gritty fingers
			dorsal ridge	transv.	dry bone
14	G31-42	mixed multiple burin	right	transv.	bone or antler
15	G28-243	core-shaped burin	right	transv.	wood
16	G34-27	blade with complete backing	right	longit.	gritty dry hide
17	H33-45B	blade w/ straight retouched truncation	left	transv.	ml wood

FIGURE 4.2

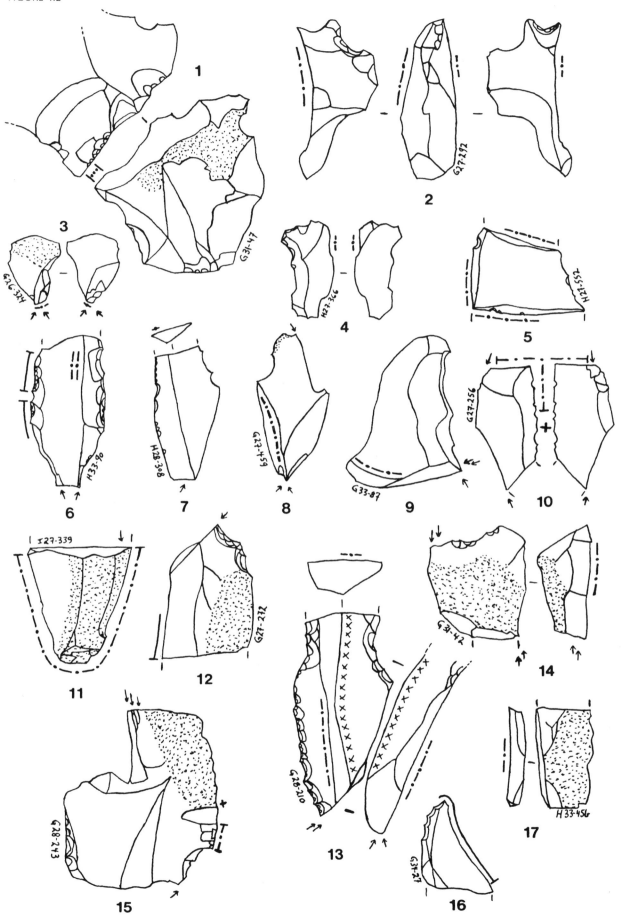

#	Piece Number	Typology	Independent Use Zones	Action	Worked Material
1	G27-251	blade w/ oblique retouched truncation	distal	transv.	gritty dry hide
2	G32-96	blade w/ oblique retouched truncation	left	longit.	gritty dry hide
3	G28-175	blade w/ continuous retouch on 1 side	left	longit.	gritty dry hide
			right	transv.	UHM
4	G28-83	blade w/ continuous retouch on 1 side	left	transv.	wood
5	G27-228	blade w/ continuous retouch on 1 side	right	transv.	dry hide
			right	longit.	gritty dry hide
6	H33-87A	blade w/ continuous retouch on 2 sides	left	longit.	gritty dry hide
			right	longit.	gritty dry hide
7	H27-577	blade w/ continuous retouch on 2 sides	distal-V	longit.	ml wood
			distal-V	longit.	gritty dry hide
			distal-D	transv.	ml bone
			right	longit.	gritty dry hide
			right	transv.	gritty dry hide
8	G27-240	notched piece	right	transv.	gritty dry hide
9	G28-182	blade w/ continuous retouch on 2 sides	proximal	rotative	dry hide
10	G27-308	blade w/ continuous retouch on 2 sides	left	longit.	gritty dry hide
			distal-V	transv.	gritty dry hide
			distal-D	transv.	dry hide
			right	transv.	ml wood
			dorsal ridge	grip	gritty fingers
11	H28-200	notched piece	right	transv.	wood
12	G34-38	notched piece	prox.-V	longit.	gritty dry hide
			prox.-D	longit.	gritty dry hide
			left	transv.	gritty dry hide
13	H28-352	notched piece	right	transv.	(undiagnostic)
14	H28-342	notched piece	proximal	transv.	UHM
15	G27-345	denticulated piece	proximal	transv.	gritty dry hide
16	G28-141	denticulated piece	left	transv.	(too abraded)

FIGURE 4.3

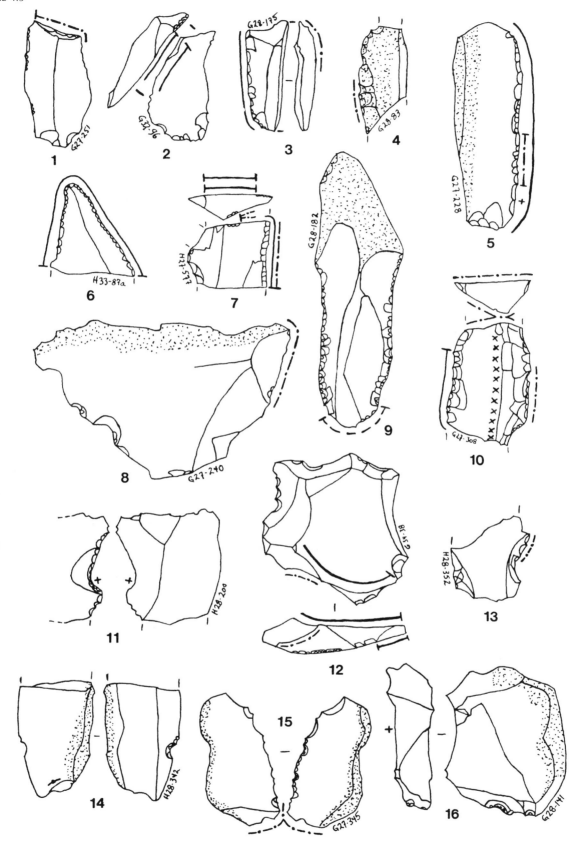

#	Piece Number	Typology	Independent Use Zones	Action	Worked Material
1	H27-293	splintered piece	left	longit.	wood
			distal	transv.	UHM
			right	longit.	wood
2	G28-136	splintered piece	right	transv.	UHM
3	I27-392	splintered piece	right	longit.	gritty dry hide
4	G27-524	splintered piece	distal	transv.	gritty dry hide
5	G27-335	splintered piece	left	transv.	gritty dry hide
6	H27-375	splintered piece	right	longit.	gritty dry hide
7	G28-244	splintered piece	left	longit.	gritty dry hide
			right	transv.	wood
8	H28-354	splintered piece	left	longit.	(undiagnostic)
			right	longit.	gritty dry hide
9	G28-76	splintered piece	left	transv.	wood
10	G27-220	splintered piece	left	transv.	gritty dry hide
11	H27-304	splintered piece	right	longit.	gritty dry hide
12	H28-310	splintered piece	left	transv.	gritty dry hide
13	H28-222	splintered piece	right	longit.	dry hide
14	H28-192	splintered piece	right	longit.	gritty dry hide

FIGURE 4.4

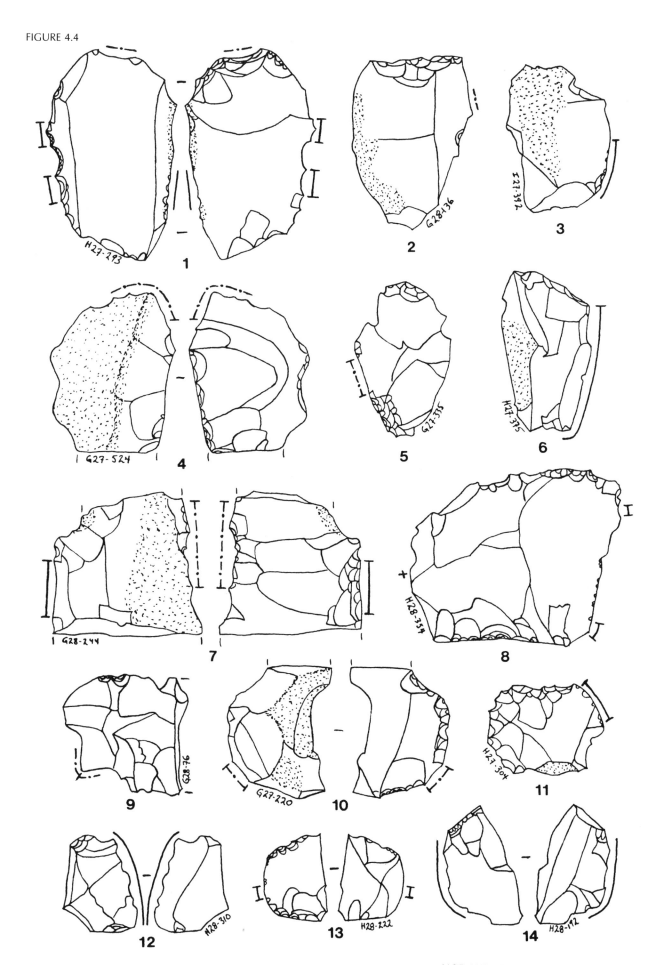

BRIEF SYNOSPIS OF FIGURE 4.5

#	Piece Number	Typology	Independent Use Zones	Action	Worked Material
1	H34-45	side-scraper	prox.-V.	transv.	gritty dry hide
			prox.-D	transv.	gritty dry hide
2	G28-170	side-scraper	left	transv.	bone
3	G27-275	side-scraper	left	transv.	UHM
			distal	transv.	bone
			right-center	transv.	gritty dry hide
			right-prox.	transv.	(too abraded)
4	G28-271	side-scraper	left	longit.	gritty dry hide
			right-dist.	uncertain	(unfamiliar)
5	H28-305	side-scraper	proximal	longit.	gritty dry hide
6	G34-42	side-scraper	distal	transv.	dry hide
			right	longit.	dry hide
7	G28-138	side-scraper	left	transv.	gritty dry hide
			right	transv.	UHM
8	I27-408	side-scraper	left	longit.	gritty dry hide
			distal	transv.	gritty dry hide
			right	longit.	gritty dry hide

FIGURE 4.5

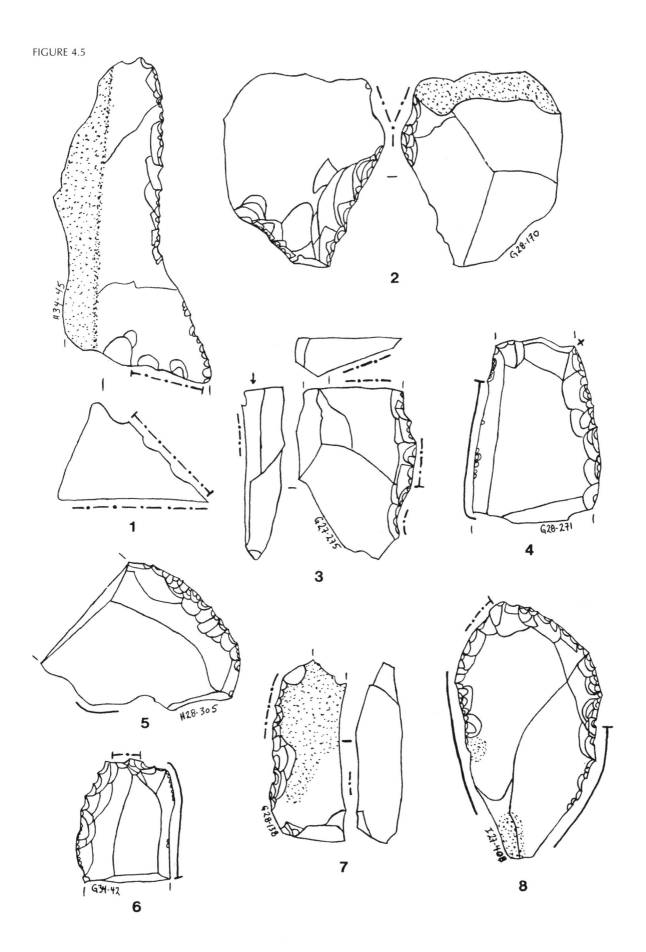

1

2

3

4

5

6

7

8

G28-170

G28-271

H34-45

H28-305

G34-42

G28-138

BRIEF SYNOPSIS FOR FIGURE 4.6

#	Piece Number	Typology	Independent Use Zones	Action	Worked Material
1	G27-493	proto-raclette	left	transv.	(too abraded)
			right	transv.	ml wood
2	H33-85	proto-raclette	distal	transv.	gritty dry hide
3	H33-105	diverse retouched	left	transv.	gritty dry hide
			right	transv.	antler
4	G26-234	diverse retouched	left	transv.	gritty dry hide
			right	longit.	gritty dry hide
5	G32-000	diverse retouched	left-prox.	transv.	UHM
			left-dist.	longit.	gritty dry hide
			distal	transv.	ml antler
6	F27-58	diverse retouched	left	uncertain	(too abraded)
7	G26-251	diverse retouched	proximal	transv.	bone or antler
			distal	transv.	gritty dry hide
			right	longit.	gritty dry hide

FIGURE 4.6

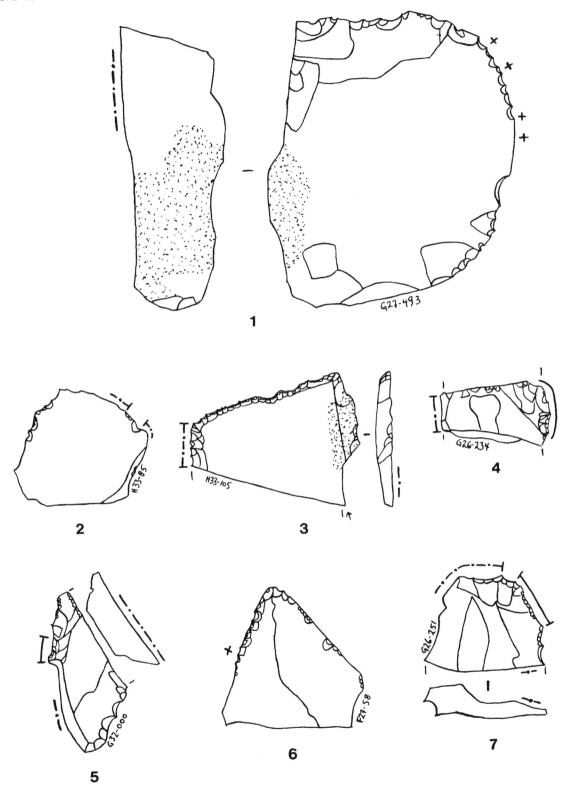

Piece Number	Typology	Independent Use Zones	Action	Worked Material
G27-497	diverse retouched	proximal	hafting	unfamiliar (wood?)
		right-dist.	hafting	plant
		right-center	transv.	wood
		right-prox.	hafting	plant

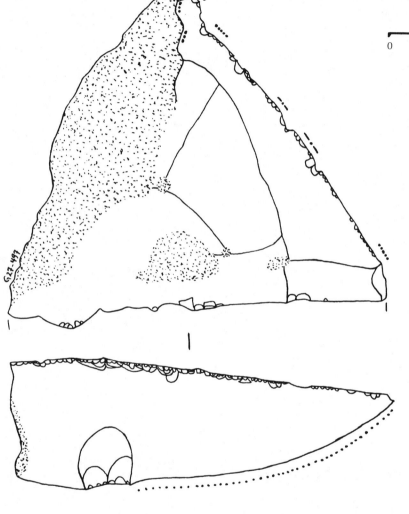

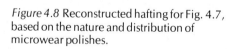

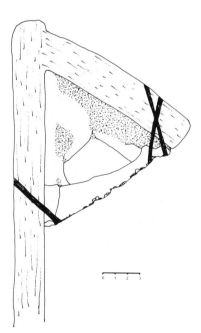

Figure 4.8 Reconstructed hafting for Fig. 4.7, based on the nature and distribution of microwear polishes.

Piece Number	Typology	Independent Use Zones	Action	Worked Material
G27-503	(core)	(distal)	transv.	gritty dry hide

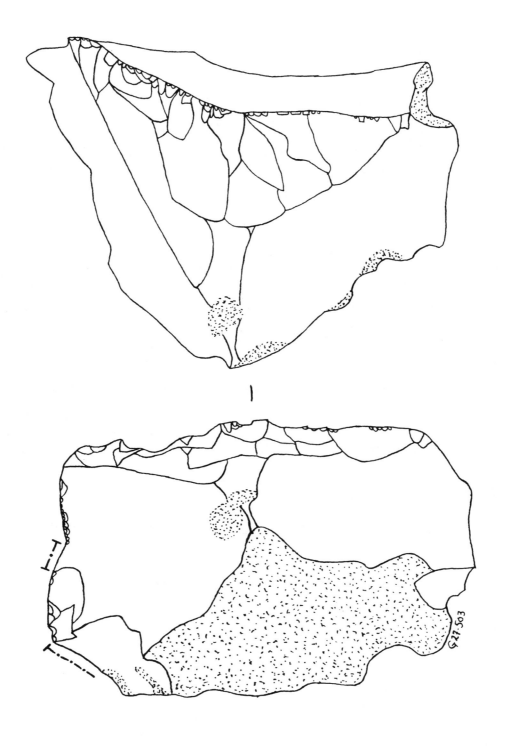

#	Piece Number	Typology	Independent Use Zones	Action	Worked Material
1	G28-174	unretouched	proximal	transv.	ml wood
2	H34-36	unretouched	right	transv.	wood
3	H33-76	unretouched	left	transv.	wood
4	G28-260	scarred piece	prox.-right	transv.	wood
			prox.-left	transv.	UHM
			left	transv.	UHM
			right-dist.	transv.	ml wood
			right-center	longit.	bone or antler
5	G27-329	retouched-ridge piece	distal	longit.	gritty dry hide
6	G27-276	unretouched	left	uncertain	(unfamiliar)
7	G31-29	retouched-ridge piece	left	transv.	dry antler
			dorsal ridge	transv.	gritty dry hide
8	G27-160	retouched-ridge piece	left	longit.	dry hide
			right	longit.	gritty dry hide
			dorsal ridge	longit.	dry hide
9	G34-16	unretouched	left-V	longit.	gritty dry hide
			left-D	transv.	gritty dry hide
10	G27-382	retouched-ridge piece	proximal	transv.	gritty dry hide
11	H28-199	retouched-ridge piece	dorsal ridge	transv.	gritty dry hide
12	I27-443	retouched-ridge piece	dorsal ridge	transv.	gritty dry hide
13	H28-233A	retouched-ridge piece	dorsal ridge	longit.	gritty dry hide
14	H27-355	retouched-ridge piece	dorsal ridge	transv.	gritty dry hide
15	G26-253	retouched-ridge piece	left	longit.	gritty dry hide
16	G28-82	retouched-ridge piece	right	transv.	(too abraded)
17	H28-233	unretouched	proximal	uncertain	(unfamiliar)
			dorsal ridge	transv.	ml bone
18	G26-222	unretouched	left	transv.	antler
			right	transv.	antler

FIGURE 4.10

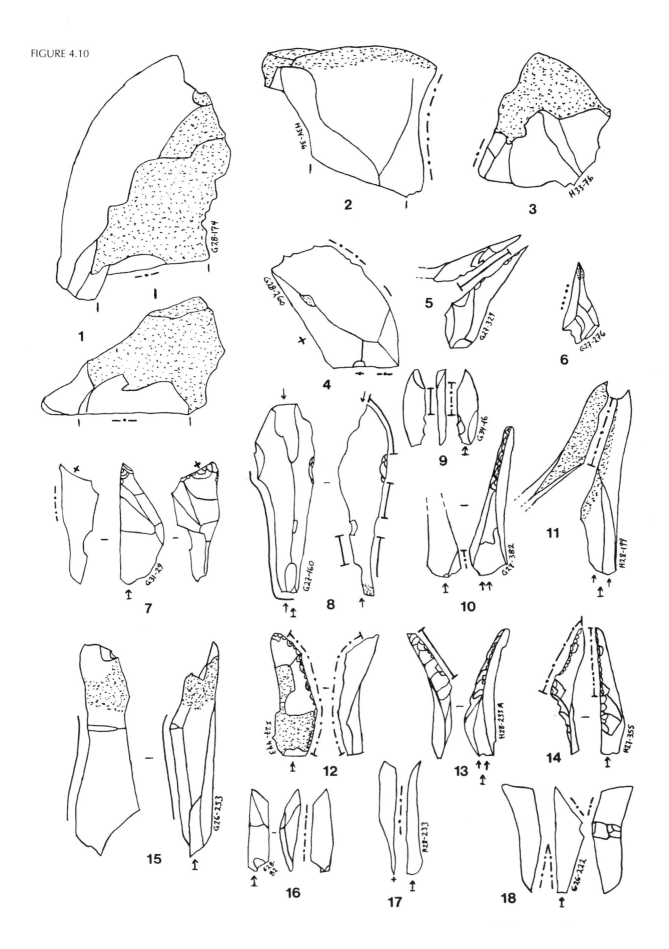

BRIEF SYNOPSIS OF FIGURE 4.11

#	Piece Number	Typology	Independent Use Zones	Action	Worked Material
1	H28-207	retouched-ridge piece	dorsal ridge	longit.	gritty dry hide
2	F27-61	scarred piece	left	longit.	gritty dry hide
			right	longit.	gritty dry hide
			right	transv.	wood
3	G28-84	scarred piece	left	transv.	gritty dry hide
			distal	transv.	gritty dry hide
			right-center	rotative	gritty dry hide
			right-prox.	transv.	gritty dry hide
5	G27-188	scarred piece	right	transv.	wood
6	H27-274	scarred piece	left	transv.	gritty dry hide
			right	grip	finger
7	G32-95	scarred piece	left	transv.	ml wood
			dorsal ridge	transv.	ml wood
8	I27-399	scarred piece	left	longit.	gritty dry hide
			right	longit.	gritty dry hide
9	G27-337	scarred piece	left	transv.	wood
			distal	longit.	gritty dry hide
10	H33-87B	scarred piece	left	longit.	gritty dry hide
			right	longit.	gritty dry hide
11	H27-254	scarred piece	left	transv.	UHM
12	G27-I72	scarred piece	distal	transv.	wood
			right	longit.	gritty dry hide
13	G27-241	scarred piece	left	longit.	gritty dry hide
14	H28-209	scarred piece	left-prox.	transv.	ml wood
			left-dist.	transv.	wood
			right	transv.	wood

FIGURE 4.11

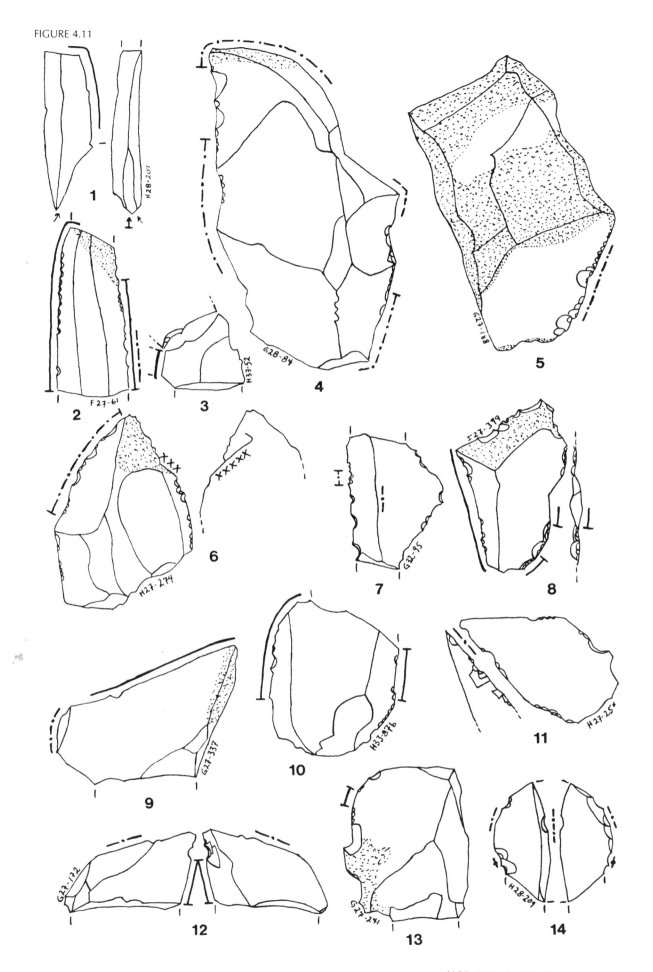

#	Piece Number	Typology	Independent Use Zones	Action	Worked Material
1	G27-357	scarred piece	left	longit.	gritty dry hide
			right	longit.	gritty dry hide
2	I27-239	scarred piece	distal	uncertain	(unfamiliar)
3	G28-224	scarred piece	left	longit.	bone or antler
4	H33-77	unretouched	left	longit.	dry hide
5	H27-354	unretouched	left-prox.	longit.	gritty dry hide
			left-dist.	longit.	gritty dry hide
6	H27-582	unretouched	left	longit.	dry hide
7	H34-37	unretouched	right	longit.	dry hide
8	G27-309	unretouched	left	longit.	gritty dry hide
			right	longit.	gritty dry hide
9	I27-429	unretouched	proximal	transv.	gritty dry hide
			right	longit.	gritty dry hide
10	G27-433	unretouched	distal	transv.	bone or antler
11	G27-331	unretouched	proximal	groove	bone
			dorsal ridge	transv.	UHM
12	H28-340	unretouched	left-prox.	transv.	wood
			left-dist.	transv.	wood
			right	longit.	gritty dry hide
13	G27-439	unretouched	left	longit.	dry hide
14	I27-409	unretouched	right-dist.	transv.	wood
			right	longit.	gritty dry hide
15	H27-348	unretouched	left	transv.	wood
16	G27-456	unretouched	distal	transv.	wood
			dist.-right	longit.	gritty dry hide
			right	longit.	gritty dry hide
17	G27-460	unretouched	distal	transv.	dry hide
			distal	longit.	dry hide
18	G33-65	unretouched	right	longit.	ml plants

FIGURE 4.12

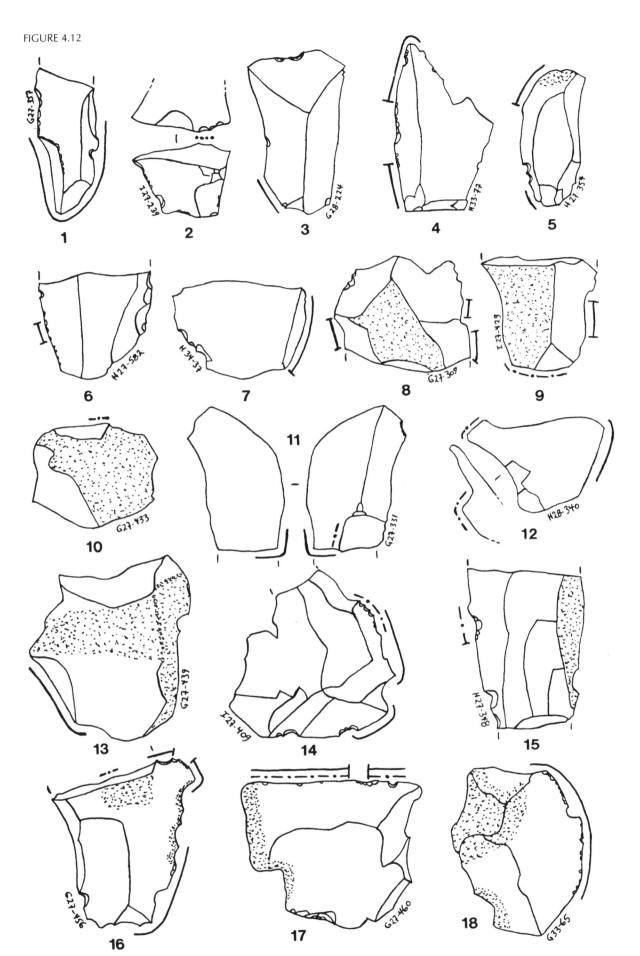

#	Piece Number	Typology	Independent Use Zones	Action	Worked Material
1	G26-311	scarred piece	left	longit.	gritty dry hide
			distal	longit.	gritty dry hide
2	G27-394	unretouched	left	longit.	gritty dry hide
3	G26-329	unretouched	proximal	longit.	gritty dry hide
			left	longit.	gritty dry hide
4	H27-532	unretouched	distal	longit.	dry hide
5	G26-265	unretouched	left	longit.	gritty dry hide
			right	grip	finger
6	G27-330	unretouched	left	longit.	gritty dry hide
7	G28-163	unretouched	dorsal ridge	transv.	bone
8	G27-429	unretouched	left	longit.	gritty dry hide
9	H33-89A	unretouched	proximal	transv.	UHM
10	H27-357	scarred piece	left	transv.	dry hide
			right	transv.	dry hide
11	H33-99	unretouched	right	transv.	UHM
12	G28-109	unretouched	left	transv.	ml wood
13	G33-47	unretouched	prox.-right	transv.	bone
			prox.-left	transv.	wood
14	H27-514	unretouched	left	grip	ml finger
			right	longit.	gritty dry hide
15	H33-46C	unretouched	prox.-V	transv.	UHM
			prox.-D	transv.	wood
16	G27-291	scarred piece	right	transv.	UHM
17	H27-268	unretouched	right	longit.	gritty dry hide
18	I27-446	unretouched	left	transv.	dry antler
19	G28-230	unretouched	right	longit.	gritty dry hide
20	H27-526	scarred piece	distal	transv.	gritty dry hide
			right	longit.	gritty dry hide
21	G27-381	scarred piece	right	longit.	gritty dry hide
22	G28-204	unretouched	prox.-V	transv.	UHM
			prox.-D	transv.	UHM
			right	transv.	ml wood
23	G28-215	unretouched	right	transv.	UHM
24	G26-204	unretouched	distal	transv.	(unfamiliar)
25	G33-63	scarred piece	dorsal ridge	transv.	bone
26	G27-273	unretouched	right	longit.	gritty dry hide
27	H27-555	unretouched	left	transv.	gritty dry hide
			right	longit.	gritty dry hide
28	G28-177	unretouched	prox.-V	transv.	gritty dry hide
			prox.-V-center	transv.	UHM
			prox.-D	transv.	gritty dry hide
29	G28-127	unretouched	left	longit.	gritty dry hide
30	H33-75	unretouched	left	transv.	gritty dry hide
31	G26-312	unretouched	left	longit.	gritty dry hide

FIGURE 4.13

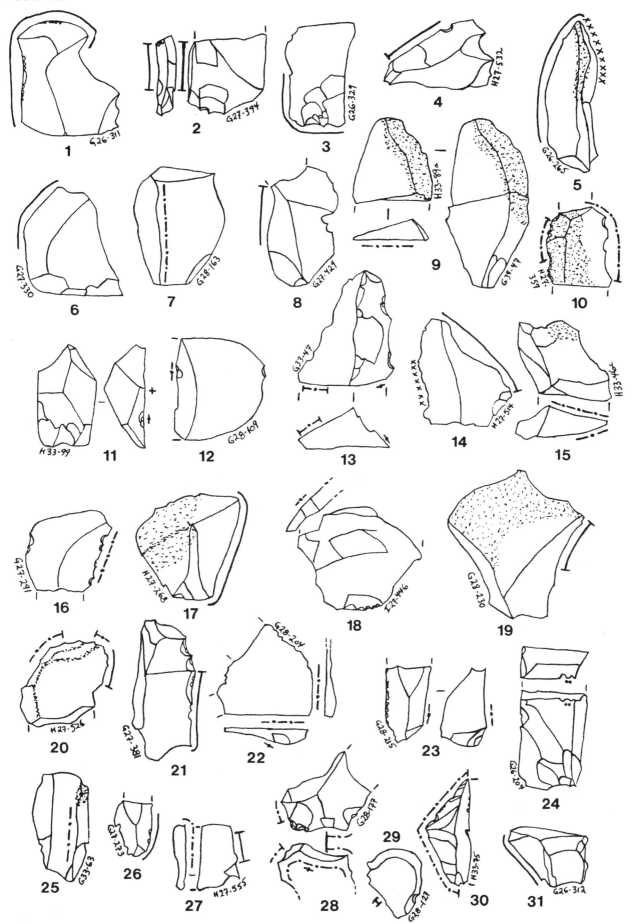

chipping on the scarred flints which lacked intentional use polishes could have been caused by accidental means in prehistoric times (e.g., rough handling, transport, dropping, trampling), by natural mechanisms in the sedimentary matrix (e.g., subsoil compaction), or even by a purposeful use motion which was sufficient to cause macroscopic edge scarring but was not prolonged enough to result in the formation of a use-wear polish and particularly one which could be distinguished from a general cover of post-depositional soil sheen over the flints.

In general, a slight majority (57%) of the used unretouched pieces displayed only one IUZ (Table 4.13). Conversely, 43% of the used unretouched flints in general bore two or more IUZ, although the proportions among the individual groups again contrasted greatly: 18% retouched-ridge pieces, 61% scarred pieces, and 40% ordinary unretouched flints showed two or more IUZ (Table 4.12). Only 11% of the ordinary unretouched pieces in general exhibited three or more IUZ, and the proportion decreases to 2% with four or more IUZ (Table 4.13). Moreover, only three used unretouched flints (4%) displayed IUZs whose positions on the pieces coincided completely: one scarred flint (Fig. 4.11:2) and two ordinary unretouched flints (Figs. 4.12:17 and 4.13:28).

In sum, retouched pieces were used more frequently and more intensively than unretouched flints. It is commonly assumed that retouched stone tools were the object of more attention or purposeful design in prehistoric times. The above findings confirm this, to a certain degree. It is also clear that unretouced stone tools *were* used, sometimes intensively (see also Moss 1983a; Cahen and Gysels 1983; Vaughan 1985a).

Actions. Three-fourths of the used retouched tools exhibited only one action (Table 4.14). Conversely, one-quarter of the used retouched tools had been involved in multiple actions, all of which consisted of a transverse motion plus a longitudinal motion (Table 4.14). In general, transverse actions, either singly or in combination, predominated among the used retouched tools. Retouched flints with a single longitudinal action were proportionally well represented only among the splintered pieces. The used unretouched pieces displayed a lower proportion (17%) of tools involved in multiple actions, but the combinations of actions were somewhat more diversified, namely, a transverse action plus a longitudinal, boring, or grooving motion (Table 4.14). The unretouched pieces were used primarily in single transverse or single longitudinal actions.

Thus retouched tools were used somewhat more often than unretouched flints for multiple actions, but for less varied combinations of motions. In contrast, unretouched pieces were used proportionally more often than retouched tools for single longitudinal actions.

Among both the retouched and unretouched used flints, the general trend was that the greater the number of IUZs per piece, the higher the proportion of pieces with multiple actions (Table 4.15). In other words, the more tasks performed with a single implement, the more likely the tool was to have been involved in *different* motions—at least one of which was a transverse action—and not just the same kind of action.

Worked Materials. The used retouched pieces displayed a greater proportion (23%) of tools with multiple worked materials than did the used unretouched flints (15%; Table 4.16). The group of side-retouched blades had the highest ratio (43%) from the retouched tools with multiple worked materials, and the splintered pieces the lowest ratio (14%) among the retouched tools. From the unretouched tool groups, the retouched-ridge pieces had the lowest percentage (9%) of multiple worked materials.

Of the retouched and unretouched flints in general that were used on only *one* kind of contact substance, nearly two-thirds (63% and 64%, respectively) involved working dry hide. The tool type groups which diverged substantially from this average two-thirds proportion of dry hide-working pieces among flints used on only one kind of material were: retouched-ridge pieces (90% on dry hide), end-scrapers (89%), side-scrapers, and splintered pieces (83% each), notches/denticulates (43%), and burin tools (44%) used on dry hide, as is further discussed below. From the retouched tools used on *more than one* kind of contact material, 89% (N = 16) involved dry hide as one of the worked substances, whereas 50% (N = 9) involved bone or antler in at least one task, and only 33% (N = 6) displayed wood polish in at least one of the multiple tasks. End- and side-scrapers, burin tools, side-retouched blades, and the group of diverse retouched tools all displayed dry hide as one of the contacted substances on pieces with multiple worked materials. From the unretouched flint groups, only 58% (N = 7) of the pieces used on more than one kind of material involved dry hide and only 25% (N = 3) involved bone and/or antler. This was due to a greater proportion of wood-working pieces (75%, N = 9) among unretouched flints used on more than one kind of contact material, giving the unretouched pieces with multiple worked materials a more diversified spread than was the case for the retouched tools used in multiple tasks. The only exception to the predominance of wood as one of the worked substances on unretouched flints used in more than one task was the group of retouched-ridge pieces, where only one piece was used in multiple tasks and that was on dry hide and antler.

Table 4.16 clearly demonstrates that *each tool type group was used on several different classes of worked materials*, singly or in combination. Some of the more notable trends from the diversity of use patterns among the tool-type groups were that: (a) end- and side-scrapers, splintered pieces, and retouched-ridge pieces were used predominantly on dry hide or in combinations with dry hide and other contact materials; (b) notches/denticulates and splintered pieces were not used on bone or antler; (c) side-scrapers and retouched-ridge pieces did not work wood; (d) becs did not work dry hide; and (e) retouched-ridge flints and the group of diverse retouched tools were not used on unspecified harder materials. Evidence for the *very diverse usages* of each tool-type group would seem to stand in contrast to the Binfords' hypothesis that individual tool types and collective tool "factors" were used in the single function or in the limited set of activities which they inferred (see Binford and Binford 1966; L. Binford 1973; S. Binford 1968).

Among both the unretouched and the retouched pieces, flints used to work bone or antler displayed only one or two IUZs, whereas pieces with a greater number of IUZs usually involved dry-hide working (Table 4.17). Again for both retouched and unretouched used pieces, a general trend was for the proportion of pieces involving multiple worked materials to increase as the number of IUZs increased. For example, among the retouched flints, 33% of the tools with two IUZs were used to work more than one kind of material, 40% of the pieces with three IUZs were involved with different contact materials, 60% of the flints with four IUZs contacted different substances, etc. The notable exceptions to this trend were the two pieces with the most IUZs (six and seven), which were used only on dry hide with added grit (Figs. 4.1: 7, 10). Nonetheless, it was generally true that if a single flint was involved in more than one task, that tool was used to work more than one kind of material, one of which was most likely to be dry hide.

Use Duration. From the relative use durations of each independent use zone on a used flint, the greatest use duration was chosen to typify the longest action accomplished with the tool. Both the used retouched and unretouched tool groups had predominantly (85%) "moderate" and "long" use durations, that is, a few minutes to one and one-half hours (Table 4.18). Still, the retouched flints as a whole had a slightly greater proportion of "short" work times, that is, a couple of minutes, than did the unretouched flints (9% vs. 1%). Nearly all of the flints which were used for a "short" duration worked bone, antler, or unspecified harder materials (Table 4.6). End- and side-scrapers, retouched-ridge pieces, and ordinary unretouched flints each displayed one example of "very extended" use (i.e., longer than one and one-half hours), but on dry hide with added grit which can skew the interpretation of use length (See Chapter 2).

Curation. Table 4.19 summarizes the presence of various curatorial activities among the used tools of the analyzed flints from Cassegros. Specifically, there were three kinds of curation noted: (1) one where the micropolish along a used edge (IUZ) terminated abruptly due to a post-use break or burin removal; (2) where use-wear polish was disrupted by intentional retouch following the utilization of an edge (IUZ); and (3) where a used edge was intentionally modified (retouched, broken, etc.) and then reused. Used edges disrupted by post-use breaks or burins were not very common (N = 15; Table 4.19), occurring on all unretouched tool groups but mainly on burin tools, side-retouched blades, and diverse retouched tools from the retouched tool type-groups (e.g., Figs. 4.1:6; 4.2:10, 11, 12; 4.3:6, 7). Use zones disrupted by retouch following the utilization (almost always dry-hide working) were more prevalent (N = 37), especially among the splintered pieces, side- and end-scrapers, and the retouched-ridge pieces (e.g., Figs. 4.1:6, 9, 11; 4.4:1, 4, 5, 6; 4.5:3, 4, 8; 4.10:13, 14). Cycles of edge modification and subsequent reuse were especially prevalent on end-scrapers, particularly along their distal ends used to scrape or soften dry hides. In some cases, the distal edge had been retouched so often that in spots the ridge of the dorsal retouch scars 'overhangs' the indented distal edge when that is viewed from the ventral surface of the end-scraper. It is well known ethnographically that the working edges of stone end-scrapers used in hide-softening were continually retouched and reused (e.g., Gallagher 1977:411; Hayden 1979b:225; Mason 1891:586).

It is important to note that the most curated tool-type groups at Cassegros—namely, end- and side-scrapers, splintered pieces, and the retouched-ridge flints (Table 4.19)—are the same groups in which dry-hide working predominated (Table 4.16). Thus the major dry-hide working tools were also the preferred objects of curatorial activities.

Burins. The functions determined for the analyzed burin tools from the Magdalenian "0" at Cassegros revealed two surprising aspects which merit discussion: the use of the side of burin facets rather than the burin tips (bevels), and the use of burin tools to work dry hide.

Thirteen of the 28 retouched flints classified as burins or end-scraper/burins exhibited use-wear polishes on some portion of the tools (Table 4.20). Dihedral burins displayed an especially high proportion of used pieces (5 out of 6), whereas the angled burins on a break and the transverse burins were for the most part lacking use-wear polishes (6 out of 8 in each group). As far as the materials worked by the burin tools, the used end-scraper/burins (N = 2), the used dihedral burins (N = 5), and the used transversal burins (N = 2) were employed on a diversity of worked materials including bone/antler, unspecified harder materials, and dry hide (Table 4.20). The two used angle burins on a break displayed only dry hide polishes; the only used multiple burin displayed a bone or antler polish, and the single core-shaped burin was the only burin to exhibit a wood micropolish.

In only one of the 13 cases of used burin tools did the burin tip or bevel bear use-wear traces, namely from a transverse motion on antler (Fig. 4.2:3, a straight dihedral burin). On 8 of the used burins, the sides of the burin facets bore use polishes: from gritty dry hide in 4 cases (Figs. 4.2:6, 8, 11, 13) and from bone, antler, or an unspecified harder material in the other four cases (Figs. 4.1:11, 12; 4.2:9, 14). Of the four remaining used burins, edges other than those formed by the burin removals bore use-wear polishes from wood (Fig. 4.2:15), dry hide (Figs. 4.2:10, 12), an unspecified harder material (Fig. 4.2:7), and from gritty finger prehension (Fig. 4.2:13).

The extremely sparse evidence for the use of the burin tip or bevel at Cassegros may only be a function of the small sample of burins bearing use-wear traces, but it is still surprising in view of the traditional emphasis on the burin tip in typological and functional studies of burins as a tool class. Since the 1860s, the central focus of attempts to classify burins has been the shape and position of the burin bevel and the method of preparing the surface from which the burin spall is removed (Brézillon 1977:615–673). L. Pradel (1966:486), for example, has been explicit in his emphasis on the morphological study of the burin tip because "c'est la partie active" (it is the active part) of the burin, in his estimation. Likewise, H. Movius et al., (1968:22) assumed that the burin tip is "functionally crucial" because "the ultimate purpose to which the various techniques of manufacture are directed is the burin edge."

Experimental studies in the use of the burin bevel by L. Leguay in the 1870s and by D. Peyrony in the early 1900s established what became the generally accepted notion of the function of the burin tip: to produce engravings and sculpture in stone, bone, and antler and to make deep grooves in bone, antler, and ivory for removal of tool blanks by the groove-and-splinter technique (Movius 1968:312–315). More recently, F. Bordes (1970a:108) and M. Dauvois (1977: 279–282) have also demonstrated experimentally that burin tips are well suited for tracing lines and making grooves in bone and antler. Wear traces such as microchipping, crushing, rounding, and polish in the area of the bevel or tip on prehistoric burins have been noted, for example, by J. Allain (1979), L. Keeley 1978a; in Audouze et al. 1981), M. Lenoir (1970, 1978), J. Massaud (1972), E. Moss (1983a), Movius and David (1970), and D. Seitzer (1977–1978).

The use of the sides of burin facets, however, is not entirely undocumented. F. Bordes (1965), D. Crabtree and E. Davis (1968:426), B. Hayden (1977:185), M. Newcomer (1974:149), and A. Rigaud (1972:106) all found experimental burin sides to be surprisingly effective in scraping or finishing the surfaces of bone and antler tools, much more so than the unretouched edge of a flake or blade. As to the use-wear which was produced in these experiments, the researchers made macroscopic observations only, but they did note the complete absence of macroscopic edge scarring in some cases and the presence of tiny microchipping along the used sides of the burin facets in others. Thus, microwear investigations relying principally upon microscarring (especially as viewed macroscopically) would be at a disadvantage in detecting the use of the sides of burin facets in comparison with microscopic examination of edge scarring in conjuncion with the high-power microscopic examinations of use polishes. Nonetheless, A. Leroi-Gourhan and M. Brézillon (1966:301–302) and L. Pradel (1973a:30; 1973b:91, 95) have found that patterned microscarring was sometimes localized on the sides of burin facets of prehistoric burin tools. In addition, edge rounding and striations visible macroscopically or at low magnification have also been employed successfully to detect the use of the sides of burin facets particularly by Bosinski and Hahn (1972), R. Feustel (1974), Peyrony et al. (1949), S. Semenov (1964: 99–100), and I. Zeiler (1981). More recently, H. Kajiwara (in Serizawa 1982: Plates 60, 61), E. Moss (1983a), G. Unrath (1982: Abb. 12), and Vaughan (1985a, b) have illustrated the positioning of use-wear polishes on the sides of burin facets investigated at 200–300x magnification.

Returning to the burins from Cassegros, another surprising aspect of their functions as detected by analysis of use-wear polishes, striations, and edge rounding was their use on dry hide. Specifically, four burin tools were used to work dry hide with sides of their burin facets (Figs. 4.2:6, 8, 11, 13) and four other burin tools worked dry hide with an edge other than those formed by the burin removals (Figs. 4.1:11, 12; 4.2:10, 12). Thus hide working was accomplished not only with edges on blanks from which burin tools were made, but also with the finished burin tool product, namely, burin facets.

Of the 28 burins analyzed from the Belgian Epipaleolithis site of Meer, L. Keeley (1978a) did not report any micropolishes from dry hide, but rather principally bone and antler use-wear polishes along with some wood and "unidentified" polishes on the burins. Keeley's analysis of 16 burins from the Magdalenian site of Verberie likewise yielded principally bone and antler use polishes (in Audouze et al. 1981: 136), as did his analysis of two burins from Pincevent (in Cahen, Karlin et al. 1980:241). E. Moss (1983a: 201f), however, found that various parts on 8 of 17 burins from Pincevent bore use polishes from working dry hide, whereas on 10 burins there were found traces of use on bone or antler. Functional analysis of Magdalenian burins from Andernach, and of Magdalenian and Late Paleolithic burins from Zigeunerfels (W. Germany), has revealed hide-working traces along with use polishes from bone, antler, and other materials on burin facet edges and on ordinary edges of the burin tools (Vaughan 1985a, b).

Splintered Pieces. The unusual type of stone tool variously known as splintered pieces, squamous pieces, *pièces esquillées*, *outils écaillés*, etc., has always posed perplexing problems of both typological and functional nature (references in Brézillon 1977: 288; Hayden 1980; Newcomer and Hivernel-Guerre 1974). There is general agreement among researchers such as J-G. Rozoy (1978:942), Semenov (1964:149), J. Tixier (1963:146–147), R. Vanderwall (1977), and J. P. White (1968a) on the fact that the splintered edges were produced by very forceful percussion, which seems undeniable given the size and number of edge removals on such pieces (Figs. 4.4:1–14). But was it by ordinary direct percussion, bipolar percussion as with cores, use as an intermediate piece in indirect percussion for detaching blades, or the result of another utilization and not of intentional manufacture at all that the edge splintering resulted? The proposed functions of splintered pieces are diverse: grooved and wedged out strips of antler from tines; intermediate pieces struck with a hammerstone to split bones; use as adzes, pressureflakers, retouchers or flake-tool fabricators, cores, or for detaching sea shells from rocks; use as strike-flints for sparks, etc.

The data on the functions of the analyzed splintered pieces from level 10 at Cassegros shed some light on the issue, but by no means in any conclusive fashion. Fourteen of the 26 available splintered pieces bore

interpretable use-wear (Table 4.12), giving a total of 17 independent use zones (Table 4.21). Dry hide with added grit was the predominant worked material on the splintered pieces (11 out of 17 IUZs), with wood polish (4 IUZs) and micropolishes from unspecified harder materials (2 IUZs) also present. The splintered pieces were carefully examined a number of times under the microscope so as to document the exact relation between the areas bearing the use-wear polishes and the areas with *esquillée*-type retouch (Table 4.21). Of the 10 IUZs where the relative sequences of use and splintered retouch could be established with certainty, 6 involved dry-hide working *before* a contiguous part of the piece received the retouch (Figs. 4.4: 4, 5, 6, 8, 10, 11). The other 4 cases involved splintered edges which worked dry hide, wood, or a harder material *after* (or while?) the *esquillée* retouch was created (Figs. 4.4:1-distal, 3, 7-left and right). Unfortunately, in seven cases it was not possible to ascertain a connection between the splintered removals and the use on dry hide, wood, and a harder material (Figs. 4.4:1-left and right, 2, 9, 12, 13, 14).

The data point to certain patterns but are, at the same time, frustratingly ambiguous. The *esquillée* removals could follow or precede the utilization, but not in any consistent manner in the case of the predominant worked material, dry hide. It is unclear what dry hide working would have to do with the violent kind of percussion strokes, of manufacture or use, that are required to produce splintered retouch. It has been suggested that the dry hide polish may result from holding the splintered pieces with a leather pad in the hand (personal communication: J. Bordaz, C. Perlès). However, the distribution of the hide polishes on the concerned edges does not allow such an interpretation. Specifically, the dry hide polishes formed by longitudinal motions on edges of 8 splintered pieces (Figs. 4.4:3, 6, 7, 8, 11, 12, 13, 14) extended too far into the interior of the used edges. In other words, they indicated a longitudinal motion which penetrated the dry hide and not one which simply rubbed against the hide. Moreover, the dry hide polishes which resulted from a transverse motion with the edges of 3 splintered pieces (Figs. 4.4: 4, 5, 10) were definitely distributed in a manner that is typical of scraping hides, that is, one surface of the working edge was more rounded and polished than the other.

Perhaps hide working was not actually involved in the purpose for which the edge splintering was produced. It could be that a piece to be splintered (by whatever means) just happened to have been used to work hide at an earlier time, or that an already splintered piece was picked up and used to work dry hide.

After all, dry hide working was the predominant task among the used flints (58% of the IUZs, Table 4.1), just as it was for the splintered pieces (11 out of 17 IUZs, or 65%, Table 4.21). On the other hand, percussive action against more solid materials would account for the edge splintering and the general absence of their micropolishes. That is, as the splinters flew off the tool edges from hard contact with solid materials, so did the use-wear polishes which formed on the tips of the splinter chips. Such is what we would expect. But certainly prehistoric workers knew much more about the various aspects of hide working, or about uses of hide, than we do today. Perhaps there was a function connected with the preparation or use of dry hides which needed, or resulted in, splintered flint edges. The fact that nearly two-thirds of the analyzed splintered pieces were made of the best-quality flints found at the site may indicate that there was indeed a connection between flints with good flaking qualities and the functions of tools which came to bear splintered edges.

Clearly, comparable functional data from a greater sample of prehistoric splintered pieces are required. But it would not be surprising if "the" function of such tools turned out to be multifaceted and in some respects too complex to be reconstructed completely by present microwear techniques.

Summary. Of the 532 retouched and unretouched flints that were studied from the Magdalenian "0" assemblage at Cassegros, 158, or 30%, bore microwear polishes which could be attributed to specific intentional utilizations. The retouched tools in general were used more frequently (41%) than the unretouched flints as a general class (24% used). Nevertheless, the functional data from Cassegros make it amply clear that prehistoric unretouched tools did serve 'useful' purposes to an extent that is not traditionally attributed to them.

The retouched flints on the whole displayed more intensive use, in that 51% exhibited two or more independent use zones or IUZs (vs. 43% among the used unretouched pieces), 27% bore three or more IUZs (vs. 11%), and 14% were found with four or more IUZs (vs. 2%). Likewise, 26% of the used retouched tools executed more than one kind of use motion, whereas only 17% of the used unretouched pieces displayed more than one action. However, the combination of motions performed with the retouched tools was limited to one transverse plus one longitudinal action, whereas multiple-action unretouched pieces were more diversified to include a longitudinal, boring, or graving motion along with at least one transverse action. The general trend among all used flints, whether retouched or not, was that the greater the number of

IUZs per piece, the higher the proportion of pieces with multiple actions. Single-action tools tended to be predominantly connected with transverse actions in the case of the retouched flints but divided more evenly between transverse and longitudinal actions among the unretouched pieces.

The predominant material worked by the general classes of retouched and unretouched flints was, by far, dry hide, mostly with added grit. Among both the retouched and unretouched flints, nearly two-thirds of the pieces used on only one kind of contact material involved dry hide. The used retouched tools exhibited a greater proportion (23%) of pieces with more than one kind of microwear polish from intentional use than did the used unretouched flints (15%). Most (89%) of the retouched tools used on more than one kind of contact substance involved dry hide as one of the materials worked. A considerably lower proportion (58%) of the multiple-task unretouched pieces involved dry hide as one of the contact materials, since there was a greater proportion (75%) of wood-working pieces among unretouched flints used on more than one kind of contact substance. As a trend among both retouched and unretouched flints as general categories, the greater the number of IUZs per piece there were, the higher the proportion of tools used on more than one kind of contact material.

Table 4.22 summarizes the patterns of the frequency and the intensity of use, the actions, the worked materials, and the presence of curation among each of the individual groups of typologically defined tools within the more general categories of retouched and unretouched flints. There were wide variations in the relative proportions of used to unused pieces among individual tool-type groups. For example, only 18% (N = 7) of the notches/denticulates were used, as opposed to 70% (N = 7) of the side-retouched blades; or 17% (N = 48) of the ordinary unretouched flints were used vs. 79% (N = 11) of the retouched-ridge pieces. Likewise, the proportion of pieces in each tool-type group that was used in more than one task varied considerably, from a high of 92% (N = 11) among the end-scraper group to a low of 14% (N = 1) among the notches/denticulates. Similarly, the proportion of flints involved in at least two different kinds of use actions ranged from 57% (N = 4) among the side-retouched blades to no multiple-action tools among the becs or the retouched-ridge pieces. The relative proportions of flints used on more than one variety of contact material varied greatly from a high of 43% (N = 3) on side-retouched blades to no examples of pieces used on more than one variety of contact substance among the notches/denticulates.

Although dry hide was the major type of material

worked by nearly every tool-type group, some examples of almost every typological tool group were used to work at least two other kinds of contact substances, such as bone, antler, wood, and unspecified harder materials (Table 4.22). Thus, each typologically distinct group of flint tools was used to work several different varieties of contact materials. The most curated groups of tool types were the end- and side-scrapers, splintered pieces, and the retouched-ridge pieces. These heavily curated tool groups were also the groups in which hide working predominated at its highest levels (83–90%), at least among the pieces used on one kind of worked material. *Thus the major emphasis in the use and curation of stone tools among the analyzed flints from the Magdalenian "0" at Cassegros seems to have been directed toward the working of dry hides.* In particular, the various utilized end-scrapers (Fig. 4.1:1–12) were predominantly employed to work dry hides and to do so in an intensive fashion, judging from the large number of IUZs on the end-scrapers which exhibited dry hide polish (N = 34), the high proportion (92%, N = 11) of end-scrapers which bore from two to seven IUZ, and the prevalence of IUZs displaying modification-reuse cycles (N = 7), all involving the working of dry hides.

Function and Lithic Raw Materials, Technological Classes, Dorsal Ridges, and Cortex

Lithic Raw Materials. The stone tool assemblage from level 10 at Cassegros is composed of a very wide diversity of flints which for purposes for the use-wear analysis were divided into the following seven groups:

(1) White-patinated Tertiary flints of medium-fine to medium-coarse grain, found in limestone layers in the immediate area of the cave. They comprise 11% of the analyzed pieces (Table 4.23).
(2) Spotted yellow jaspoid flint of medium-fine texture, found 80 km to the northeast of the site but also in the River Lot adjacent to the site. Patinated portions are yellow (Munsell 2.5Y 8/6) or pale yellow (2.5Y 8/4) and are spotted white or yellowish brown (10YR 5/6 and 10YR 5/8). Nonpatinated areas are the same yellowish brown. Comprised 9% of the flints studied.
(3) Blue-grey Senonian flint of fine to very fine grain size, found 15 km to the north of the cave. Color banding and spotting make for individual cores and pieces which vary from light grey (7.5YR N7) to very dark grey (7.5YR N3) and dark blue-grey. Comprised 28% of the analyzed flints.

(4) Dark grey-black Senonian flint of medium-coarse grain, found 15 km to the north of the cave. The color is uniform very dark grey (7.5YR N3) which passes to black. Comprised 5% of the studied pieces.
(5) Grey-banded Senonian flint of medium-fine grain, found 15 km to the north of the site. The alternating color bands consist of grey (7.5YR N6) and white (7.5YR N8). Comprised 4% of the analyzed flints.
(6) Ivory to brown Tertiary flints of medium-coarse texture, found in limestone layers in the immediate area of the site. Patinated areas vary from a very pale brown (10YR 8/3, 10YR 8/4) to a tan-yellow; and nonpatinated portions are a dark brown (10YR 4/3, 10YR 3/3). Comprised 17% of the flints studied.
(7) A large number of miscellaneous flints of a wide range of dark and light colors and of various grain sizes. Each individual type was present in very small quantities, but taken together the miscellaneous flints constituted 25% of the analyzed flints.

The single most numerous flint type (no. 3, at 28%) was also the best quality flint (fine- to very fine-grained texture) and a distinctive grey to dark blue-grey in color. Nearly three-fourths of the pieces studied, however, were comprised of varying but small percentages of other flint types such as ivory to brown-colored flints (no. 6, 17%) and white-patinated flints (no. 1, 11%) (Table 4.23). The Tertiary flints of known *local origin* (nos. 1 and 6) made up 28% of the pieces studied. The darker-colored Senonian flints (nos. 3, 4, and 5) which come from 15 km to the north of the cave comprised a total of 38% of the flints. And the yellow jaspoid flint, which is found both in the alluvial deposits of the local river and also 80 km northeast of the site, comprised 9% of the analyzed pieces. Whatever the origin of the flints, judging from the débitage patterns in level 10, the size of the available nodules was generally small. Only the yellow jaspoid flint exhibited a few examples larger than 10 cm (e.g., Figs. 4.7 and 4.9). It is, therefore, probable that the yellow jaspoid flint was imported to the site as nodules that were considerably larger than those which would have been obtainable locally in the Lot River. If this is the case, then a total of 47% of the analyzed pieces consisted of imported flints (nos. 2, 3, 4, and 5).

The proportion of retouched pieces in each flint type varied from 24% (no. 4) to 42% (no. 2; Table 4.23). The flints from distant sources (nos. 2–5) displayed an average of 33% retouched pieces, which is only slightly greater than the 30% retouch ratio for the flints of known local origin (nos. 1 and 6). While the imported flints on the whole were not retouched to any substantially greater degree than the local flints, individual types of imported flint showed higher retouch ratios (nos. 2 and 3, at 42% and 38%) or smaller ratios (nos. 4 and 5, at 24% and 27%) than the average 33% retouch ratio. The flint types that were most retouched (nos. 2 and 3) are, in fact, the best quality flints, judging principally by their grain size and the débitage patterns.

The use ratios mark a range of variation that is almost identical to that of the retouch ratios: 22% (no. 7) to 42% (no.3) used pieces. It is remarkable how close the retouch and the use ratios are, particularly for individual flint types numbers 2, 3, 4, 5, and 6 (Table 4.23). The local Tertiary flints (nos. 1 and 6) showed an average of 26% used pieces, whereas an average 32% of the flints from distant sources (nos. 2–5) bore use traces. But again, some imported flints were proportionally more used (nos. 2 and 3, 38% and 42%) and others were used proportionally less (nos. 4 and 5, 24% and 23%) than the average 32% use ratio. As with the retouch ratios, the best-quality flints (nos. 2 and 3) were also proportionally the most utilized flint types (38% and 42%). The same two flints also exhibited the highest proportions (53%, 48%) of pieces used in more than one task, along with the collective group of miscellaneous flints (48%). Also, the imported flints exhibited a greater proportion of pieces used in multiple tasks (53% and 48% for nos. 2 and 3) than did the flints of known local origin (31% for no. 1; 40% for no. 6).

Among the individual tool-type groups there was also generally a wide spread of flint types (Table 4.24). Side-retouched blades and retouched-ridge pieces, however, were made mostly (90% and 80%) of the best imported flints (nos. 2 and 3). In each case, there would seem to be a specific technological reason: with good-quality flint it is easier to produce successful blades (i.e., side-retouched blades) and burin spalls (i.e., retouched-ridge pieces). In fact, one-half the burin spalls among those studied were of a fine-grained blue-grey flint (no. 3) alone, and just under half (43%) of the blades were also made of the blue-grey flint (Table 4.25). In the same way, 65% of the splintered pieces were of the best flints (nos. 2 and 3; Table 4.24). This preference for flints with good flaking qualities might be related in some way to the function of the enigmatic splintered pieces *if* splintered edges were the desired end result because the best-quality flints would splinter the most easily.

Table 4.26 clearly shows that the blue-grey flint (no. 3) made the single largest contribution in working all major categories of contact materials. For all flint types, hide-working edges generally made up the majority of the IUZs, except in the case of the yellow jaspoid flint (no. 2) where 51% of the IUZs were found to bear polishes from bone/antler, wood, and unspecified harder materials. The yellow and blue-grey flints (nos. 2 and 3) accounted for about three-fourths of the "short" use durations of a couple of minutes (Table 4.27), from which the majority (72%) involved working hard substances such as bone/antler and unspecified harder materials (Table 4.6). Furthermore, the longest use durations (over one and one-half hours) also took place on the yellow and blue-grey flints, and on miscellaneous flint types (no. 7; Table 4.27). Finally, the blue-grey flint (no. 3) was by far the single most curated type of flint (Table 4.28), even taking into account its being the largest flint type numerically.

In sum, the 532 flints studied were composed of a variety of types, of which those known to be from distant sources made up nearly half (47%) of the series. The imported flints were used to a somewhat greater degree (32%) and more intensively than the flints of known local origin (26% use ratio). The two best quality flints (nos. 2 and 3) were both from distant sources and displayed the highest ratios of retouch, use, and curation of the individual flint types. These general trends are perhaps not too surprising in that they would seem to reflect the logical behavior of working with the best raw materials even if they are not available in the immediate area.

Technological Classes. Almost 80% of the analyzed flints consisted of flakes (Table 4.29): 20% small flakes (under 18 x 24 mm) and nearly 60% larger flakes (over 18 x 24 mm). Blades totaled only 8% of the pieces, which is truly an unusual state of affairs for a Magdalenian stone-tool assemblage. The manufacture of the débitage and of retouched tools seems to have been accomplished at the site during level 10, given the presence of minute retouch chips and the high proportion (46%) of flints that bore cortex (see section entitled "Cortex" below). Nonetheless, there were only a couple of cases where flints from the excavated portion of level 10 could be refitted in the laboratory (e.g., Fig. 4.1:9).

The highest retouch ratio was among the blades (60%), and about half the larger flakes and the debris pieces were retouched (Table 4.29). The highest *use* ratio was found, again, among the blades (about 60%). The lowest use ratios were among the small flakes and the bladelets (6% each), indicating that the smallest flints were also the most infrequently used (or they were used in tasks which left insufficient wear traces). The burin spalls showed the second highest use ratio after the blades (42%), but it must be stressed that the burin spalls were nearly always used before a burin blow removed them from the edge of a larger tool. Only around a third (35%) of the larger flakes (over 18 x 24 mm), which constituted the most common technological class (57% of all pieces), were used. Among the used larger flakes was an equal proportion of retouched and unretouched pieces, whereas three-fourths of the used blades were retouched examples. Whereas 60% of the utilized blades were involved in more than one task, only 47% of the larger flakes exhibited more than one IUZ.

Slightly more than half (54%) of the tasks on larger flakes involved hide working (Table 4.30). However, a greater proportion of hide-working tasks were performed on less numerous technological types such as small flakes, blades, and burin spalls (60% to 90%). Blades and burin spalls also were curated to a greater degree, relative to their numerical importance, than were the larger flakes (Table 4.31).

Thus, blades were few in the stone-tool series from level 10 at Cassegros, but they were the most retouched, used, and curated of all the technological classes. Burin spalls were also few but showed a high use ratio from utilization before detachment, thus reflecting a basic curatorial technique. On the other hand, the larger flakes, which were numerically the most important class, displayed only a one-third use ratio. And, not surprisingly, the technological classes smallest in size—namely, bladelets and small flakes under 18 x 24 mm—were the most infrequently used.

Dorsal Ridges. Ten pieces (6 retouched, 4 unretouched flints) displayed clear traces of use on their dorsal ridges. In all cases, the ridge angles measured over 110°. The uses were varied: gritty finger prehension (Figs. 4.1:7; 4.2:13; 4.3:10), an uncertain action (prehension?) with dry hide (Fig. 4.1:10), dry-hide scraping plus gritty finger prehension (Fig. 4.1:11), and transverse actions on bone and antler (Figs. 4.2:6, 13; 4.13:7, 25), wood (Fig. 4.11:7), and an unspecified harder material (Fig. 4.12:11). Certain unusual cases deserve brief comment.

The dorsal ridge of the end-scraper in Fig. 4.1:10 bore polish that is typical of dry hide with added grit along with striations running mainly parallel to the ridge. As the edge angle of the ridge was 120°, it can hardly be a case of true longitudinal motion such as cutting or incising hide. Perhaps the microwear pattern was caused by manual prehension with a leather hand pad. The dorsal ridge measuring 130° on end-scraper/burin Fig. 4.1:11 was used to scrape dry hide with grit, but in parts of the ridge, traces of gritty finger prehension were seen superimposed over the dry hide polish. This may indicate that one or more of the four

tasks involving the edge of the tool was executed after the dorsal ridge was used to scrape hide. The ridge (115°) of the dorsal surface of the straight dihedral burin in Fig. 4.2:6 was used first to scrape bone and then afterwards antler on more or less the same part of the ridge.

The most interesting example of the use of dorsal ridges is a double one, on a flint typed as a transversal burin on a notch (Fig. 4.2:13). The right dorsal ridge (140°) showed continuous traces of gritty finger prehension. The left dorsal ridge (130°) bore a polish which I had not produced in use-wear tests, but which is identical to that created by M. Newcomer in scraping old but not dried-out bone (Keeley 1980:75, Plate 64). One would generally expect that there was always access to fresh bone, but apparently old bone was worked, if only rarely.

Cortex. A total of 243 pieces bore cortex, or 46% or the total 532 flints studied (Table 4.32). Chi-square tests were performed to detect significant differences in observed and expected frequencies of cortex pieces with respect to the variables of retouch, general use, intensity of use, worked materials, and flint variety. As in the previous use of the chi-square test in context of experimental microchipping, significance limits were set here at the .05 level (see p. 20).

No significant differences were found by the chi-square test between the observed and expected frequencies of cortex pieces with regard to retouch, general use, or intensity of use (Table 4.32). The presence of cortex on a flint apparently did not significantly alter the choice of the piece for retouch or use. Nor were any significant differences found in the observed and expected totals for cortex pieces with respect to contact materials worked (Table 4.33) or kinds of flint employed (Table 4.34). Once again, the presence of cortex does not seem to have significantly affected the overall choice of a piece in respect to the material it worked or the variety of flint of which it was made.

Moreover, no significant difference was found in the frequency of local and imported flints with cortex, irrespective of use (Table 4.35). Thus, it cannot be shown that imported flints were under-represented among the cortex pieces. If they were significantly under-represented, it might be suggested that the imported flint nodules arrived at the site already partially worked, or at least decorticated (e.g., Torrence 1979). As it was, the imported flints seem to have undergone the same decortication process at the site as did the flints of local origin. This would then accord with the highly significant difference ($p < .001$) found between the observed and expected frequencies of cortex pieces in the technological classes (Table 4.36). In normal core-reduction sequences (e.g., Collins 1975), larger flakes and cores would bear cortex more often than smaller flakes, bladelets, and burin spalls, as was the case in flint series studied from Cassegros (Table 4.36). However, there was not a significant difference in the expected vs. observed usage of the various technological types which bore cortex.

Summary. The analyzed pieces from Cassegros were very heterogeneous with respect to flint types, with a substantial proportion (47%) of the flint coming from known distant sources. The imported materials were utilized somewhat more often (32% use ratio) and more intensively than the flints of known local origin (26% use ratio). In particular, the two best-quality flints were both from distant sources and exhibited the highest ratios of retouch, utilization, intensity of use, and curation of the individual flint types. Judging from the finds of minute retouch chips in the sedi-ments of level 10 and the presence of cortex on the various flint types and technological classes, both the imported and the local flints seem to have undergone the full reduction sequence at the site.

The presence of cortex on a flint does not seem to have significantly affected the choice of the piece for retouch or use. However, not all technological classes were treated alike in regard to utilization and retouch. Even though almost 60% of the studied flints was comprised of larger flakes (over 18 x 24 mm), only one-half of this class was retouched and only one-third bore intentional use-wear polishes. Blades, on the other hand, were few (8% of the series) but displayed the highest retouch, use, and curation ratios of all the technological classes. The lowest use ratios were found among the smallest flints, namely, the bladelets and the smaller flakes (under 18 x 24 mm).

Activities Performed at Cassegros, Level 10

Functional Aspects of Tool Distribution

Soundings in the gallery behind the first chamber at Cassegros (Fig. 3.3) have revealed very little cultural material, and even within the excavated squares of the first chamber the finds become less dense toward the back (northern part) of the cave. It is necessary also to recall that the analyzed material from the terrace area in front of the cave came from all three sublevels (a, b, c) of level 10, whereas for the most part only sublevel 10a material from squares within the first chamber could be included in the study. For the following discussions, therefore, three assumptions are made. First, the flints from sublevel 10a inside the cave's entrance will eventually prove to be a representative sample of those from the sublevels 10a, 10b, and 10c within the first chamber. Second, the back portion of the first chamber will not yield significant amounts of cultural material, which means that the excavated portions closer to the cave's entrance are representative of the cultural deposits of the entire cave. Third, the distinctive stratigraphical nature of level 10 (i.e., the ocher staining) is a reflection of (a) the repeated frequentation of the site by members of the same 'cultural group', known by their lithic industry as Magdalenian "0", and/or (b) the repeated practice of the same kind of activities, by whatever people.

There was a distinct contrast in the proportions of flints recovered from the excavated area inside the cave entrance (75% of the pieces studied) and those from the squares on the terrace in front of the entrance (25%; Table 4.37). Unfortunately, the transition area between these two flint concentrations—namely, squares G29–30 and H29–31 (Fig. 3.3)—was destroyed by neolithic or protohistoric burial pits and by recent clandestine diggings. Nonetheless, if one assumes that the find-spot of a tool is indicative of its *general* place of but not necessarily the *exact* spot of utilization, then the excavated area inside the cave entrance seems to have been the focus of the majority of the activities involving stone tools during the period represented by level 10. Specifically, the excavated squares inside the first chamber contained 73% of the retouched tools, 81% of the used flints, 93% of the tools most intensively used (three or more IUZ), 83% of the tools utilized on two or more worked materials, 84% of the flints employed in more than one action, and 76% of the curated flints (Table 4.37). The proportion of curated pieces found on the terrace (24%) would seem to indicate a slightly different spatial pattern of use and/or discard for some curated tools in comparison with utilized but noncurated tools which were much less common (11%) in the excavated squares on the terrace in front of the cave.

The distribution of used pieces by major groups of contact materials (Table 4.38) reveals that dry hide working tools displayed the greatest proportion of pieces found inside vs outside the cave entrance (83% inside). Similarly, three of the four tool-type groups in which hide working was especially predominant (end-scrapers, splintered pieces, and retouched-ridge pieces; Table 4.16) were found exclusively or almost

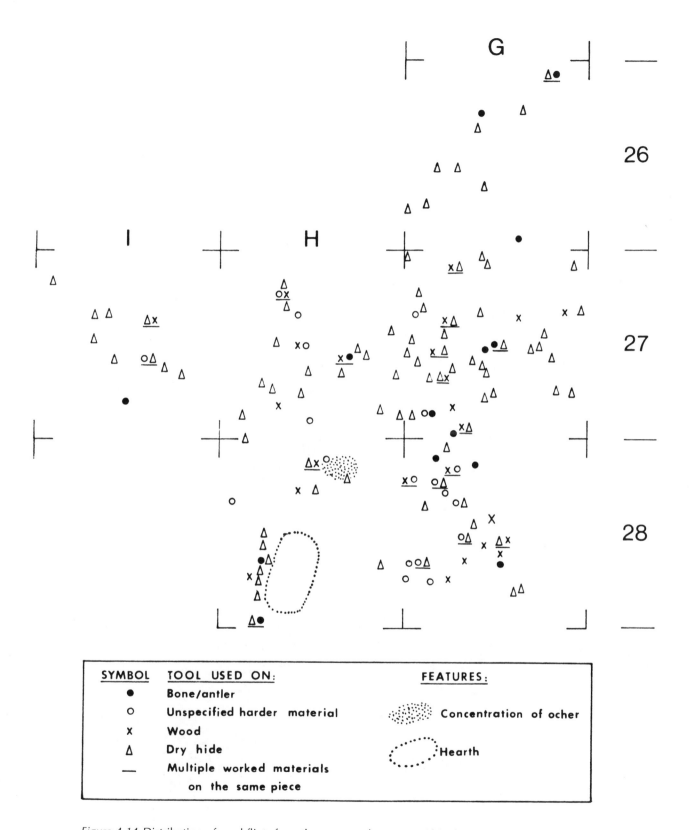

Figure 4.14 Distribution of used flints from the excavated squares within the cave of Cassegros (level 10).

exclusively within the first chamber of the cave (Table 4.39). Tools which worked unspecified harder materials and those used on wood exhibited similarly high proportions inside the first chamber (81% and 80%, Table 4.38). Comparatively fewer bone- and antler-working flints were located inside the cave entrance (67%).

Squares G27 and G28 inside the cave contained the densest concentrations of flints both in general (Table 4.37) and in the case of most of the individual flint types (Table 4.40). The exception was a concentration of primarily unused flakes of a very distinctive local flint (number 6, ivory-brown) in one square of the terrace area (H33; Table 4.40). This could perhaps represent a small tool-knapping area. Squares G27 and G28 inside the first chamber also yielded the greatest number of tools used on more than one worked material (Table 4.37; Fig. 4.14). In squares G27, H27, and I27 were found 8 of the 9 tools with superimposed mutliple use zones (Figs. 4.1:3, 7, 10; 4.3:5, 7; 4.11: 2; 4.12:14, 17). As for specific find-spots of the used flints within the first chamber (Fig. 4.14), there do not seem to be any mutually exclusive distributions according to worked materials, except that wood-working tools were rare or absent in two squares (I27 and G26). Note, however, that used tools were found around but not within the hearth of square H28 (Fig. 4.14). Thus, squares G27, G28, H27, and H28 together constitute the principal concentration of used tools within the excavated area of the Magdalenian "0" at Cassegros (Fig. 4.15).

Finally, the distribution of flints with damaged use-wear polishes corresponded to expected frequencies (Table 4.41). This implies that prehistoric, post-depositional, and post-excavation damage mechanisms were no more harmful to the flints inside the cave than to the flints on the terrace in front of the cave.

Site Activities

In recent years, archaeologists have begun to confront the issue of how representative the excavated record is of the activities actually performed at a site and of the artifacts and material remains which actually resulted from those activities. Ammerman and Feldman (1974), F. Bordes (1975, 1980a, b; Bordes et al. 1972), B. Hayden (1978, 1979a), M. Schiffer (1976), and Speth and Johnson (1976), for example, have paid

Figure 4.15 Proportion of used flints per excavated square at Cassegros (level 10). Percentages refer to the portion of the total 158 used flints which were recovered from each excavation square.

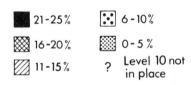

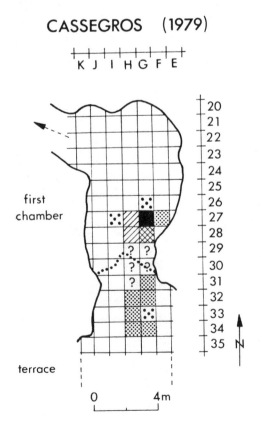

special attention to the representativeness and distribution of chipped-stone tools from excavated sites. It is especially important that the functional attributes of stone tools be subjected to the same scrutiny, since they provide one of the most direct sources of information on prehistoric activities.

The major patterns of edge and tool usage on the 532 flints studied, along with aspects of the spatial distribution of the utilized flints, indicate that working dry hide was the principal activity within the excavated portions of level 10 at Cassegros and that the work was conducted primarily inside the cave entrance within the first chamber.

The presence of stone tools used on bone, antler, and wood is not incongruous with the full range of tasks that are actually involved in preparing hides. Ethnographic evidence from various North American Indian groups (Mason 1891; McGrath 1970; Steinberg 1966), and from Ethiopia (Gallagher 1977), for example, indicates the use of wooden racks, frames, pegs, and sharpened stakes in the various stages of stretching, drying, scraping, and softening of animal skins. Among the Eskimos and the American Indian groups of the Great Basin and the Southwest, tools made of bone, antler, or horn were very commonly employed in dehairing and defleshing the fresh animal hides before drying or tanning began, as documented by H. Driver (1961:173), C. Hallock (1877:657), O. Mason (1891), K. McGrath (1970:95–100), L. Pfeiffer (1910), J. Steinbring (1966), and J. Witthoft (1958:97).

Stone tools would have been employed at Cassegros to produce and maintain any implements of wood, bone, and antler that were involved in the hide-preparation activities. Although the site has to date yielded sparse remains of manufactured bone tools (1973–1978 excavations: 20 bone tools out of 2330 bone fragments), one polished bone *lissoir* ("polisher") 10.5 cm long and four bone needles and fragments of needles found in level 10 attest to the fabrication of implements at least out of bone which could have served important functions in hide preparation. Specifically, the "polisher" could have been used to dehair fresh hides, and the needles for sewing pelts together. In fact, the hypothesized use of bone and antler tools to work the skins in their fresh state would also explain the absence of use-wear traces from fresh hide on the analyzed flints from the Magdalenian "0". Thus, the wear traces found on the flint tools from Cassegros may tell only part of the story, namely, dry-hide working and preparation of accessory implements. The *entire* range of hide-processing activities on fresh, dried, and tanned skins may well have been carried out at the site in level 10 by means of

a tool kit which included stone, bone, antler, and wooden implements.

The heavy ocher staining of the entire extent and depth of level 10 at Cassegros may be yet another indication of hide preparation. L. Keeley (1978a: 76–77, 1980:170–172) has noted that there is a very strong connection between red ocher and hide working. Some Magdalenian and Epi-Paleolithic end-scrapers with hide wear have also yielded traces of red ocher in microscopic cracks on the working edge (Keeley 1980:171; Moss 1983a:337; Rosenfeld 1970). Red ocher may act as a natural preservative for the collagen in animal skins (Audouin and Plisson 1982; Mandl 1961). And ethnographic accounts from Australia and Tasmania mention the use of a mixture of red ocher and grease as an effective protection against vermin (Bonwick 1898:24; Solas 1924:277). Traces of red ocher were not noticed microscopically on the Cassegros flints, but the tools had been thoroughly cleaned a number of times before examination on the microscope. However, it will be possible to check for such evidence on the hide-working flints from the portions of level 10 which remain to be excavated.

The very cold climate which reigned during the occupation of level 10 at Cassegros understandably would have created the need for an abundance of hides and furs for clothing, bedding, and shelter. But the cold climate may also explain why the principal area of activity at Cassegros appears to have been *inside* the cave entrance and why there was a hearth inside the cave as well (Figs. 4.14 and 4.15). J. Yellen (1977:92, 145) has reported that hide preparation among the !Kung Bushmen is carried out in an area behind the circle of huts so as to keep the stench and vermin associated with such work away from the main habitation area. In a severe periglacial climate, however, an enclosed working area such as Cassegros which could be heated would be of considerable advantage in a long and arduous job such as hide preparation.

Assuming that the excavated and analyzed samples of flint tools from level 10 of the cave are representative of the stone tools present over the entire site, one can ask whether during the period represented by level 10 the cave was a habitation site where hides were also prepared, or whether it was exclusively a hide-working site for which the main camp was located elsewhere. As explained above, the functional composition of the analyzed flints can be accounted for solely in terms of hide-preparation activities. The cave could thus have served as a hide-working location during the seasonal hunts, for instance. According to A. Spiess's study of reindeer-hunting societies, the best time of the year to take reindeer skins for clothing is in the fall, September and October (Speiss 1979:29). Detailed analysis of the faunal remains from Cassegros, and in particular the reindeer mandibles and molars, may furnish independent information on the season at which the Magdalenian "0" folk hunted their game.

But perhaps the *choice* between a habitation site *or* a hide-preparation site would constitute an anachronistic and false dichotomy for a Magdalenian hunting-gathering society. The few people engaged in working the hides within the cave could have lived at or next to the site while the other members of the group resided down in the valley closer to the game and flora that were available during the various seasons. Or

perhaps the cave was used as a 'regular' habitation site—however, that would be defined functionally with respect to stone tools in particular—during the nonhunting, or at any rate nonhide-processing, seasons of the year. The cumulative effect of a number of distinct activities being performed at a site over a long period of time is an apparent masking of most activities by the single activity which happens to involve a very large number of stone tools (Hayden 1978:199). Whether or not people lived in the cave of Cassegros, it is certain that hide working was the principal tool-related activity as attested by the functions of the stone tools and also probably by the ocher-stained sediments of level 10.

Comparisons, Trends, and Implications

Table 4.42 provides a listing of the various sites whose chipped, stone-tool assemblages have been studied in part for microscopic use traces by application of the high-power method of use-wear analysis. The diverse patterns of tool usage which have become apparent from these chronologically disparate sites—from ca. 2.7 Mi BP to ca. A.D. 1500—allow certain generalizations to be made.

(1) *Tool groups defined on morpho-typological criteria were used in a variety of tasks, especially on a variety of contact substances, although some tool-type groups displayed a strong correlation with a certain task or combination of tasks.* For example, end-scrapers were used for working mainly hides but also other materials, particularly wood, according to micropolish studies conducted by P. Genel (in Vermeersch 1982:49−51), H. Jensen (1982), L. Keeley (1978a; in Audouze et al. 1981:138−40), E. Moss (1983a; Moss and Newcomer 1982), H. Plisson (1982b), H. Kajiwara (in C. Serizawa 1982:ii), and P. Vaughan (1985a and this volume). There is a danger, however, at this early point in microwear research, in accepting as fact currently established associations between tool form and function. Stone tool types which do not at present show strong patterns of preferential usage may only be the temporary victims of inadequate sampling. After all, who has not used an ordinary kitchen knife for all sorts of odd jobs for which it was never intended? Stone tools must surely have been subjected to the same kinds of misuse (e.g., Bordaz 1970:45−46; Hayden 1977, 1979a). Therefore, we should not draw hard and fast conclusions now concerning the relationship between stone tool typology and utilization, given the present small sample of functionally analyzed stone tools.

Likewise, it is premature to conclude that there is no functional significance to subtle typological difference between tool types of the same general tool class which all appear to have been used in the same manner. For example:

It is obvious that [end] scrapers as a class were primarily hide-working implements and that the great majority were used on dry hide. It would therefore seem that the typological distinctions made within the scraper class have no functional significance. . . . The explanation for the existence of different types of scrapers must lie with some other variable than utilization. . . . While it cannot be determined whether the different proportion of end-scraper types recovered at Meer reflect ethnic preferences, hafting arrangements, length of occupation or the constraints of the available lithic raw material, it can be confidently concluded that these proportions do not reflect *discernibly different uses or activities* (Keeley 1978a:78−79, emphasis added).

It cannot be denied that factors such as ethnic or religious values and raw materials played a part in determining the overall role or function of a stone tool within an economy or society. But such factors should not be invoked *a priori* simply because a use-wear analysis cannot detect "discernibly different uses or activities" for a given tool class.

There are certain fine aspects and mechanics of stone tool utilization which *cannot* be reconstructed by present techniques of use-wear analysis. For example, making a spear in wood involves a number of tasks. The stone tools used in some of these tasks will certainly be distinguishable on the level of wood-chopping vs wood-whittling or planing implements. But the microanalyst would not be capable of detecting the use of typologically different tools for subtle yet meaningful differences, for example, in the planing/ scraping/whittling tasks alone—namely, getting through the hard outer bark, removing the stringy bast, roughing out the general shape of the spear, making the point, and giving a smooth finish. To return to our ordinary kitchen knife, who would ever deny that some degree of functional significance exists among the different types known as the bread knife, the butter knife, the butcher knife, or the carving knife, even though *all* of these types of knives are used in longitudinal actions under normal circumstances? Perhaps it was as well known to any Late or Epi-Paleolithic person that end-scraper type A was best for working redampened tanned hides, end-scraper type B for thick hides, end-scraper type C for slightly gritty hides, or end-scraper type D for softening delicate fur pelts. Such distinctions may not be "discernible" to the microanalyst, but they were certainly of functional importance to the prehistoric tool user, or to anyone who has tried working various kinds of animal hides with stone tools. Furthermore, continued modification and reuse of certain types of stone tools could have been extensive enough to leave us a record of only the *last* use of each implement. Stone-tool assemblages consisting of a large percentage of heavily curated tools would then "not be truly representative of the complete range of activities carried on by a group of prehistoric people" (Bordez 1970:45).

Thus, the limitations of use-wear reconstructions should not be equated with the lack of functional significance behind subtle morpho-typological distinctions.

(2) *Unretouched flints and unretouched edges on retouched tools were used in the full range of tasks for which retouched stone edges and implements were employed.* There has really never been any doubt that unretouched flakes and blades were utilized in prehistoric times (Bordaz 1970:45; Evans 1872). But unretouched stone tools have traditionally been relegated to the fringes of typological studies because the latter are based by necessity on techniques of edge modification by retouch which result in recognized characteristic forms. In French lithic terminology, unretouched pieces are even excluded from the class termed *outils*, (tools) (Brézillon 1977: 277), or they are qualified as a different kind of tool (e.g., *outils a posteriori*) from retouched flints (*outils façonnés*; Bordes 1970b:200). At best, unretouched flints are assimilated through a typological back door if they bear *retouche d'utilisation*, (use retouch). But since the purpose of typological classification is not to arrive at functional determinations per se, it is futile to reproach the typological system for failing to incorporate entities for which is was not constructed.

Ethnoarcheological research among stone tool users in Australia and New Guinea has demonstrated that in those regions and cultures secondary edge modification in the form of retouch was performed prior to and during tool use so as to facilitate prehension, to create a suitable working edge, and to rejuvenate worn edges, but not to create the *ideal* tool form for a task (Gould 1980; Hayden 1979a; White and Thomas 1972). This analogy is not imposed as an explanation that is necessarily valid for the Paleolithic of Western Europe, nor for the Stone Age of any other region of the world. However, that the use and retouch ratios of most of the flint types are surprisingly close (Table 4.23), should be considered as a hypothesis for future testing, given the evidence from Cassegros. On the other hand, it is undeniable that the retouched pieces from the Magdalenian "0" at Cassegros (Table 3.3) conform to many of the well-defined Upper Paleolithic tool types which recur with surprising regularity and in certain proportions from certain periods. Furthermore, not all retouched flints from Cassegros bore evidence of intentional utilization (Table 4.12). But the analogy still has merits to be considered for testing on a large sample of Paleolithic chipped-stone tools. For example, are retouched edges related to specific discernible functions which are consistently associated with individual typologically defined tool types or classes in a number of similar industries?

(3) *Despite strongly negative ethnographic evidence for the use of chipped-stone tools other than sickle elements in gathering and processing plants (Hayden 1977:182–183, 1978:184, 187; McGrath 1970:79–86), plant-cutting tools have been identified from Lower Paleolithic through Mesolithic assemblages in the Old World and thus represent antecedents to the well-known sickle elements from Neolithic sites.* Given the problem of soil sheen and the fact that plant micropolishes are slow to form on flint edges in comparison with working harder materials, the actual number of prehistoric plant knives is most likely very underrepresented in the archaeological record. For example, use-wear analysis of chipped-stone tools from Bandkeramik sites near Cologne, West Germany, has revealed that 25% of the flint edges with *micro*scopically identifiable plant polish did not bear *macro*scopically detectable sickle gloss and would, therefore, not be classified on typological grounds as 'sickle elements' (Vaughan 1985a). The role of "man the gatherer" in prehistoric economies (D. Clarke 1976) can be elucidated in part by microwear evidence for the use of stone tools in plant exploitation.

(4) Interesting as these initial functional results are, it is also quite obvious that no use-wear research

has been undertaken on a carefully controlled regional and chronological basis to document the functional aspect of technological variability and change within the context of broader questions such as the physical evolution of the human species, adaptation to strikingly diverse environments, or the change from hunting-gathering to food-producing economies. But such projects will certainly be among the second generation of use-wear studies.

In planning use-wear analyses of lithic assemblages, microanalysts and excavators need to exercise caution with respect to a number of points. The temporal, spatial, and cultural associations of the stone tools must be well controlled so that the functional data will fit into a meaningful time-space matrix. Tool samples to be analyzed should be representative of the entire tool assemblage of the site (or level) as a whole so that the resulting functional data is representative of the range of modes of stone tool usage. Not all stone tools were subsistence oriented, and not all subsistence activities required the use of stone implements; therefore, use-wear analyses should not stand alone in paleoeconomic reconstructions but rather serve as a complement to paleobotany, palynology, and paleozoology. Very specific programs of tool-use experimentation, based on many lines of available evidence from a site, constitute the optimal approach to the functional reconstruction of the technology employed in a given place at a given period (Moss and Newcomer 1982). But the credibility of any publication which contains use-wear data can be assured only if mention is made of the *specific* method of microwear analysis which was applied and of what tool-use experimentation the microanalyst undertook. Vague reference to a mixture of various use-wear analytical techniques and publications can hardly inspire confidence in the results of a functional study (e.g., Stapert 1979; Hulthén and Welinder 1981). PLEASE NOTE: stone tools suffer *considerable, irreversable damage* when scrubbed to remove adhering soil or if packed too tightly in the same bag or box.

Finally, use-wear analysis can hope to contribute to anthropological and prehistoric research only if functional lithic studies are properly done:

> Another point that soon becomes apparent is that microwear analysis is not for the dilettante. The techniques of examination are time consuming and demand attention to technical details, and the methodology behind any good microwear study must be specially constructed and carefully implemented. These considerations argue for microwear analysis being regarded as a specialist activity to be undertaken, hopefully, in special laboratories (Keeley 1974: 334).

The Cassegros Microwear Project in Perspective

The study of the functions of prehistoric stone tools has undergone a slow but steady development over the years since S. Nilsson (1838–1843) first advocated the examination of worn tool edges to interpret how they were used. Over the past century and a half, investigations into the functions of archaeological stone implements have progressed from the stage of educated but untested inference to the stages of sophisticated microscopes that allow detailed examination both of prehistoric microwear patterns and the wear traces produced in systematic tool-use experimentation.

The present use-wear project has also encompassed the experimental use of stone tools and the analysis of wear patterns on prehistoric stone implements. The experimental research was begun in 1978 with two goals. First, it sought to combine and further develop the so-called low-power and high-power microwear approaches which had recently been published. Second, the framework of controlled tool-use experiments was designed to test on a systematic basis a wider range of lithic and contact materials than had been reported by previous researchers. The test variables were chosen to gather information on each experimental tool and its manner of use (lithic material, edge angle, action, worked material, contact angle, use length in strokes and minutes) and on a number of attributes of the resulting use-wear traces, namely, edge microchipping, striations, rounding, and polishes. The results of a total of 249 tests with flakes of three varieties of flint demonstrated that the attributes and patterning of edge microscarring exhibit too much variability to be used as reliable indicators of the variables of use motion and worked material, which are of primary concern in functional analyses. On the other hand, the current experimental project verified the basic results of L. Keeley's research, that is, that diagnostic microwear polishes result on flint edges used to work certain classes of materials such as stone, bone, antler, wood, dry hide, plants, fresh hide, meat, and carcasses. In addition, the present experimental results have expanded the high-power analytical method by (a) firmly demonstrating a direct relationship between the formation of microwear polishes and the grain-size or texture of a flint variety; (b) documenting a sequence of three stage of polish development for all materials worked by flint tools; (c) establishing the existence of a previously unreported group of polishes from working reeds; and (d) greatly amplifying the details and the implications of grit polishes or soil sheen which are produced over flint edges and surfaces by natural and accidental wear mechanisms.

The experimental results were applied in a use-wear analysis of 532 retouched and unretouched flint tools from the Lower Magdalenian of the cave of Cassegros in southwestern France. The restricted size of the site and of its lithic assemblages presented an opportunity to undertake a complete functional study of all flints recovered during seven seasons of excavation (1973–1979), excluding only the pieces which were too small to manipulate on the microscope. The Magdalenian "0" assemblage from level 10 at Cassegros was specifically chosen for wear analysis because the heavy red ocher staining of its sediments makes level 10 a clearly demarcated stratigraphical entity. Thus the analyzed sample of flint tools from Cassegros was fully representative of the excavated portions of the site and was situated within a single well-defined stratigraphical unit. The study was conducted by examining the distribution, attributes, and patterning of microwear polishes, striations, edge rounding, and some aspects of edge microflaking on the flints so as to document patterns of tool utilization with reference to two basic functional units: the individual used edge (termed the "independent use zone" or IUZ) and the entire tool as a typological and technological entity. Data were collected on a total of 25 variables which covered aspects of the discernible functions, technology, typology, and provenience of the tools. Furthermore, the functional aspects of the flints were plotted according to the horizontal coordinates of the pieces so as to locate activity areas within the excavated portions of level 10.

Of the 532 flints examined, 158, or 30%, displayed microwear that was assignable to specific intentional use. The study also revealed a consistent pattern among the used tools: a variety of usages was found to be associated with each variable investigated, but in each case there was nonetheless a definite predominance of a certain manner, or certain manners, of utilization. In other words, no one function was exclusively linked to any variable studied, but still each variable displayed a clear preference for one or more functional possibilities. In regard to the basic functional unit of the independent use zones on the tools, almost 60% of the 238 IUZs displayed use-wear from dry hide, principally with added grit. Microwear from wood, bone and antler, and unspecified harder materials were found on far fewer IUZs (13%, 11%, 9%,

respectively). The variable of edge angle showed that transverse actions, such as scraping and planing, on harder materials were executed predominantly with solid flint edges measuring more than 75°, whereas wood and dry hide were worked transversely with both acute and thicker edges. While each of the various edge states—such as unretouched, retouched, broken, and scarred edges—revealed uses in a variety of different tasks, there were some preferences (e.g., harder materials were usually worked with unretouched edges or with break edges). A certain degree of intensive use of available flint resources was indicated by the many cases in which IUZs overlapped or completely coincided with one another along a tool edge, that is, the same edge was used more than once. Intensive usage was also reflected by those IUZs which displayed curatorial activities and even reuse following reshaping after an initial utilization. The greatest part of these intensively used IUZs was involved in working dry hide.

Likewise, the functional study of the flint tools as typological and technological entities revealed a variety of usages but also certain preferences with respect to each variable investigated. The highest ratios of retouch, utilization, intensity of use, and curation among the six individual flint types present in the series were exhibited by the two best-quality flints, even though these were both imported to the site from known distant sources and comprised only 37% of the examined pieces. Despite the fact that nearly two-thirds of the analyzed flints were unretouched pieces, the retouched tools on the whole displayed a higher use ratio (41%) than did the unretouched flints (24%). And although retouched tools were also used more intensively (51% vs. 43% in executing two or more tasks per piece), unretouched flints were definitely found to have served 'useful' purposes to an extent that is not traditionally attributed to them. Each typologically distinct tool-type group (e.g., side-scrapers, burins, splintered pieces, and ordinary unretouched pieces) was used to work several different kinds of contact materials, but dry hide was the major type of material worked by nearly every tool group. The most curated groups of tool types (end- and side-scrapers, splintered pieces, and retouched-ridge pieces) were also the groups in which hide-working predominated at its highest levels. This was especially evident on the utilized end-scrapers: their distal and proximal ends and even some lateral edges were intensively used and reused to scrape or soften dry hides, and their side edges were employed to cut dry hide. Thus, the functional data from both the independent use zones and from the tool-type groups clearly indicated that although the flints were involved in a variety of different functions, the major emphasis in the use and curation of stone tools from the Magdalenian "0" at Cassegros seems to have been directed toward the working of dry hides.

Ethnographic evidence from stone-tool using cultures in North America and Africa shows that various implements and accessories made from bone, wood, and antler also play a major role in the processing of animal skins. Cassegros has yielded so far remains of a few bone tools which correspond to ethnographically known bone implements which serve in various stages of hide working. Since stone tools would have been used to fabricate and maintain any wooden, bone, or antler implements used in hide-preparation activities, the presence on various flints of use-wear from wood, bone, and antler is not incongruous with the wide variety of tasks which are actually involved in preparing finished hides and furs from fresh animal skins. Thus, the entire range of hide-processing activities on fresh, dried, and tanned pelts may well have been carried out at Cassegros by means of a tool kit which included flint, bone, antler, and wooden implements.

The very cold climate which sedimentological analyses have documented for the period of level 10 at Cassegros (the beginning of Würm IV, within the seventeenth millennium B.C.) would understandably have created the need for an abundance of hides and furs for clothing, bedding, and shelter. Furthermore, distributional aspects of the tool functions at Cassegros pointed overwhelmingly to a localization of these hide-working activities within the first chamber of the cave. The terrace area in front of the cave entrance yielded only 19% of the used flints and only 7% of the most intensively used tools (those with three or more IUZs). Given this distributional data and the presence of a hearth inside the cave entrance in level 10, one may conclude that in a severe periglacial climate an enclosed working area which could be heated would have been a prime location for the long and arduous activities involved in hide preparation. If the strong association between red ocher and hide working as proposed by L. Keeley (1980:170–172) is indeed true, then the heavy ocher staining of the sediments of level 10 at Cassegros would corroborate the conclusion based on use-wear and distributional evidence that during Magdalenian "0" times Cassegros was the site of hide-preparation activities.

Part III

Plates

NOTE: Unless otherwise indicated, all micrographs were taken at 280x magnification and are printed on a scale of 4 cm = 0.1 mm.

Plates of microwear on prehistoric flints are denoted with an asterisk (*).

1. Edge row of microchipping within larger scars of a flint edge affected by spontaneous retouch (34x; 2.5 cm = 0.5 mm).

2. Deep striation on a flint dragged along a ground surface consisting of hardened loamy soil.

3. Superficial striation created by percussion strokes with an antler tine.

4. Detailed view of a superficial striation, showing linearly arranged components of smooth-type grit polish (cf. Plates 122, 124, 125); 5.5 cm = 0.1 mm.

5. Unused ventral surface of a fine-grained experimental flint.

6. Unused ventral surface of a medium-fine-grained experimental flint.

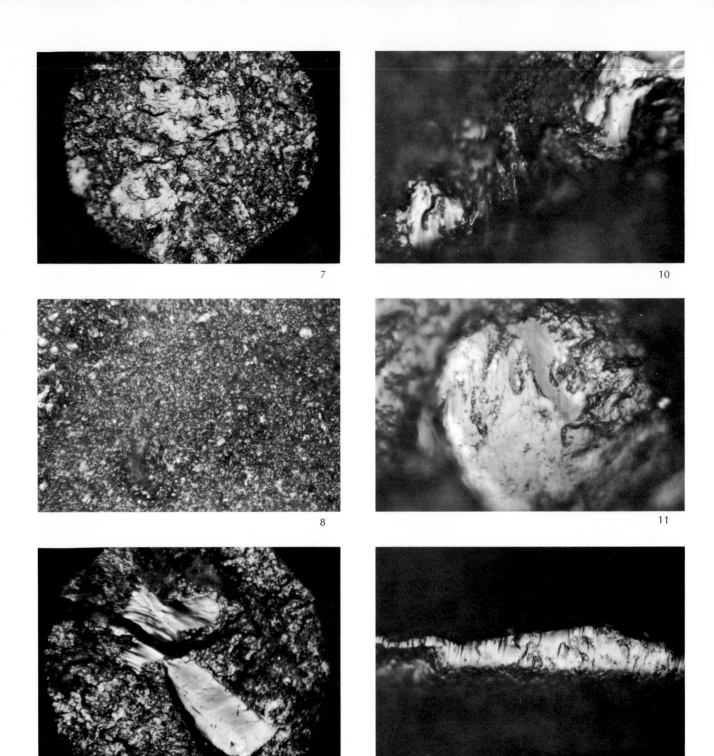

7. Larger natural reflective areas consisting of finer-grained silicate inclusions, as in Plate 6.

8. Unused dorsal surface of a medium-coarse-grained experimental flint.

*9. Quartz crystal faces on dorsal surface of Cassegros flint in Fig. 4.3: 7 (140x; 5.5 cm = 0.2 mm).

10. Worn quartz crystals in the flint matrix of the contact side of a flint edge used to plane soaked-seasoned cypress wood for 1000 strokes, 10 min.

*11. Naturally worn quartz crystal on a flint from the open-air Magdalenian site of Orville, France (Perlès 1982); 5.5 = 0.1 mm.

12. Polish bevel on the contact surface of an edge of fine-grained flint used to scrape fresh cow bone for 1200 strokes, 9 min.

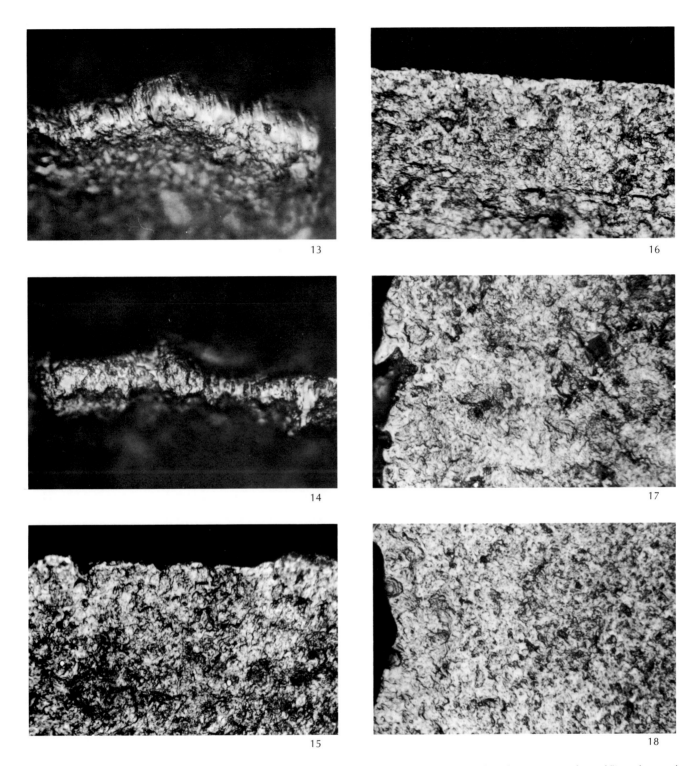

13

14

15

16

17

18

13. Polish bevel on the contact surface of an edge of medium-fine-grained flint used to scrape fresh cow bone for 1200 strokes, 11 min.

14. Poorly developed polish bevel on the contact surface of an edge of medium-coarse-grained flint used to scrape fresh cow bone for 1200 strokes, 9 min.

15. Generic weak polish on the contact surface of a flint edge used in defleshing the inside of a fresh calf hide for 1200 strokes, 13 min.

16. Generic weak polish in the contact surface of flint edge used to scrape moistened tanned deer hide for 800 strokes, 8 min.

17. Generic weak polish on the contact surface of a flint edge used to whittle fresh almond wood for 1500 strokes, 24 min., edge to left. More developed wood polish elsewhere on the same edge: Plate 47.

18. Smooth-pitted polish on the contact surface of a flint edge used to whittle fresh almond wood for 2500 strokes, 31 min., edge to left. More developed wood polish elsewhere on the same edge: Plate 51.

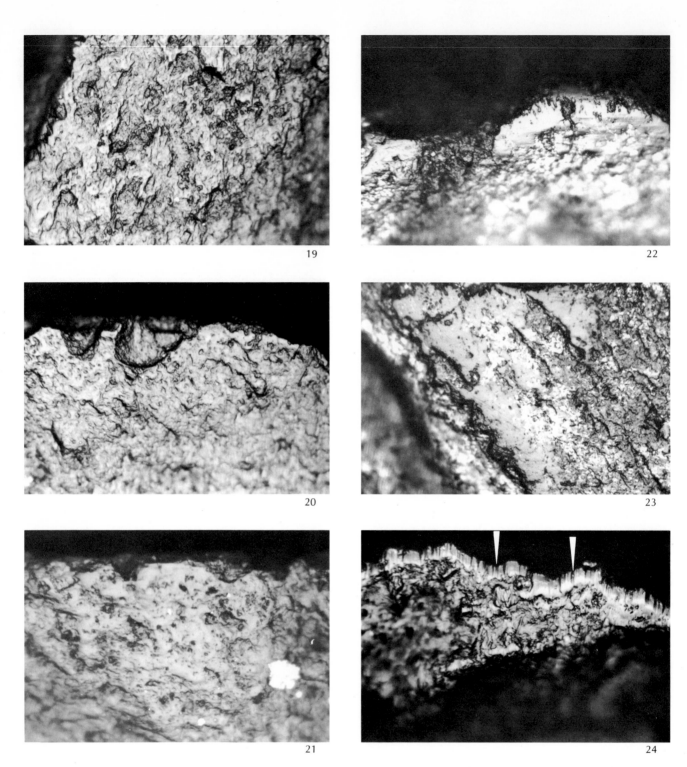

19. Smooth-pitted polish from sawing fresh reeds (*Pseudosasa*) for 2400 strokes, 19 min., edge to left; see also Plate 53.

*20. Smooth-pitted polish from a longitudinal motion in bone or antler, on the right edge of a Cassegros flint as in Fig. 4.1: 11.

21. Smooth-pitted polish from sawing soaked cow bone for 1000 strokes, 8 min.

*22. Raised polish with vague paralled troughs from prolonged bone-sawing, on the edge of a flint blade from the Preceramic Neolithic site of Mesad Mazzal, Israel (see Taute 1981).

*23. Bright flat-surfaced polish from intensive bone-sawing, on the same tool as in Plate 22.

24. Polish bevel from grooving soaked cow bone for 600 strokes, 3 min. Arrow: ''comet-tail'' linear indicators in the polish surface.

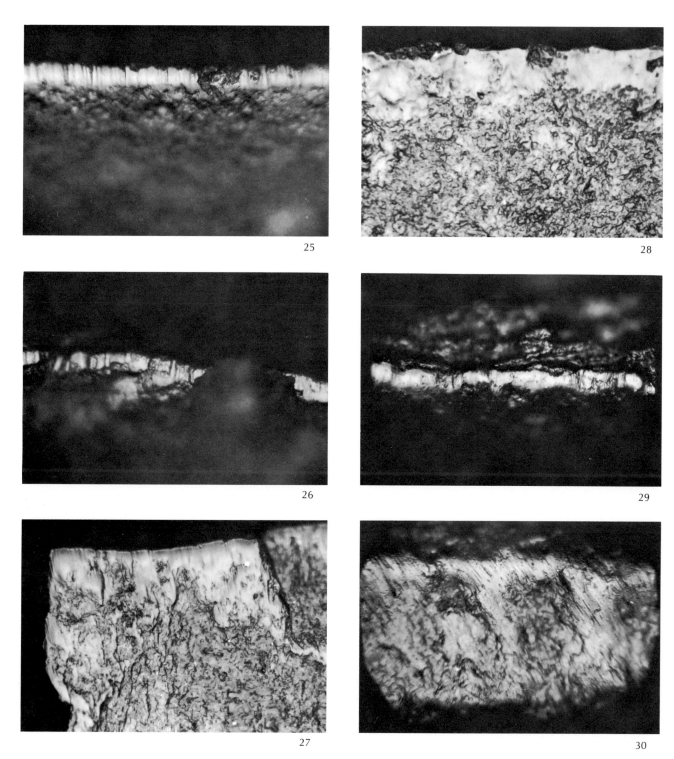

25

28

26

29

27

30

*25. Polish bevel from scraping bone, on the contact surface of the right burin-facet edge of Cassegros flint in Fig. 4.1: 11 (168x; 2.5 cm = 0.1 mm). Polish on the opposite (noncontact) surface of the same edge: Plate 28.

*26. Polish bevel from scraping bone, on the contact surface of the proximal break edge of Cassegros flint in Fig. 4.13: 13; 5.5 cm = 0.1 mm.

27. Polish bevel from grooving soaked cow bone for 600 strokes, 6 mm.

*28. Bone polish of the "flat" variety found on the noncontact side of bonescraping edges, on the right burin-facet edge of Cassegros flint in Fig. 4.1: 11. Polish on the opposite (contact) surface of the same edge: Plate 25.

29. Polish bevel on the contact surface of a flint edge used to scrape boiled then dried-out cow bone for 300 strokes, 3 min.

*30. Polish from scraping old bone, on the left dorsal ridge of Cassegros flint in Fig.4.2: 13 (168x; 3.3 cm = 0.1 mm). Determined on analogy with an identical polish reported by L. Keeley (1980: 75, Plate 64).

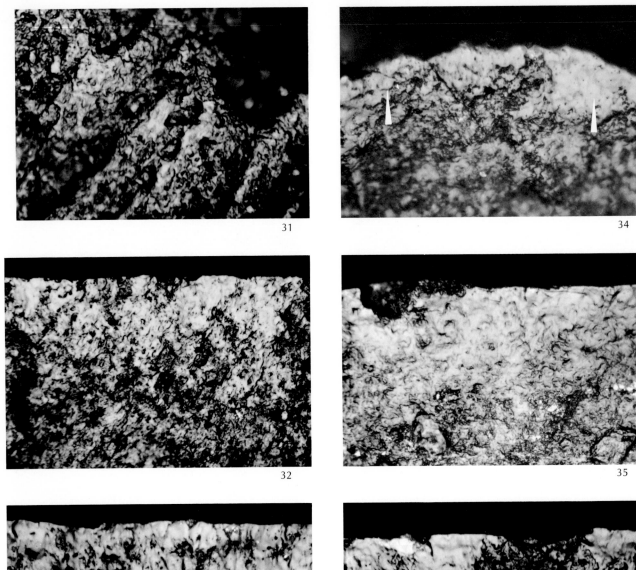

31

34

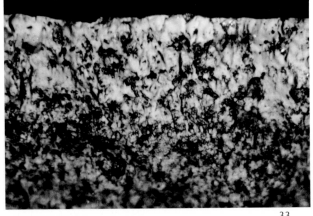

32

35

33

36

31. Smooth-pitted polish from sawing soaked antler for 1000 strokes, 9 min.; 5.5 cm = 0.1 mm.

32. Smooth-type antler polish in its initial stages of development, on the noncontact surface of a flint edge used to plane soaked antler for 600 strokes, 5 min. Polish on the contact surface of the same edge: Plate 37.

33. Smooth-type antler polish on the noncontact surface of a flint used to plane soaked antler for 1200 strokes, 9 min. Polish on the contact surface of the same edge: Plates 38 and 39.

34. Smooth-type antler polish on the noncontact surface of a flint edge used to scrape soaked antler for 600 strokes, 4 min. Arrows: "diffuse depressions" in the polish surface.

*35. Smooth-type antler polish from a transverse motion on the noncontact surface of the proximal burin-facet edge of Cassegros flint in Fig. 4.2: 9. Polish on the opposite (contact) surface of the same edge: Plate 40.

*36. Smooth-type antler polish from a transverse motion, on the noncontact surface of an edge on an Upper Mesolithic flint from Franchthi Cave. Polish on the opposite (contact) surface of the same edge: Plate 41.

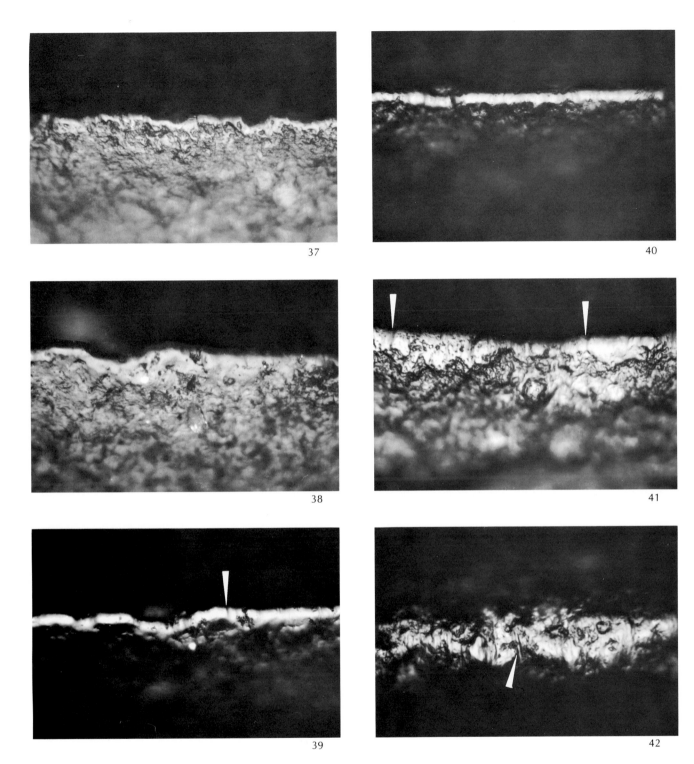

37. Initial development of a polish bevel on the contact surface of a flint edge used to plane soaked antler for 600 strokes, 5 min. Polish on the opposite (noncontact) surface of the same edge: Plate 32.

38. Polish bevel on the contact surface of a flint edge used to plane soaked antler for 1200 strokes, 9 min. Polish on the opposite (noncontact) surface of the same edge: Plate 33.

39. As Plate 38, photographed at a higher angle. Arrow: ''comet-tail'' linear indicators in the polish surface.

*40. Polish bevel from scraping antler, on the contact surface of the proximal burin-facet edge of Cassegros flint in Fig. 4.2: 9. Polish on the opposite (noncontact) surface of the same edge: Plate 35.

*41. Polish bevel from scraping antler, on the contact surface of an edge on an Upper Mesolithic flint from Franchthi Cave. Arrow: vague perpendicular trough in the polish surface. Polish on the opposite (noncontact) surface of the same edge: Plate 36.

42. Polish bevel on the contact surface of a flint edge used to scrape hard dry antler for 1200 strokes, 7 min. (5.5 cm = 0.1 mm). Arrow: deep-narrow striation through the polish bevel.

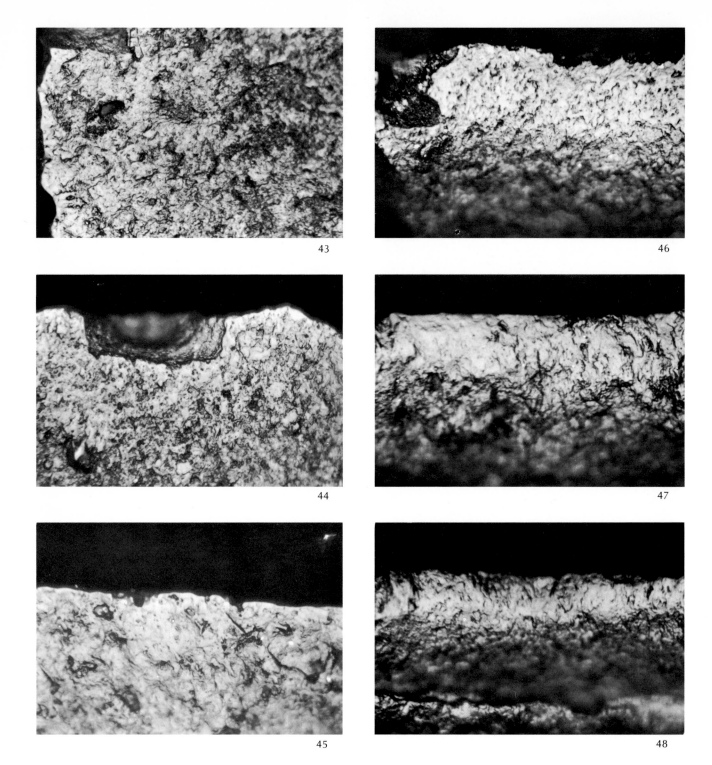

43. Contact surface of a flint edge used to whittle soaked-seasoned cypress wood for 600 strokes, 7 min: at the very edge (left) is a thick band of developed wood polish domes, whereas the interior (center) displays generic weak polish.

44. Initial stages of developed wood polish on the contact surface of a flint edge used to whittle fresh almond wood for 1600 strokes, 33 min.

45. Wood polish on the noncontact surface of a flint edge used to whittle fresh cypress wood for 1600 strokes, 26 min.

*46. Wood polish from a transverse motion on the noncontact surface of an edge on an Upper Mesolithic flint from Franchthi Cave.

47. Wood polish on the contact surface of a flint edge used to whittle fresh almond wood for 1500 strokes, 24 min. Generic weak polish elsewhere in the same edge: Plate 17.

*48. Wood polish from a transverse motion, on the contact surface of the distal edge of Cassegros flint in Fig. 4.11: 12 (5.5 cm = 0.1 mm).

49

52

50

53

51

54

*49. Most likely wood polish from a transverse motion, on the contact surface of the distal break edge of Cassegros flint Fig. 4.3: 7.

*50. Wood polish from a transverse motion, on the contact surface of an edge on an Upper Mesolithic flint from Franchthi Cave.

51. Wood polish on the contact surface of a flint edge used to whittle fresh almond wood for 2500 strokes, 31 min. Smooth-pitted polish elsewhere on the same edge: Plate 18.

*52. Wood polish from a transverse motion, on the contact surface of an edge on an Upper Mesolithic flint from Franchthi Cave. Arrows: "valleys" between wood polish domes.

53. Smooth-pitted polish from sawing fresh reeds (*Pseudosasa*) for 2400 strokes, 19 min. (see also Plate 19).

54. Very developed polish from sawing fresh reeds (*Phragmites*) for 800 strokes, 8 min.

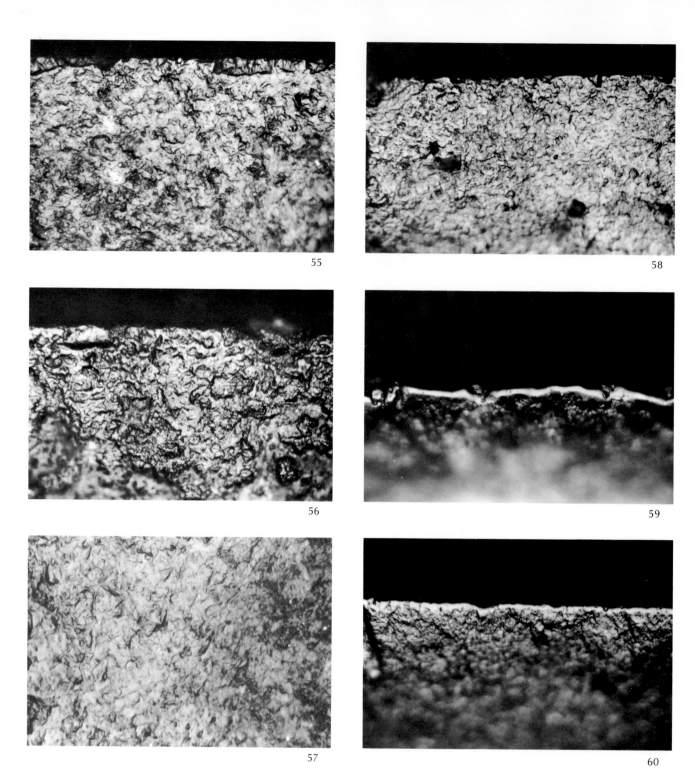

55
58
56
59
57
60

55. Transverse-motion reed polish ("terraced-bumpy") on the noncontact surface of a flint edge used to plane fresh reeds (*Pseudosasa*) for 800 strokes, 7 min. (see also Plate 57). Polish on the opposite (contact) surface of the same edge: Plates 61 and 62.

*56. Transverse-motion reed polish ("terraced-bumpy"), on the noncontact surface of an edge on an Upper Mesolithic flint from Franchthi Cave.

57. As Plate 55, but edge to left.

*58. Transverse-motion reed polish ("terraced-bumpy"), on the noncontact surface of an edge on an Upper Mesolithic flint from Franchthi Cave. Polish on the opposite (contact) surface of the same edge: Plate 60.

59. Polish bevel on the contact surface of a flint edge used to plane fresh reeds (*Phragmites*) for 600 strokes, 6 min. (cf. Plates 37–41).

*60. Polish bevel from a transverse motion on reeds, on the contact surface of an edge on an Upper Mesolithic flint from Franchthi Cave (cf. Plates 37–41). Polish on the opposite (noncontact) surface of the same edge: Plate 58.

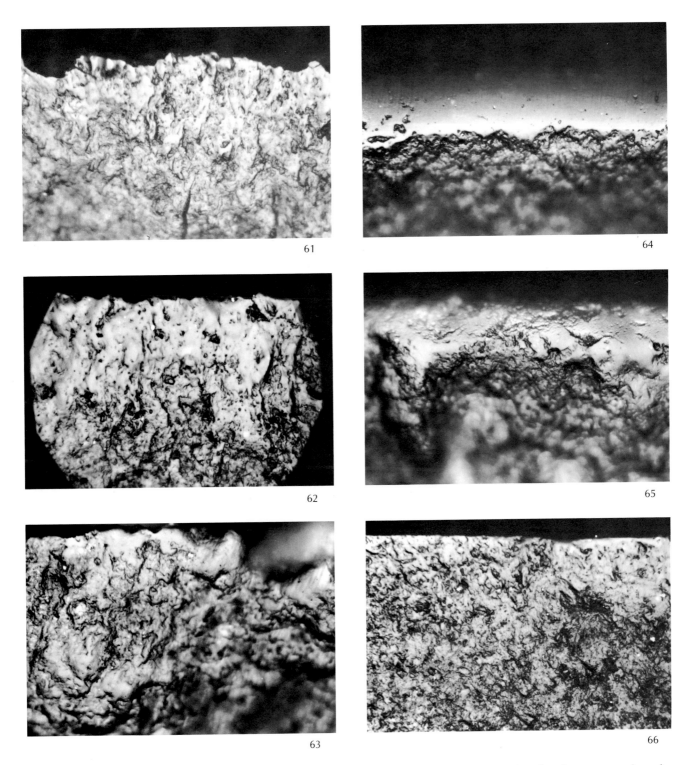

61

64

62

65

63

66

61. Polish on the contact surface of flint edge used to plane fresh reeds (*Pseudosasa*) for 800 strokes, 7 min. (see also Plate 62, but cf. Plates 43 and 44). Polish on the opposite (noncontact) surface of the same edge: Plates 55 and 57.

62. Polish on another section of the same edge as in Plate 61, just more developed (but cf. Plates 50–52). Polish on the opposite (noncontact) surface of the same edge: Plates 55 and 57).

*63. Reed polish from a transverse motion, on the contact surface of an edge on an Upper Mesolithic flint from Franchthi Cave.

64. Well developed, flat polish bevel on the contact surface of flint edge used to plane fresh reeds (*Phragmites*) for 800 strokes, 8 min. Polishes on the opposite (noncontact) surface of the same edge: Plates 66 and 67.

*65. Well-developed though damaged bevel from a transverse motion on reeds, on the contact surface of an edge on an Upper Mesolithic flint from Franchthi Cave.

66. Two varieties of transverse-motion reed polish on the noncontact surface of a flint edge used to plane fresh reeds (*Phragmites*) for 800 strokes, 8 min.: on the left half, the special "terraced-bumpy" reed polish; on the right half, the initial development of the reed polish which resembles smooth-type antler polish (cf. Plates 32 and 33). Polish on the opposite (contact) surface of the same edge: Plate 64.

67. Transverse-motion reed polish on another, more developed section of the same noncontact surface as in Plate 66. Note the resemblance with smooth-type antler polish with its "diffuse depressions" (cf. Plate 34). Polish on the opposite (contact) surface of the same edge: Plate 64.

68. Well-developed polish bevel on the contact surface of a flint edge used to scrape dried reeds (*Phragmites*) for 300 strokes, 3 min.

69. Smooth-pitted polish (left) and generic weak polish (center) from harvesting ripe barley for 3 hours (edge to left). More developed plant polish elsewhere on the same edge: Plates 73 and 79.

70. Smooth-pitted polish from slicing fresh cattail plants for 1500 strokes, 12 min.

*71. Most likely smooth-pitted plant polish, on the right edge of Cassegros flint in Fig. 4.12: 18.

*72. Smooth-pitted plant polish, on an edge of a Mousterian flint from Pech de l'Azé IV, France (identification courtesy of P. Anderson-Gerfaud).

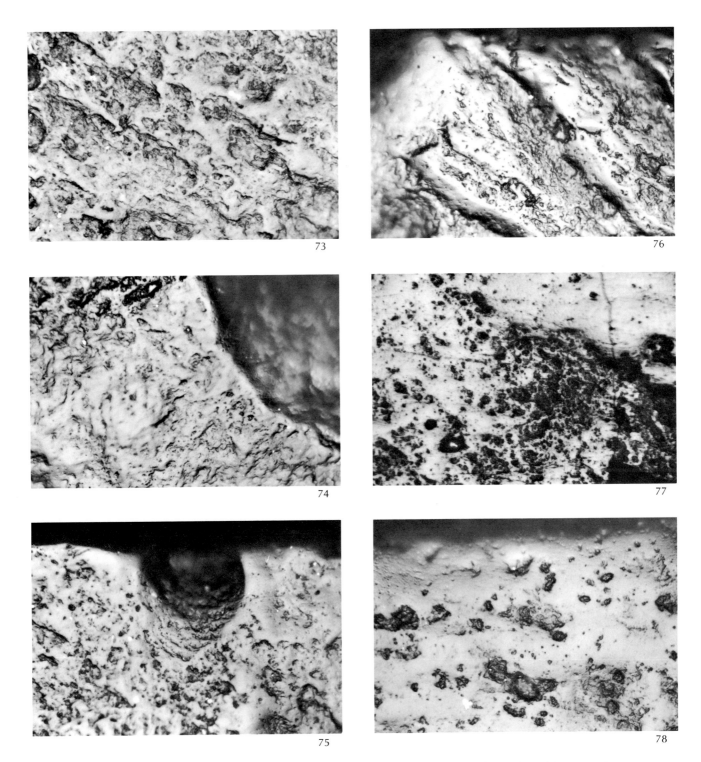

73. Plant polish in its initial stages of linkage, from harvesting ripe barley for 3 hours (edge towards the top). Lesser developed plant polish elsewhere on the same edge: Plate 69. More developed plant polish: Plate 79.

74. Plant polish with "pockmarked" aspect from cutting fresh cattail for 4 hours (edge towards the top).

75. Plant polish with "pockmarked" aspect from cutting fresh wild *Gramineae* for 3 hours (see also Plate 76).

76. As Plate 75, in another section of the same edge.

*77. Plant polish with "pockmarked" aspect on an edge of a Neolithic sickle flint from Franchthi Cave (edge towards the top); (140x; 4 cm = 0.2 mm). Note how the polish towards the right appears raised above the level of the darker, unaltered flint. More developed plant polish ("sickle gloss") elsewhere on the same edge: Plate 80.

*78. Plant polish with a "pockmarked" aspect on an edge of a Late Neolithic sickle flint from Franchthi Cave. Note the heavy rounding at the working edge (top).

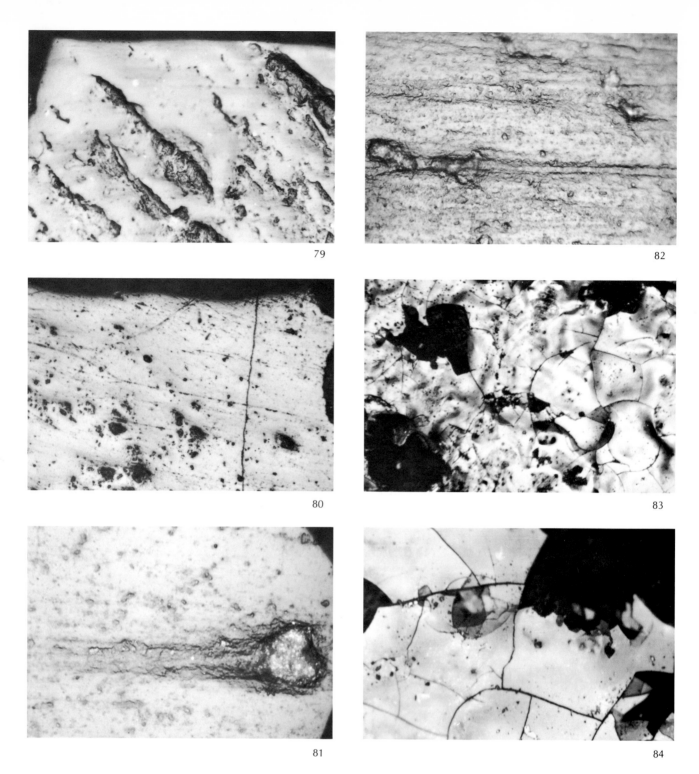

79. Plant polish, at maximum development known as "sickle gloss," from harvesting ripe barley for 3 hours. Lesser developed plant polishes elsewhere on the same edge: Plates 69 and 73.

*80. Plant polish at maximum development known as "sickle gloss," on an edge of a Neolithic sickle flint from Franchthi Cave (140x; 4 cm = 0.2 mm). Lesser developed plant polish elsewhere on the same edge: Plate 77.

*81. Comet-shaped pit within "sickle gloss" plant polish, on an edge of a Neolithic sickle flint from Franchthi Cave (5.5 cm = 0.1 mm).

*82. Comet-shaped pits within grit-influenced "sickle gloss" plant polish, on an edge of a Neolithic sickle flint from Franchthi Cave.

83. Very thin layer of highly reflective, very smooth-surfaced, glasslike material, cracking and exfoliating from the rusted surface of an iron sickle blade known to have been used to harvest cereal crops from ca. 1870 to 1930 (140x; 4 cm = 0.2 mm).

84. Same glossy layer as in Plate 83, but under higher magnification (280x; 4 cm = 0.1 mm).

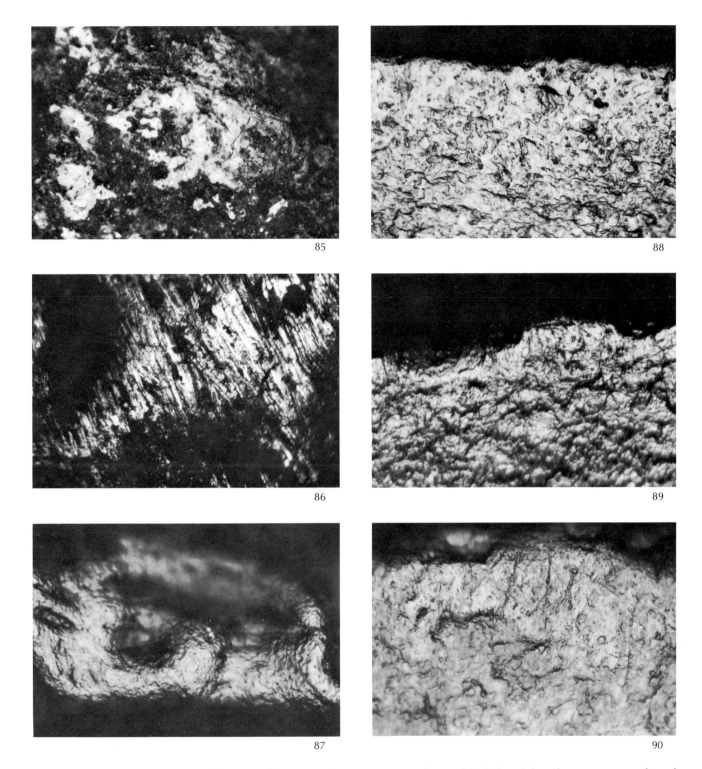

85. Minute, barely formed patches of the vitreous layer situated at the outer limit of the glossy band described for Plates 83 and 84.

86. Patches of striations within the surface of the antique iron sickle in an area which did not exhibit the glossy band described for Plates 83–85 (140x; 4 cm = 0.1 mm).

87. Dry hide polish and edge rounding from scraping dry tanned cowhide for 3000 strokes, 28 min. (dorsal retouch scars toward the top; ventral surface facing toward the bottom).

88. Grit-influenced dry hide polish on the noncontact surface of a flint edge used to scrape lightly moistened tanned deer hide, to which sand particles were added, for 2000 strokes, 14 min.

*89. Grit-influenced dry hide polish from scraping on the contact surface of the left edge of Cassegros flint in Fig. 4.2:11 (140x; 5.5 cm = 0.2 mm). See also Plate 90.

*90. Grit-influenced dry hide polish and edge rounding from scraping on the contact surface of the left edge of Cassegros flint in Fig. 4.2:11 (see also Plate 89). Polish and rounding on the opposite (noncontact) surface of the same edge: Plate 91.

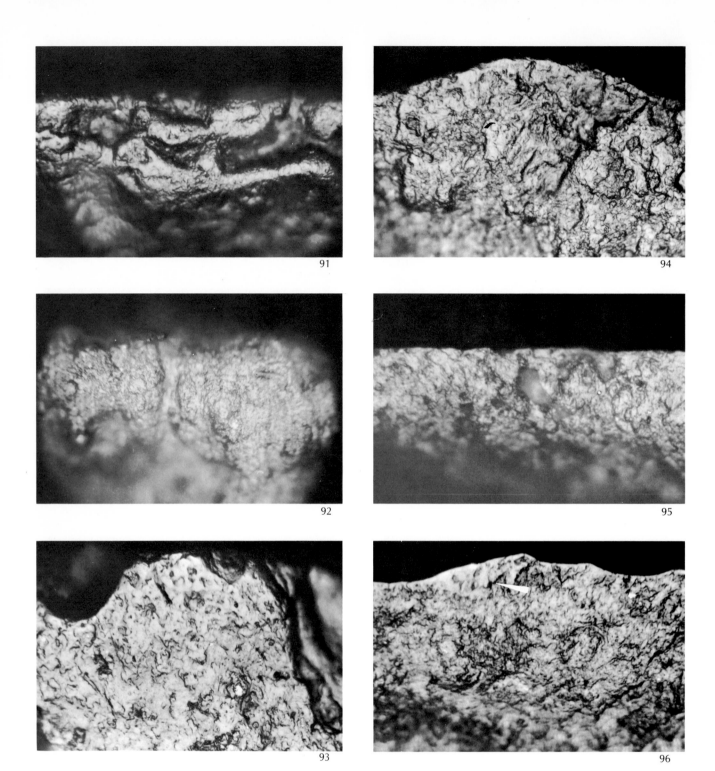

91

94

92

95

93

96

*91. Dry hide polish and rounding from scraping on the noncontact surface of the left edge of Cassegros flint Fig. 4.2:11 (5.5 cm = 0.1 mm). Polish and rounding on the opposite (contact) surface of the same edge: Plate 90.

*92. Grit-influenced dry hide polish and edge rounding from scraping, on the contact surface of an edge on an Upper Mesolithic flint from Franchthi Cave (168x; 3.3 cm = 0.1 mm).

93. Dry hide polish on the noncontact surface of a flint edge used to scrape moistened tanned deer hide for 2000 strokes, 17 min.

*94. Dry hide polish from cutting on the distal edge of Cassegros flint in Fig. 4.13:4. The hide must have been in a moistened state, as the polish lacks the extreme pitting typical of working unmoistened dry hides (e.g., Plate 87).

95. Meat polish as generic weak polish on a flint edge used to cut meat without bone contact for 1600 strokes, 18 min. (5.5 cm = 0.1 mm).

96. Fresh hide polishes from defleshing the inside of fresh calf hide for 2000 strokes, 40 min. (5.5 cm = 0.1 mm). Note the narrow polish band on the crest of the working edge, patches of smooth-pitted polish under the band (arrow), and wider areas of generic polish away from the edge.

97

100

98

101

99

102

97. Fresh hide polish as smooth-pitted polish from defleshing the inside of fresh calf hide for 1200 strokes, 13 min. (5.5 cm = 0.1 mm).

98. Small patches of smooth-pitted polish from butchering (removing meat from cow vertebrae) for 1000 strokes, 27 min.

99. Small patch of smooth-pitted polish from butchering (removing meat from cow vertebrae) for 1000 strokes, 20 min. (5.5 cm = 0.1 mm). Arrow: a diagonal trough in the polish surface, which is indicative of bone contact.

100. Bone residue from butchering (removing meat from cow vertebrae) for 1000 strokes, 20 min. (5.5 cm = 0.1 mm). The parallel orientation of the residue indicates a longitudinal motion into bone.

101. Same area as in Plate 100 (5.5 cm = 0.1 mm), but after a 15% HCl bath removed the bone residue, leaving just the natural reflective spots in the flint matrix (cf. Plate 6).

*102. Grit-influenced dry hide polish, on the contact side of the left edge of Cassegros flint in Fig. 4.2: 11. Effects of grit particles are seen in the heavy edge rounding and the dark grooves in the polish surface (see also Plates 90 and 92).

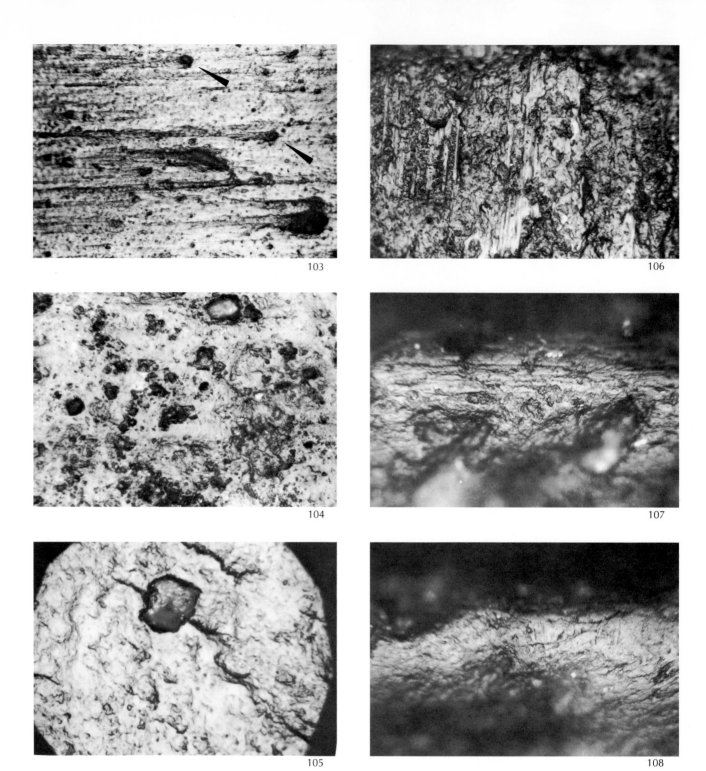

103

106

104

107

105

108

*103. Grit-influenced plant polish, on an edge of a Neolithic sickle flint from Franchthi Cave (140x, 4 cm = 0.2 mm). The heavy pitting of the polish surface and the numerous lengthy grooves in the polish are the effects of grit particles (see also Plate 82).

104. Wood polish, very much influenced by grit, on a flint edge used to groove fresh almond wood, with considerable added grit, for 800 strokes, 12 min. Notice the very pitted and rough aspect in comparison with normal wood polish (cf. Plate 51), and the ''microcraters'' (arrows).

105. ''Microcrater'' with embedded grit particle and surrounding rough-type grit polish or soil sheen on the rolled external surface of a flint nodule from an open-air source (5.5 cm = 0.1 mm).

106. Patterned deep and superficial striations on a flint surface held with purposely dirtied fingers.

*107. Rough, flat grit polish with parallel striations and ridge rounding, on the dorsal ridge of Cassegros flint Fig. 4.3:10 (168x, 3.3 cm = 0.1 mm). All features, typical of grit influence, would indicate prehension with dirty fingers.

*108. As in Plate 107, in another section of the same ridge.

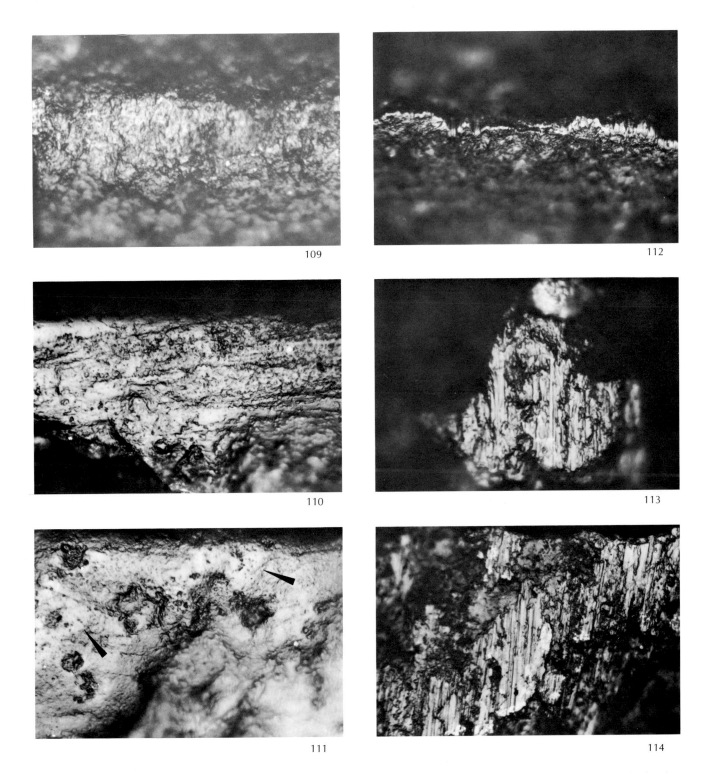

109. Generic weak polish from finger prehension on the dorsal ridge of a flint used to saw bone (5.5 cm = 0.1 mm).

*110. Pitted polish and parallel grooves from cutting gritty dry hide (right) superimposed over well-developed plant polish (left) on an edge of a Middle Neolithic sickle flint from Franchthi Cave.

*111. Pitted polish and a few dark grooves from cutting gritty dry hide, and only remnants of a developed plant polish (arrows) which preceded the hide cutting.

112. Hammerstone polish bevel on a flint edge retouched with a limestone pebble.

113. Heavily scored hammerstone polish on a flattened dorsal retouch ridge of an edge retouched with a limestone pebble.

114. Hammerstone polish and grooves on the striking platform of a flint knapped with a limestone pebble.

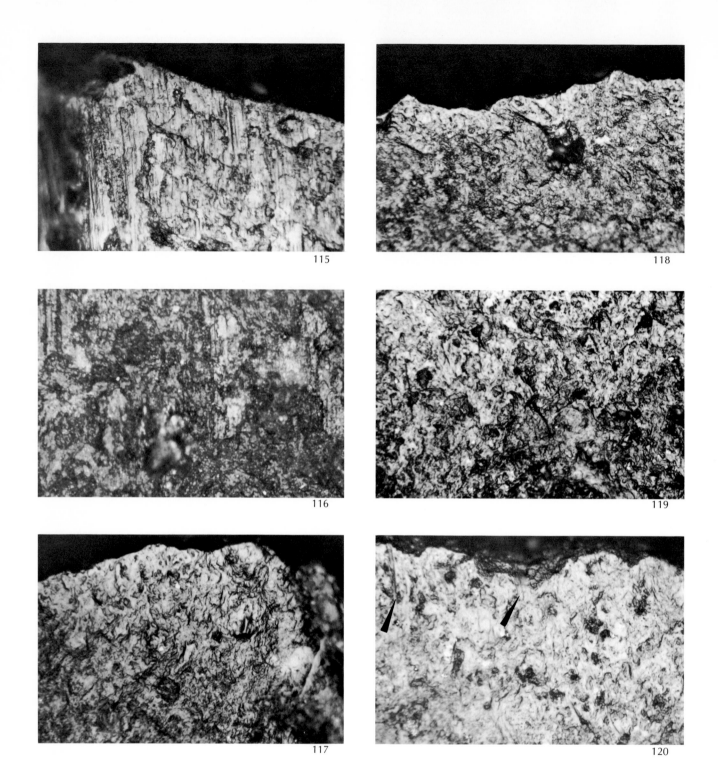

115. As in Plate 114, on another flint.

*116. Weak remnants of hammerstone polish and grooves in the striking platform of a Lower Mesolithic flint from Franchthi Cave (5.5 cm = 0.1 mm).

117. Smooth-pitted polish on a flint edge retouched by percussion with dry antler.

118. Smooth-pitted polish on a flint edge retouched by percussion with a dried cow bone.

119. Smooth-type grit polish (similar to smooth-pitted polish) on a flint edge scrubbed with a toothbrush and added grit particles.

120. Smooth-type grit polish, with perpendicular grooves through some polish areas (arrows), on a flint edge dragged across a hardened ground surface for 25 strokes.

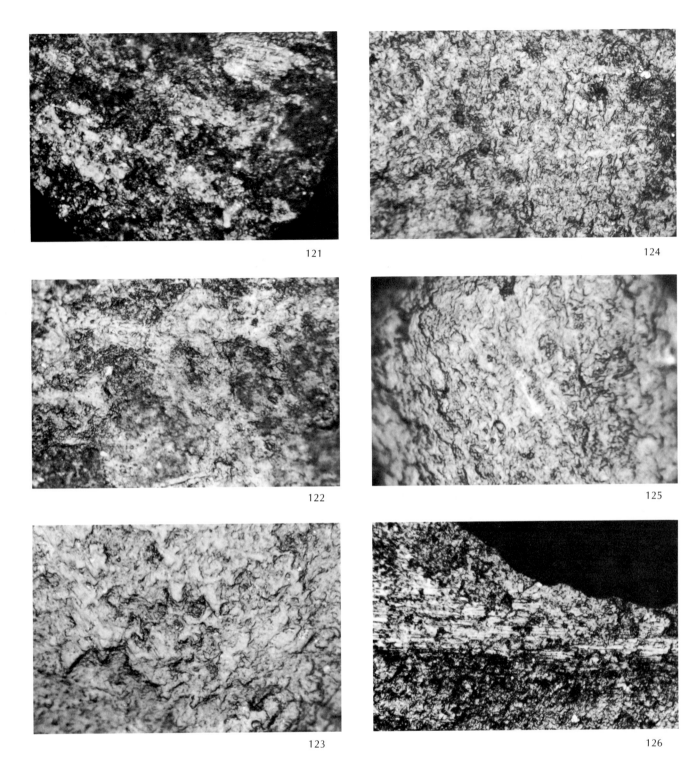

121. Small spots of smooth-type grit polish on the rolled external surface of a riverbed flint nodule (5.5 cm = 0.1 mm).

*122. Smooth-type grit polish in vague linear arrangements as superficial striations on the ventral surface of an Upper Mesolithic flint from Franchthi Cave.

*123. Smooth-type grit polish, with some grooves (left), on the dorsal surface of a flint from the Magdalenian open-air site of Orville, France (Perlès 1982).

124. Smooth-type grit polish in linear arrangements as superficial striations on a flint edge scrubbed with a toothbrush and added grit particles for 50 strokes.

125. Smooth-type grit polish on the bulbar protrusion of a flint dragged across a hardened ground surface (5.5 cm = 0.1 mm).

*126. Superficial striations made of smooth-type grit polish with grooves, most likely caused by a hard accidental blow against a rock, at the edge of an unretouched and unused flint from Cassegros (140x, 4 cm = 0.2 mm).

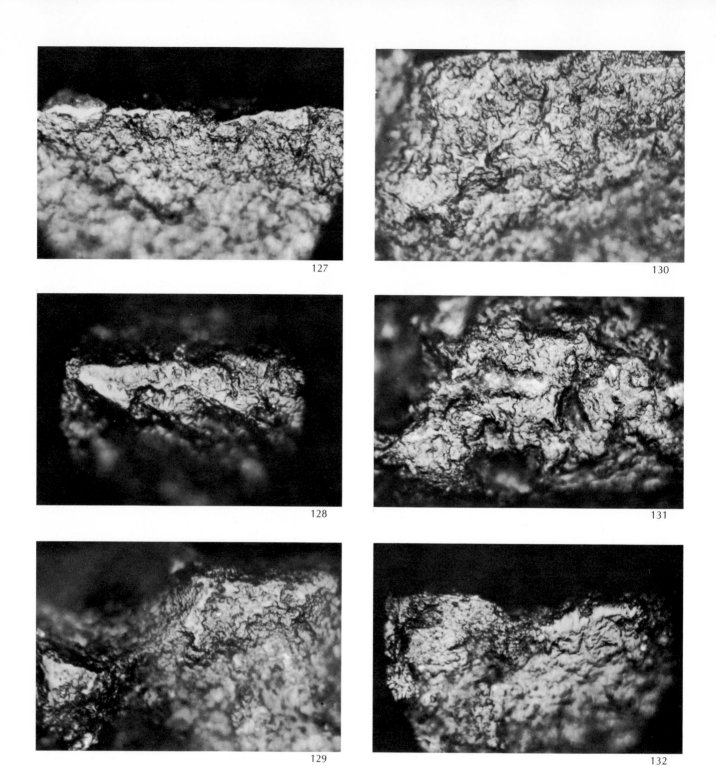

127. A few spots of smooth-type grit polish on the dorsal ridge of a flint submitted to a series of trampling-screening tests.

*128. Smooth-type grit polish on the dorsal ridge of an unused flint from Cassegros (5.5 cm = 0.1 mm).

*129. Smooth-type grit polish on the left edge of Cassegros flint in Fig. 4.1:5 (5.5 cm = 0.1 mm).

*130. Smooth-type grit polish on an elevated portion of the left edge of an unused flint from Cassegros (5.5 cm = 0.1 mm).

*131. Smooth-type grit polish on the dorsal ridge of an unused flint from Cassegros.

*132. Spot of smooth-type grit polish with grooves on the dorsal ridge of Cassegros flint in Fig. 4.3:11 (5.5 cm = 0.1 mm). The polish could resemble a fragment of bone polish bevel (cf. Plate 14).

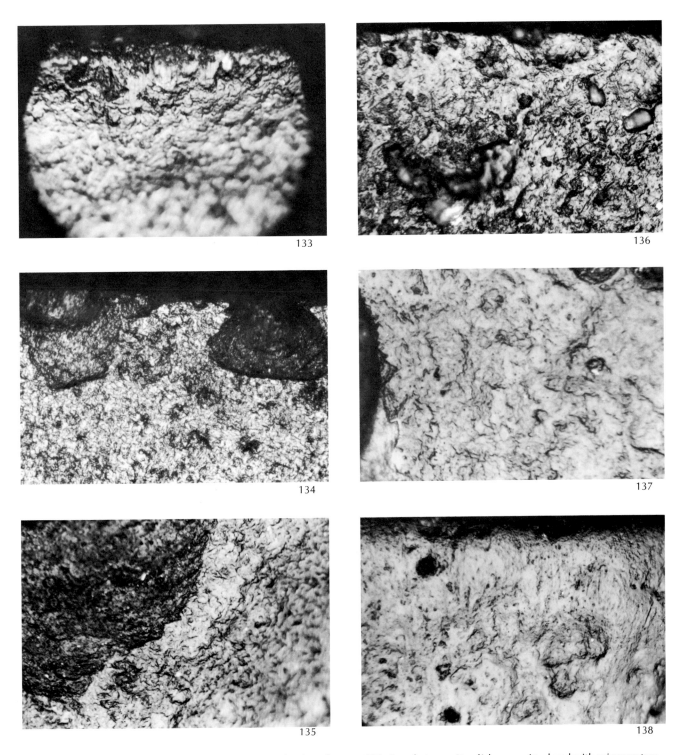

133

136

134

137

135

138

*133. Spot of smooth-type grit polish with grooves on the dorsal ridge of an unused flint from Cassegros (5.5 cm = 0.1 mm). The polish could resemble a fragment of bone polish bevel (cf. Plate 14).

*134. The interior of the post-excavation scar to the right reveals the unaltered state of the flint, whereas the surrounding flint surface and even the interior of the microscar to the left exhibit a uniform cover of soil sheen caused by natural wear mechanisms in the ground (140x, 4 cm = 0.1 mm). Proximal edge of Cassegros flint in Fig. 4.6:3.

*135. The interior of the post excavation scar (left half of micrograph) reveals the unaltered state of the flint, whereas the surrounding flint surface exhibits soil sheen in the form of generic weak polish (cf. Plates 17, 43, 69, 95, 109). Right edge of Cassegros flint in Fig. 4.10:10.

136. Rough-type grit polish, very pitted and with microcraters (see Plates 104 and 105) on a flint edge scrubbed with toothbrush and added soil for 150 strokes.

137. Rough-type grit polish and rounding on the rolled external surface of a flint nodule from an open-air source (5.5 cm = 0.1 mm).

138. Rough-type grit polish, a few grooves, microcraters and edge rounding on the ventral surface of a flint onto which was rubbed mud from loamy soil for 800 strokes.

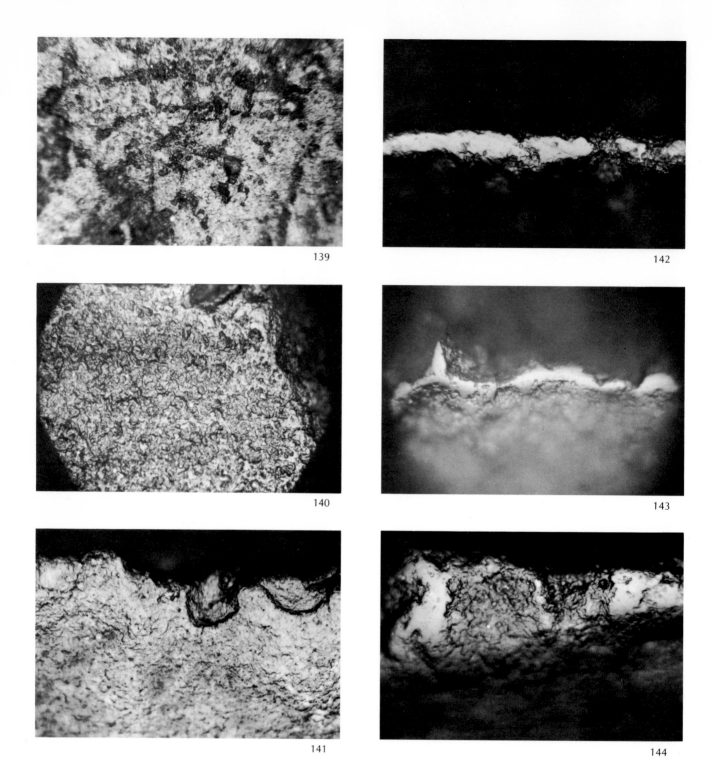

*139. Rough-type grit polish, microcraters, and intersecting deep striations on a rolled portion of the dorsal surface of an unused flint from Cassegros (168x; 3.3 cm = 0.1 mm).

*140. Rough-type grit polish on the ridges of retouch scars on an edge of a Late Neolithic flint from Franchthi Cave.

*141. Rough-type grit polish and considerable edge rounding on an edge of an Upper Mesolithic flint from Franchthi Cave.

*142. Remnant of a polish bevel from an unspecified harder material on the proximal-dorsal edge of Cassegros flint in Fig. 4.13:22.

*143. Remnants of a polish bevel from an unspecified harder material on the right edge of Cassegros flint in Fig. 4.13:16.

*144. Remnants of a once substantial polish bevel from an unspecified harder material on an edge of a Middle Neolithic flint from Franchthi Cave.

145

148

146

149

147

150

*145. Remnants of a polish bevel from an unspecified harder material on the right dorsal edge of Cassegros flint in Fig. 4.13:22.

146. Bone residue on the contact surface of a flint edge used to scrape soaked rabbit bone for 600 strokes, 4 min.

147. Bone residue with linear orientation from grooving soaked cow bone for 50 strokes, 1 min.

148. Bone residue with linear orientation from grooving soaked cow bone for 600 strokes, 3 min.

149. Residue from cutting dried beef (jerky) for 2000 strokes, 21 min.

150. Dried beef residue after application of medicinal alcohol on an edge used to cut beef jerky for 3000 strokes, 33 min.

151

152

153

151. Hammerstone residue on the contact surface of flint edge retouched by percussion with a limestone pebble.

152. Hammerstone residue on the contact surface of a flint edge which was pressure-retouched with a pointed limestone pebble.

153. The cave of Cassegros (Lot-et-Garonne, France). Excavated terrace area is in the foreground; entrance to the first chamber of the cave is in the background (1976 season).

154

155

156

154. Cassegros: excavated squares within the first chamber of the cave (1977 season).

155. Cassegros: stratigraphy of Würm IV and postglacial levels within the first chamber of the cave, as seen from the balk forming the north side of square I27 (1976 season).

156. Cassegros: recording positions of objects by quarter squares, in square H27, level 10 (1976 season).

157

160

158

161

159

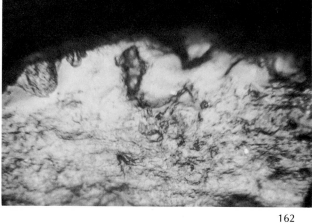

162

*157. Ripply polish on the dorsal surface of Cassegros flint Fig. 4.4:5 (140x; 4 cm = 0.2 mm).

*158. Ripply polish draped over rough flint topography on an unused flint from Cassegros.

*159. Flat polish spots on the left edge of Cassegros flint Fig. 4.3:1 (140x; 4 cm = 0.2 mm).

*160. A more detailed view of the flat polish spots in Fig. 159 (5.5 cm = 0.1 mm).

*161. Combination of ripply polish (left) and flat polish (far right) on the proximal edge of Cassegros flint in Fig. 4.3:15 (140x; 4 cm = 0.2 mm).

*162. Ripply polish spot superimposed over micropolish from cutting gritty dry hide, on the right side of Cassegros flint in Fig. 4.11:10.

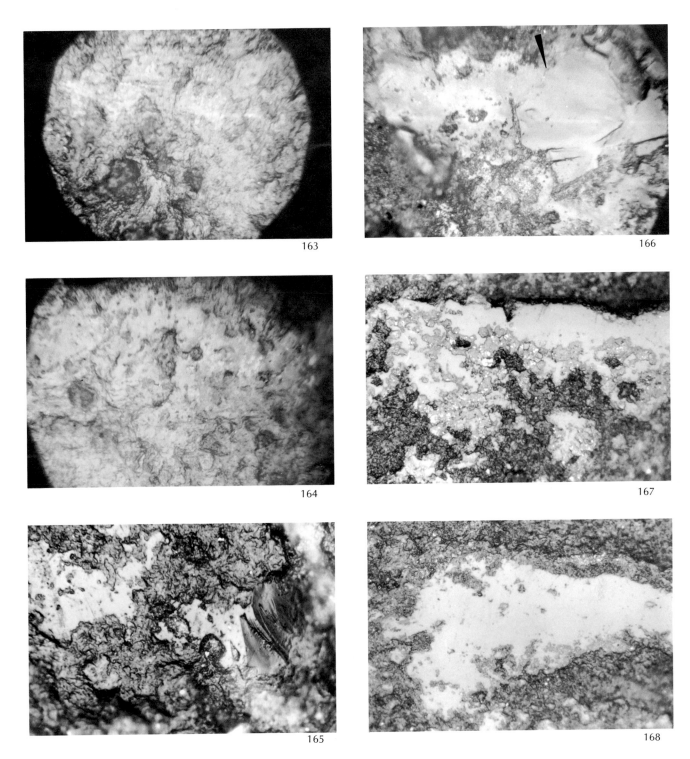

163

166

164

167

165

168

*163. Use-wear polish from cutting gritty dry hide superimposed over ripply polish spots, on the left edge of Cassegros flint in Fig. 4.10:15 (168x; 3.3 cm = 0.1 mm).

*164. Another section of the same edge as in Plate 163 (168x; 3.3 cm = 0.1 mm).

*165. Flat polish spot at the right is a very smooth fracture face of a large quartz crystal in the flint matrix, on the proximal edge of Cassegros flint in Fig. 4.3:7.

*166. Flat polish spot (left) and a crystal face (right) contiguous yet distinct from one another (arrow) on the edge of an unused flint from Cassegros.

167. Flat polish spot produced by rubbing flint onto a moistened flint surface for 5 minutes.

168. Flat polish spot produced by rubbing a glass object onto a moistened flint surface for 5 minutes.

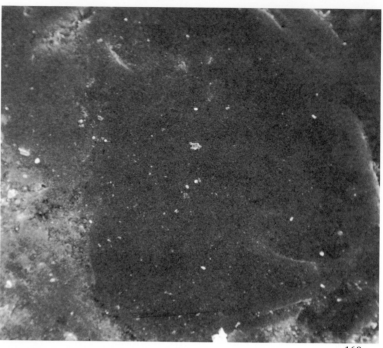

169

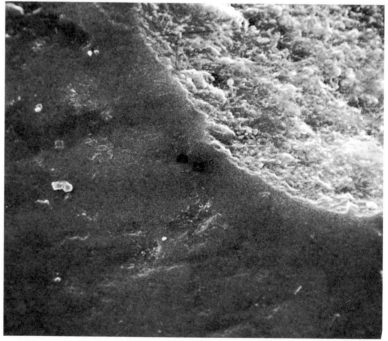

170

*169. Smooth surface of a flat polish spot on an unused flint from Cassegros magnified 1000x in the scanning electron microscope.

*170. Very smooth surface of a ripply polish spot on an unused flint from Cassegros, magnified 2000x in the scanning electron microscope. Note the sharp contrast between the polish surface and the rough texture of the interior of a post-excavation microscar (upper right).

Part IV

Reference Material

Appendix A / Tables 1.1 to 4.42

TABLE 1.1   NUMBER OF EXPERIMENTAL TESTS

EXPERIMENTER	TOTAL	STONE	BONE	ANTLER	WOOD	HIDE	FISH SKIN	MEAT + CARCASS	REED + PLANT	PROJEC-TILE	NATURAL FACTORS	TRAMPLE	SOFT HAMMER	MISCEL-LANEOUS [*]
THIS PROJECT	249 (453)	2 (2)	18 (43)	16 (36)	50 (167)	35 (46)	-	20 (29)	30 (45)	-		24 (24)	20 (20)	34 (41)
TRINGHAM et al., 1974	91	-	12	8	36	8	4	5	3	-	5	10	-	-
ODELL 1977, 1978, 1980b	71	-	6	-	13	-	2	9	11	30	-	-	-	-
KEELEY 1980	127	-	32	10	56	16	-	11	2	-	-	-	?	-
ANDERSON-GERFAUD 1981	131	4	16	31	38	11	-	15	4	-	5	3	4	-

Parentheses indicate the number of observations per test, e.g., at 100, 500, 1000 strokes.

[*] Hardhammer retouch, spontaneous retouch, soil contact, plastic bag contact, plastic bristles contact.

TABLE 2.1   CHI-SQUARE TEST FOR DIFFERENCES IN SCORES OF MICROCHIPPING
AMONG THE THREE EXPERIMENTAL FLINT TYPES

VARIABLES CORRELATED	REFER TO TABLE No.	ACTIONS OR MATERIALS	CHI-SQUARE	df	p	SIGNIFICANT DIFFERENCE **
Action and Surface of scarring	2.2	transverse	4.52	8	.8	-
		longitudinal	9.25	8	.3	-
Action and Distribution of scarring	2.3	transverse	16.44	8	.035	**
		longitudinal	5.45	8	.75	-
Action and Scarring in edge row	2.4	transverse	6.25	8	.6	-
		longitudinal	8.77	8	.4	-
Material and Distal cross-section of scars	2.5	hard	6.97	11	.8	-
		medium-hard	29.30	11	.001	**
		medium-soft	8.35	11	.75	-
		soft	13.32	11	.25	-
Material and Proximal cross-section of scars	2.6	hard	11.28	11	.4	-
		medium-hard	28.38	20	.1	-
		medium-soft	14.00	14	.5	-
		soft	11.51	11	.4	-
Material and Scar size	2.7	hard	10.11	14	.75	-
		medium-hard	16.40	17	.5	-
		medium-soft	23.14	17	.15	-
		soft	27.17	11	.004	**
Material and Presence of edge row scarring	2.8	hard	4.35	8	.85	-
		medium-hard	14.87	5	.01	**
		medium-soft	3.22	5	.65	-

TABLE 2.2   MICROCHIPPING: ACTION AND PREDOMINANT SURFACE OF SCARRING

ACTION	EXPECTED PATTERNS *	PATTERNS NOT EXPECTED **	NO SCARRING	% NO SCARRING ON EDGES ABOVE 66°	% NO SCARRING ON MEDIUM OR HARD MAT'LS	OBSERVATIONS ON RETOUCHED EDGES	TOTAL OBSERVATIONS
TRANSVERSE	60 38%[a]	73 46%	26 16%	92%	54%	28	187
LONGITUDINAL	89 65%[a]	23 17%	25 18%	20%	44%	25	162

NB: TRANSVERSE = whittle, plane, scrape.   LONGITUDINAL = cut, slice, saw, groove, fleshing.

[a] Percentage of observations on unretouched edges.

* Expected Scarring Patterns:
   i. Transverse actions:
     --with ventral side in contact: scarring on dorsal side only, or on dorsal more than ventral side.
     --with dorsal side in contact: scarring on ventral side only, or on ventral more than dorsal side.
   ii. Longitudinal actions: scarring equal on ventral and dorsal sides, more on ventral than dorsal side, or more on dorsal than ventral side.

** Scarring Patterns Not expected:
   i. Transverse actions:
     --with ventral side in contact: scarring on ventral side only, on ventral more than dorsal side, or equal on ventral and dorsal sides.
     --with dorsal side in contact: scarring on dorsal side only, on dorsal more than ventral side, or equal on dorsal and ventral sides.
   ii. Longitudinal actions: scarring on ventral side only, or on dorsal side only.

TABLE 2.3   MICROCHIPPING: ACTION AND DISTRIBUTION OF SCARRING ALONG USED EDGES

ACTION	EXPECTED PATTERNS *	PATTERNS NOT EXPECTED **	NO SCARRING	OBSERVATIONS ON RETOUCHED EDGES	TOTAL OBSERV.
TRANSVERSE	51 32%[a]	82 52%	26 16%	28	187
LONGITUDINAL	91 66%[a]	21 16%	25 18%	25	162

[a] Percentage of observations on unretouched edges.

* Expected Scarring Patterns:
   i. Transverse actions: run-together.
   ii. Longitudinal actions: close, wide, uneven, too few scars.

** Scarring Patterns Not Expected:
   i. Transverse actions: close, wide, uneven, too few scars.
   ii. Longitudinal actions: run-together.

TABLE 2.4   MICROCHIPPING: ACTION AND EDGE ROW SCARRING

ACTION	EXPECTED PATTERNS *	PATTERNS NOT EXPECTED **	NO EDGE ROW	OBSERVATIONS ON RETOUCHED EDGES	TOTAL OBSERV.
TRANSVERSE	25 16%[a]	17 11%	117[b] 73%	28	187
LONGITUDINAL	3 2%[a]	21 15%	113[b] 83%	25	162

[a] Percentage of observations on unretouched edges.

[b] Observations include complete range of edge angles and use durations.

* Expected Scarring Patterns:
   i. Transverse actions:
     --with ventral side in contact: edge row on dorsal side only.
     --with dorsal side in contact: edge row on ventral side only.
  ii. Longitudinal actions: edge row on both ventral and dorsal sides.

** Scarring Patterns Not Expected:
   i. Transverse actions:
     --with ventral side in contact: edge row on ventral side only,
                       or on both ventral and dorsal sides.
     --with dorsal side in contact: edge row on dorsal side only, or
                      on both ventral and dorsal sides.
  ii. Longitudinal actions: edge row on ventral side only, or on dorsal
                      side only.

TABLE 2.5   MICROCHIPPING: WORKED MATERIALS AND DISTAL CROSS-SECTION OF SCARS

WORKED MATERIALS *	CRESCENT BREAK	FEATHERED	HINGE/ STEP	FEATHERED = HINGE/ STEP	CRESCENT BREAK = FEATHERED	TOO FEW	NO SCARRING	NO SCARRING ABOVE 66°	OBSERV. ON RETOUCHED EDGES	TOTAL OBSERV.
HARD	-	10 15%[a]	42 63%	11 16%	-	-	4 6%	(33%) N=2	4	71
MEDIUM-HARD	-	31 25%[a]	40 33%	33 27%	1	4	13 11%	62%	28	150
MEDIUM-SOFT	1	22 37%[a]	16 27%	7 12%	1	2	10 17%	80%	13	72
SOFT	17 25%	7 10%	12 18%	3	2	-	26 39%	42%	8	75

[a] Percentage of observations on unretouched edges.

* HARD: fresh/soaked:dry bone, dry antler, dry almond and cypress woods, butchering; MEDIUM-HARD: fresh and soaked almond wood, soaked antler; MEDIUM-SOFT: fresh and soaked cypress wood, reeds, barley, wild Gramineae, dried beef; SOFT: meat without bone, hide, green plant stems, cattail.

TABLE 2.6   MICROCHIPPING: WORKED MATERIAL AND PROXIMAL CROSS-SECTION OF SCARS

WORKED MATERIALS	CRESCENT BREAK	SHALLOW	BREAK- SHALLOW	STEEP	SHALLOW = BREAK- SHALLOW	BREAK- SHALLOW = STEEP	SHALLOW = STEEP	TOO FEW	NO SCARS	EDGE ROW SCARRING INTERFERS	OBSERV. ON RET. EDGES	TOTAL OBSERV.
HARD	-	46 69%[a]	1	2	6 9%	-	4 6%	2	4 6%	2	4	71
MEDIUM- HARD	-	34 28%[a]	5 4%	30 25%	3	16 13%	17 13%	4	13 11%	-	28	150
MEDIUM- SOFT	1	11 19%[a]	14 24%	14 24%	-	5 8%	2	1	10 17%	1	13	72
SOFT	17 25%[a]	9 13%	1	9 13%	1	1	2	1	26 39%	-	8	75

[a] Percentage of observations on unretouched edges.

TABLE 2.7   MICROCHIPPING: SCAR SIZE

WORKED MATERIALS	VERY LARGE (w/ eyes)	LARGE (w/ 10x lens)	MEDIUM (34x)	SMALL (84x)	MINUTE (+100x)	WIDELY VARIABLE	NO SCARRING	OBSERVATIONS ON RETOUCHED EDGES	TOTAL OBSERVATIONS
HARD	26 39%[a]	16 24%	10 15%	1	-	10 15%	4 6%	4	71
MEDIUM-HARD	3	17 14%[a]	41 34	25 20%	14 11%	9 7%	13 11%	28	150
MEDIUM-SOFT	7 12%[a]	7 12%	16 27%	10 17%	5 8%	4	10 17%	13	72
SOFT	1	5 7%[a]	25 37%	10 15%	-	-	26 39%	8	75

[a] Percentage of observations on unretouched edges.

TABLE 2.8   MICROCHIPPING: WORKED MATERIAL AND EDGE ROW SCARRING

WORKED MATERIALS	COMPLETE EDGE ROW	PARTIAL EDGE ROW	SPECIAL* EDGE ROW	NO EDGE ROW	OBSERVATIONS ON RETOUCHED EDGES	TOTAL OBSERV.
HARD	12 18%[a]	24 36%	-	31 46%	4	71
MEDIUM-HARD		18 15%[a]	4	100 82%	28	150
MEDIUM-SOFT	2[b]	11 19%[a]	-	46 78%	13	72
SOFT	-	-	-	67 100%[a]	8	75

[a] Percentage of observations on unretouched edges.

[b] From working fresh cypress wood.

* Combination of complete and partial edge rows.

TABLE 2.9   STRIATIONS: ORIENTATION IN RELATION TO THE WORKING EDGE

ACTION	PERPEN-DICULAR	DIAGONAL	DIAGONAL = PERPEN.	PARALLEL	DIAGONAL = PARALLEL	PERPEN. = PARALLEL	INTER-SECTING	NO STRIAE	FRESH WOOD: NO STRIAE*	TOTAL OBSERV.
TRANSVERSE	52 60%[a]	12 14%	5 6%	-	-	-	-	17 20%	101	187
LONGITUDINAL	-	11 9%	2[b]	33 27%	6 5%	2[c]	3	67 54%	38	162

[a] Percentage of observations excluding those for fresh wood.

[b] Grooving resulted sometimes in striations oriented perpendicular to the leading edge but diagonal to the main working edge.

[c] Perpendicular striations were caused by a "down stroke" (i.e., transverse motion) at the end of a basically longitudinal action.

* Data not collected since the striation attributes had not been finalized when the fresh wood experiments were conducted.

TABLE 2.10   STRIATIONS: SURFACE OF EDGE

ACTION	EXPECTED PATTERNS *	PATTERNS NOT EXPECTED **	NO STRIAE	FRESH WOOD: NO STRIAE ***	TOTAL OBSERV.
TRANSVERSE	64 74%[a]	5[b] 6%	17 20%	101	187
LONGITUDINAL	32 26%[a]	25 20%	67 54%	38	162

[a] Percentage of observations excluding those for fresh wood.

[b] High or obtuse edge angles held at a high angle of contact.

* Expected Striation Patterns:
   i. Transverse action:
      --with ventral side in contact: striations on ventral side only, on ventral more than dorsal, or equally on dorsal and ventral sides.
      --with dorsal side in contact: sitriations on dorsal side only, on dorsal more than ventral, or equally on ventral and dorsal sides.
   ii. Longitudinal action: striations equally on ventral and dorsal sides, on ventral more than dorsal side, or on dorsal more than ventral side.

** Striation Patterns Not Expected:
   i. Transverse action:
      --with ventral side in contact: striations on dorsal side only, or on dorsal more than ventral side.
      --with dorsal side in contact: striations on ventral side only, or on ventral more than dorsal side.
   ii. Longitudinal actions: striations on ventral side only, or on dorsal side only.

*** Data not collected since the striation attributes had not been finalized when the fresh wood experiments were conducted.

TABLE 2.11   ROUNDING: SURFACE OF EDGE

ACTION	EXPECTED PATTERNS *	PATTERNS NOT EXPECTED **	EQUAL ROUNDING	NO ROUNDING	TOTAL OBSERVATIONS
TRANSVERSE	118 63%[a]	7[b] 4%	28[b] 15%	34 18%	187
LONGITUDINAL	101 62%[a]	18 11%	(101) (62%)	43 27%	162

[a] Percentage of all observations.

[b] Caused by very high contact angles.

* Expected Rounding Patterns:
   i. Transverse actions:
     --with ventral side in contact: rounding greater on ventral than on dorsal side.
     --with dorsal side in contact: rounding greater on dorsal than on ventral side.
   ii. Longitudinal actions: rounding on perpendicular edge crest only, or equal rounding on dorsal and ventral.

** Rounding Patterns Not Expected:
   i. Transverse actions:
     --with ventral side in contact: rounding greater on dorsal than on ventral side.
     --with dorsal side in contact: rounding greater on ventral than on dorsal side.
   ii. Longitudinal actions: rounding greater on dorsal than on ventral side, or rounding greater on ventral than on dorsal side.

TABLE 2.12   ROUNDING: INTENSITY

DEGREE OF ROUNDING	FLINT VARIETY*	BONE	ANTLER	REEDS	WOOD	TANNED HIDE	FRESH HIDE	PLANTS
NONE	f	1 min.	1 min.	1-5 min.	1-2 min.	-	41 min.	-
	mf	1	1	2	1-3	-	40-41	2-4
	mc	1-2	2	2	1-5	-	51	-
LIGHT **	f	1-11	1-10	1-8	1-31	2-16	10-44	7-35
	mf	1	1-10	1-12	2-22	3	22-39	14-31
	mc	1-10	2-9	7-8	5-24	4-7	14-60	4-41
MODERATE ***	f	2-12	3-9	3-9	5-25	7-46	13	120-240
	mf	3-15	2-10	2	5-33	15	-	42
	mc	3-9	2-10	-	2-13	17-47	46	-

* f = fine-grained; mf = medium-fine grained; mc = medium-coarse grained flint.

** light rounding: ridges and edges are rounded on crests only.

*** moderate rounding: ridges and edges are flattened or blurred.

TABLE 2.13   POLISHES: POTENTIAL DIFFERENCES IN SMOOTH-PITTED
POLISHES AS PRODUCED BY SAWING SOLID MATERIALS

ATTRIBUTE	BONE	ANTLER	WOOD	REEDS
CREST OF SAWING EDGE	No solid band of polish, but very short broken stretches of polish band on f and mf. *	No solid band of polish, but short stretches of polish band on f and mf.	Usually a solid band of polish (only in sections on mc).	A solid band of polish, or stretches of polish band on coarser flints.
LINEAR INDICATORS IN POLISH SURFACE	Many troughs and grooves; perhaps some comet-tails (few on mc).	Few troughs or grooves on f and mf, rare on mc.	Vague "valleys" between polish domes; no troughs unless grit interfers.	Possible vague "valleys" between polish domes.
POLISH IN USE SCARS	No polish within microchipping.	Polish not usual within use scars.	Polish forms inside use scars if they are not too deep.	
COVERAGE OF POLISH OVER FLINT TOPO-GRAPHY	Polish development greatly favored on elevations, giving light to moderate linkage at most.	Some localized, moderately to heavily linked areas with diffuse depressions on f and perhaps mf.	More even, widespread coverage of higher and lower topography (not so on mc).	
ADDITIONAL	On mc flints, bone- and antler-sawing polishes are very similar if not indistinguishable.		Polish domes show volume and a smooth surface texture.	Initially as from wood; but with more contact: large domed polish agglomerates.

* f = fine-grained flint; mf = medium-fine grained flint; mc = medium-coarse grained flint.

TABLE 2.14   POLISHES: SURFACE OF EDGE WITH GREATEST
DEGREE OF POLISH DEVELOPMENT

ACTION	EXPECTED PATTERNS *	PATTERNS NOT EXPECTED **	EQUAL DEVELOPMENT	NO POLISH	TOTAL OBSERVATIONS
TRANSVERSE	150 82%[a]	6[b] 3%	27[b] 15%	4	187
LONGITUDINAL	128 83%	26 17%	(128) (83%)	8	162

[a] Percentage of observations displaying micropolish.

[b] Caused by very high contact angles.

* Expected Patterns of Greatest Deptree of Polish Development:
   i. Transverse actions:
     --with ventral side in contact: polish develops on edge crest
     only, on ventral side only, or on ventral more than on
     dorsal side.
     --with dorsal side in contact: polish develops on edge crest
     only, on dorsal side only, or on dorsal more than on
     ventral side.
   ii. Longitudinal actions: polish develops on ventral more than on
     dorsal side, on dorsal more than on ventral side, or equally
     on dorsal and ventral sides.

** Patterns of Greatest Degree of Polish Development Not Expected:
   i. Transverse actions:
     --with ventral side in contact: polish develops on dorsal side
     only, or on dorsal more than on ventral side.
     --with dorsal side in contact: polish develops on ventral side
     only, or on ventral more than on dorsal side.
   ii. Longitudinal actions: polish develops on dorsal side only, or on
     ventral side only.

TABLE 3.1   SUMMARY OF CLIMATE AND LITHIC INDUSTRIES OF THE
WÜRM IV AND POSTGLACIAL LEVELS AT CASSEGROS

LEVEL	PERIOD	CLIMATE	LITHIC INDUSTRY
1-5	Post-glacial	increasingly milder, wetter	Neolithic to Middle Ages
6		very intensely cold, dry climate	Lower or Middle Magdalenian
7	W Ü R M	significantly milder climate	Lower Magdalenian
8		very cold, rather dry conditions	
9		·milder, wetter climate	Magdalenian I
10a	IV	very cold, drier climate	
10b		wet, only moderately cold climate	Magdalenian "0"
10c		sudden intense cold, moderate wetness	

Source: Compiled from Le Tensorer 1981:295-338.

TABLE 3.2   GENERAL CHARACTERISTICS OF DEBITAGE
FROM LEVEL 10 AT CASSEGROS

Retouched tools *	172	) 194	22.69%
"Utilized or lightly retouched" flakes	22		
Flakes	189	)	
Small flakes (under 24 x 18 mm)	181	) 594	69.47%
Small débris and retouched flakes	224	)	
Unretouched blades	14		1.64%
Unretouched bladelets	17		1.99%
Cores	8		0.93%
Burin spalls	28		3.27%
	TOTAL: 855		

* 35 (or 20.35%) on blades, and 137 (or 79.65%) on flakes.

NB: Counts are on material from the 1973-1978 excavations.
Source: After Le Tensorer 1981:295-338.

TABLE 3.3   TYPE LIST OF MAGDALENIAN "O" (LEVEL 10) OF CASSEGROS

*1. End-scraper on end of blade	5	2.91%
3. Double end-scraper	1	0.58%
5. End-scraper on retouched blade	2	1.16%
8. End-scraper on flake	5	2.91%
11. Carinated end-scraper	5	2.91%
12. Atypical carinated end-scraper	2	1.16%
17. End-scraper/burin	3	1.74%
24. Bec	24	13.95%
27. Straight dihedral burin	2	1.16%
29. Angled dihedral burin	1	0.58%
30. Angled burin on a break	6	3.49%
37. Burin on convex retouched truncation	1	0.58%
38. Transversal burin on lateral retouch	6	3.49%
39. Transversal burin on a notch	3	1.74%
41. Mixed multiple burin	1	0.58%
43. Core-shaped burin	1	0.58%
60. Blade with straight retouched truncation	1	0.58%
61. Blade with oblique retouched truncation	2	1.16%
62. Blade with concave retouched truncation	2	1.16%
65. Blade with continuous retouch on one side	9	5.23%
66. Blade with continuous retouch on two sides	4	2.33%
74. Notched piece	28	16.28%
75. Denticulated piece	7	4.07%
76. Splintered piece	18	10.47%
77. Side-scraper	18	10.47%
78. Raclette	1	0.58%
78-A. Proto-raclette	9	5.23%
93. Miscellaneous	5	2.91%

TOTAL: 172

* Tool-type numbers following de Sonneville-Bordes and Perrot 1953-1956.

NB: Counts are on material from the 1973-1978 excavations, after
    Le Tensorer 1981: Tableau XXXVIII.

ACTION	BONE	MOST LIKELY BONE	BONE OR ANTLER	ANTLER	MOST LIKELY ANTLER	TOTAL BONE + ANTLER	WOOD	MOST LIKELY WOOD	TOTAL WOOD	DRY HIDE	DRY HIDE + GRIT	TOTAL DRY HIDE	UNSPEC- IFIED HARDER MATERIAL
TRANS- VERSE*	10[a]	4	3	8[b]	1	(26)	23	12	(35)	7	65	(72)	24
LONGITU- DINAL**	-	-	3	-	-	(3)	3	-	(3)	11	79	(90)	-
GROOVE	1	-	1	-	-	(2)	-	-	-	-	-	-	-
BORE	-	-	-	-	-	-	-	-	-	1	1	(2)	-
FINGER GRIP	-	-	-	-	-	-	-	-	-	-	1	(1)	-
HAFTING	-	-	-	-	-	-	-	-	-	-	-	-	-
UNCERTAIN	-	-	-	-	-	-	-	-	-	-	-	-	1
COLUMN TOTAL	11	4	7	8	1	(31)	26	12	(38)	19	146	(165)	25
COLUMN %	3.89	1.41	2.47	2.83	0.35	(10.95)	9.19	4.24	(13.43)	6.71	51.59	(58.30)	8.83

TABLE 4.1 (continued)

FRESH HIDE OR MEAT	MOST LIKELY MEAT	PLANTS	MOST LIKELY PLANTS	GRIT	INSUFFI- CIENTLY DEVELOPED	POLISH TOO ABRADED	POLISH UNFA- MILIAR	ROW TOTAL	ROW %	ACTION
-	-	-	-	-	1	4	1	163	57.60	TRANSVERSE
-	-	-	1	-	1	-	1	98	34.62	LONGITUDINAL
-	-	-	-	-	-	-	-	2	0.71	GROOVE
-	-	-	-	-	-	-	-	2	0.71	BORE
3	1	-	-	3	-	-	-	8	2.83	FINGER GRIP
-	-	2	-	-	-	-	1	3	1.06	HAFTING
-	-	-	-	1	-	1	4	7	2.47	UNCERTAIN
3	1	2	1	4	2	5	6	283		COLUMN TOTAL
1.06	0.35	0.71	0.35	1.41	0.71	1.77	2.12			COLUMN %

* Includes whittle, plane, scrape.   ** Includes cut, slice, saw.

[a] Nine cases of soaked/fresh bone, one case of dried bone.

[b] Five cases of soaked antler, three cases of dried antler.

TABLE 4.2   NUMBER OF INDEPENDENT USE ZONES BY ACTIONS

ACTION	N	% OF ALL 283 IUZs	WORKED MATERIAL	N	% IUZs FOR THE ACTION
TRANSVERSE	162	57.60%	dry hide	72	44.17%
			wood	35	21.47%
			bone/antler	26	15.95%
			UHM *	24	14.72%
			insuf. devel.	1	0.61%
			too abraded	4	2.45%
			unfamiliar	1	0.61%
LONGITUDINAL	98	34.62%	dry hide	90	91.84%
			wood	3	3.06%
			bone/antler	3	3.06%
			plants	1	1.02%
			insuf. devel.	1	1.02%
GROOVE	2	0.71%	bone/antler	2	100%
BORE	2	0.71%	dry hide	2	100%
FINGER GRIP	8	2.83%	meat	4	50.00%
			grit	3	37.50%
			dry hide (pad)	1	12.50%
HAFTING	3	1.06%	plants	2	66.67%
			unfamiliar	1	33.33%
UNCERTAIN	7	2.47%	UHM *	1	14.29%
			grit	1	14.29%
			too abraded	1	14.29%
			unfamiliar	4	57.14%

* UHM = Unspecified harder material (e.g., bone, antler, reeds).

TABLE 4.3   CONTACT SURFACES USED IN TRANSVERSE ACTIONS

A) VENTRAL SIDE AS CONTACT SURFACE:
116 IUZs OR 73% OF TRANSVERSE ACTIONS

CONTACT ANGLE	BONE/ ANTLER	WOOD	DRY HIDE	UHM*	OTHER	TOTAL
LOW-MEDIUM (0-75°)	8	14	30	6	2	60
HIGH (76-90°)	8	3	27	8	2	48
INDETERMINABLE	-	2	2	2	2	8
TOTAL	16	19	59	16	6	116
% TOTAL DORSAL AND VENTRAL	64.00%	57.56%	83.10%	66.66%	100%	72.96%

B) DORSAL SIDE AS CONTACT SURFACE:
43 IUZs OR 27% OF TRANSVERSE ACTIONS

CONTACT ANGLE	BONE/ ANTLER	WOOD	DRY HIDE	UHM*	OTHER	TOTAL
LOW-MEDIUM (0-75°)	3	9	8	6	-	26
HIGH (76-90°)	6	5	4	1	-	16
INDETERMINABLE	-	-	-	1	-	1
TOTAL	9	14	12	8	-	43
% TOTAL DORSAL AND VENTRAL	36.00%	42.44%	16.90%	33.34%	0	27.04%

* UHM = Unspecified harder material (e.g., bone, antler, reeds).

TABLE 4.4   EDGE ANGLE GROUPS FOR IUZs USED IN TRANSVERSE ACTIONS

A) MAXIMUM EDGE ANGLE GROUPS

ANGLE GROUP	BONE/ANTLER	UHM**	WOOD	DRY HIDE	OTHER	TOTAL	ROW %
30° ± 5°	-	-	2	2	-	4	2.45%
40° ± 5°	-	1	4	1	-	6	3.68%
50° ± 5°	-	1	4	8	-	13	7.98%
60° ± 5°	1	3	6	8	1	19	11.66%
70° ± 5°	1	1	7	6	-	15	9.20%
80° ± 5°	2	6	2	9	-	19	11.66%
90° ± 5°	10	5	8	17	-	40	24.54%
above 96°	12	7	2	21	5	47	28.83%
TOTAL	26	24	35	72	6	163	
*PERCENTAGE SETS	84.62%	75.00%	88.57%	95.83%			

B) MINIMUM EDGE ANGLE GROUPS

ANGLE GROUP	BONE/ANTLER	UHM**	WOOD	DRY HIDE	OTHER	TOTAL	ROW %
30° ± 5°	-	-	2	3	-	5	3.07%
40° ± 5°	-	1	5	8	-	14	8.59%
50° ± 5°	-	1	4	11	-	16	9.82%
60° ± 5°	1	3	6	12	1	23	14.11%
70° ± 5°	1	2	7	10	-	20	12.27%
80° ± 5°	2	5	2	12	1	22	13.50%
90° ± 5°	10	5	7	6	-	28	17.18%
above 96°	12	7	2	10	4	35	21.47%
TOTAL	26	24	35	72	6	163	
*PERCENTAGE SETS	84.62%	70.83%	88.57%	95.83%			

** UHM = Unspecified harder material (e.g., bone, antler, reeds).

TABLE 4.5   EDGE ANGLE GROUPS FOR IUZs USED IN LONGITUDINAL ACTIONS

A) MAXIMUM EDGE ANGLE GROUPS

ANGLE GROUP	BONE/ ANTLER	WOOD	DRY HIDE	OTHER	TOTAL	ROW %
30° ± 5°	-	-	6	-	6	6.12%
40° ± 5°	1	-	11)	1	13	13.27%
50° ± 5°	-	1	15) *	-	16	16.33%
60° ± 5°	1	1	20)	-	22	22.45%
70° ± 5°	1	-	16)	1	18	18.37%
80° ± 5°	-	-	7	-	7	7.14%
90° ± 5°	-	-	7	-	7	7.14%
above 96°	-	1	8	-	9	9.18%
TOTAL	3	3	90	2	98	

*PERCENTAGE SET   68.89%

B) MINIMUM EDGE ANGLE GROUPS

ANGLE GROUP	BONE/ ANTLER	WOOD	DRY HIDE	OTHER	TOTAL	ROW %
20° ± 5°	-	-	3	-	3	3.06%
30° ± 5°	-	-	13)	-	13	13.27%
40° ± 5°	1	-	18) *	1	20	20.41%
50° ± 5°	-	1	18)	-	19	19.39%
60° ± 5°	1	1	21)	-	23	23.47%
70° ± 5°	1	-	6	1	8	8.16%
80° ± 5°	-	-	6	-	6	6.12%
90° ± 5°	-	-	3	-	3	3.06%
above 96°	-	1	2	-	3	3.06%
TOTAL	3	3	90	2	98	

*PERCENTAGE SET   77.78%

TABLE 4.6   USE DURATIONS OF THE INDEPENDENT USE ZONES

USE DURATIONS	BONE/ ANTLER	UHM**	WOOD	DRY HIDE	OTHER	TOTAL	ROW %
SHORT (couple of minutes	12	6	-	5	2	25	8.83%
MODERATE (few to ± 20 min.)	13	10	27	91	-	141	49.82%
LONG (up to one and a half hrs.)	5	4	10	63	7	89	31.45%
VERY EXTENDED (more than 90 min.)	-	-	-	4	-	4	1.41%
UNCERTAIN DURATION	1	5	1	2	15	24	8.48%
TOTAL	31	25	38	165	24	283	
*PERCENTAGE SETS	80.65%	80.00%	97.37%	93.33%			

**UHM = Unspecified Harder Material (e.g., bone, antler, reeds).

TABLE 4.7   OVERLAPPING OF INDEPENDENT USE ZONES (IUZs)

TYPE OF IUZ	N	% OF ALL IUZs	
Isolated IUZ	239	84.45%	
Overlapping slightly or continuing into another IUZ	28	9.89%	} 15.54%
Completely coinciding IUZs	16	5.65%	
TOTAL	283		

TABLE 4.8   EDGE STATES OF THE INDEPENDENT USE ZONES (IUZs)

A) WITH REGARD TO ACTION

ACTION	UNRE-TOUCHED	RETOUCHED	SCARRED	BREAK EDGES	SIDES OF BURIN FACETS	RETRO-FLEXED	TOTAL
TRANS-VERSE	53 32.51%*	43 26.38%	24 14.72%	31 19.02%	11 6.75%	1 0.61%	163
LONGITU-DINAL	47 47.96%*	22 22.45%	22 22.45%	5 5.10%	2 2.04%	-	98
OTHER	11	6	3	2	-	-	22
TOTAL	111	71	49	38	13	1	283
% ALL IUZs	39.22%	25.09%	17.31%	13.43%	4.59%	0.35%	

B) WITH REGARD TO WORKED MATERIAL

WORKED MATERIAL	UNRE-TOUCHED	RETOUCHED	SCARRED	BREAK EDGES	SIDES OF BURIN FACETS	RETRO-FLEXED	TOTAL
BONE + ANTLER	13 41.94%*	3 9.68%	-	10 32.25%	5 16.13%	-	31
UHM**	10 40.00%*	3 12.00	2 8.00	8 32.00	2 8.00	-	25
WOOD	10 26.32%*	9 23.68%	12 31.58%	7 18.42%	-	-	38
DRY HIDE	65 39.39%*	50 30.30%	32 19.39%	8 6.66%	6 3.63%	1 0.61%	165
OTHER	13	6	3	2	-	-	24
TOTAL	111	71	49	38	13	1	283
% ALL IUZs	39.22%	25.09%	17.31%	13.43%	4.59%	0.35%	

 * Percentage calculated across the row.

** UHM = Unspecified harder material (e.g., bone, antler, reeds).

TABLE 4.9   NUMBER OF IUZs PER TOOL-TYPE GROUP BY WORKED MATERIAL

TOOL-TYPE GROUP	BONE/ ANTLER	UHM**	WOOD	DRY HIDE	OTHER	TOTAL
END-SCRAPERS	3	1	2	34 20.12%*	4	44
BECS	4	3	1	-	-	8
BURINS	8 24.24%*	3	1	13	1	26
SIDE-RETOUCHED BLADES	1	1	3	12	1	18
NOTCHES AND DENTICULATES	-	1	1	5	2	9
SPLINTERED PIECES	-	2	4	11	1	18
SIDE-SCRAPERS	2	2	-	11	2	17
DIVERSE RETOUCHED TYPES	3	1	3	10	5	22
RETOUCHED-RIDGE PIECES	1	-	-	12	-	13
SCARRED PIECES	3	4	11 28.95%*	24 14.20%*	2	44
ORDINARY UNRE-TOUCHED PIECES	8 24.24%*	8 30.77%*	12 31.58%*	37 21.89%*	6	71
TOTAL	33	26	38	169	24	290***

* Percentage calculated down the column.

** UHM = Unspecified harder material (e.g., bone, antler, reeds).

*** The counts differ slightly from the actual IUZ total of 283 (cf Table 4.1) since the seven IUZs from two used end-scrapers/burins (H28-359 and I27-220; Figs. 4.1:11, 12) were counted twice, with both the end-scrapers and the burins.

TABLE 4.10   EFFECTS OF NONUSE WEAR ON THE IUZs

DEGREE OF CERTAINTY OF POLISH DETERMINATION	N	% OF ALL IUZs
Definite	225	79.51%
Most likely	20)	7.07%)
Unspecified harder material	25)∗	8.83%)∗
Too abraded	5)	1.77%)
Insufficiently developed	2	0.71%
Unfamiliar	6	2.12%
∗ TOTAL IUZs reflecting damage by nonuse wear	50	17.67%

TABLE 4.11   SUMMARY OF THE PRINCIPAL TASKS ACCOMPLISHED BY THE INDEPENDENT USE ZONES

PRINCIPAL TASKS	N OF IUZs, % ALL IUZs	CONTACT SURFACE, CONTACT ANGLE	EDGE ANGLE	EDGE STATES	TOOL-TYPE GROUPS	OVERLAPPING & CURATION
DRY HIDE: LONGI-TUDINAL ACTIONS	N = 90 31.80%	(bifacial contact)	mainly above 66°	mainly unre-touched edges, retouched edges, and scarred edges	almost all types, esp. ordinary unre-touched pieces, end-scrapers, and scarred flints	most cases involved working hides
DRY HIDE: TRANS-VERSE ACTIONS	N = 72 25.44%	mainly ventral contact surface; low-medium or high contact angles	mainly 46° to above 96°			
WOOD: TRANSVERSE ACTIONS	N = 35 12.37%	ventral or dorsal contact surface; mainly low-medium contact angles (0 to 75°)	mainly 46° to above 96°	wide range: scarred edges, unretouched & retouched edges, and break edges	most types, esp. ordinary unre-touched pieces and scarred flints	rare
BONE & ANTLER: TRANSVERSE ACTIONS	N = 26 9.19%	mostly ventral contact surface; low-medium or high contact angles	mainly above 86°	mainly unre-touched edges & break edges	mainly ordinary unretouched, burins, & becs	few cases
UNSPECIFIED HARDER MATERIALS: TRANS-VERSE ACTIONS	N = 24 8.48%	mainly ventral contact surface; low-medium or high contact angles	mainly 76° to above 96°	mainly unre-touched edges & break edges	mainly ordinary unretouched flints, scarred pieces, becs, and burins	rare

TOTAL: N = 247, or 87.28% of all IUZs (N = 283).

TABLE 4.12   USE RATIOS OF TOOL-TYPE GROUPS

TOOL-TYPE GROUPS	TOTAL PIECES	N USED	% USED	NUMBER OF IUZs PER PIECE						
				1	2	3	4	5	6	7
A) RETOUCHED TOOLS (N = 78*)										
END-SCRAPERS	21	12	57.14%	1	3	3	1	2	1	1
BECS	27	5	18.52%	3	1	1	-	-	-	-
BURINS	28	13	46.43%	7	3	1	1	1	-	-
SIDE-RETOUCHED BLADES	10	7	70.00%	2	3	-	1	1	-	-
NOTCHES AND DENTICULATES	38	7	18.42%	6	-	1	-	-	-	-
SPLINTERED PIECES	26	14	53.85%	11	2	1	-	-	-	-
SIDE-SCRAPERS	14	8	57.14%	2	4	1	1	-	-	-
DIVERSE RETOUCHED	28	12	42.86%	6	3	2	1	-	-	-
TOTAL RETOUCHED	(192)*	(78)*	(40.62%)	(38)	(19)	(10)	(5)	(4)	(1)	(1)
B) UNRETOUCHED FLINTS** (N = 82)										
RETOUCHED-RIDGE PIECES	14	11	78.57%	9	1	1	-	-	-	-
SCARRED PIECES	54	23	42.59	9	10	2	1	1	-	-
ORDINARY UNRE-TOUCHED PIECES	275	48	17.45%	29	15	4	-	-	-	-
TOTAL UNRET.	(343)	(82)	(23.91)	(47)	(26)	(7)	(1)	(1)	-	-
OVERALL TOTAL	532***	158***	29.70%							

* Three end-scraper/burins (of which two were used) were counted twice, once with the end-scrapers and once with the burins.

** RETOUCHED-RIDGE PIECES: flints with retouched dorsal ridge (i.e., burin spalls struck off of retouched edges). SCARRED PIECES: classified by the excavator as "utilized or lightly retouched" due to macroscopically visible edge-chipping.

*** Overall totals adjusted to eliminate double counts.

TABLE 4.13   NUMBER OF INDEPENDENT USE ZONES (IUZs) PER PIECE IN
RETOUCHED AND UNRETOUCHED TOOL CLASSES

	USED RETOUCHED (N = 78)		USED UNRETOUCHED (N = 82)	
NUMBER OF IUZs	N	% OF 78	N	% OF 82
ONE	38	48.72%	47	57.32%
TWO OR MORE	40	51.28%	35	42.68%
THREE OR MORE	21	26.92%	9	10.98%
FOUR OR MORE	11	14.10%	2	2.44%
FIVE OR MORE	6	7.69%	1	1.22%

TABLE 4.14   ACTIONS DISPLAYED BY THE TOOL-TYPE GROUPS

TOOL-TYPE GROUPS	TRANS-VERSE	LONGITU-DINAL	TRANS. + LONGIT.	GROOVE	BORE	TRANS. + BORE	TRANS. + BROOVE	UNCER-TAIN
A) RETOUCHED TOOLS (N= 78)								
END-SCRAPERS	5	-	6	1	-	-	-	-
BECS	4	-	-	-	-	-	-	1
BURINS	10	1	2	-	-	-	-	-
SIDE-RETOUCHED BLADES	1	1	4	-	1	-	-	-
NOTCHES AND DENTICULATES	6	-	1	-	-	-	-	-
SPLINTERED PIECES	5	7	2	-	-	-	-	-
SIDE-SCRAPERS	4	2	2	-	-	-	-	-
DIVERSE RETOUCHED	6	2	3	-	-	-	-	1
TOTALS	(41)	(13)	(20)	(1)	(1)	-	-	(2)
PERCENTAGE OF TOTAL 78 IUZs	52.56%	16.67%	25.64%					
B) UNRETOUCHED FLINTS (N = 82)								
RETOUCHED-RIDGE PIECES	6	5	-	-	-	-	-	-
SCARRED PIECES	9	7	5	-	-	1	-	1
ORDINARY UNRE-TOUCHED PIECES	20	19	7	-	-	-	1	1
TOTALS	(35)	(31)	(12)	-	-	(1)	(1)	(2)
PERCENTAGE OF TOTAL 82 IUZs	42.68%	37.80%	14.63%*			1.22%*	1.22%*	

TOTAL % IN MULTIPLE ACTIONS: *17.07%

TABLE 4.15   PROPORTION OF MULTIPLE ACTION TOOLS
AMONG FLINTS WITH MORE THAN ONE IUZ

| NUMBER OF IUZ | SINGLE ACTION TOOLS | | | MULTIPLE ACTION TOOLS | TOTAL | MULTIPLE ACTION TOOLS AS % OF TOTAL |
	TRANS-VERSE	LONGITU-DINAL	OTHER			
A) RETOUCHED TOOLS (N = 76*)						
ONE	25	10	3	-	38	-
TWO	7	3	1	7	18	38.89%
THREE	5	-	-	5	10	50.00%
FOUR	3	-	-	2	5	40.00%
FIVE to SEVEN	-	-	-	5	5	100%
B) UNRETOUCHED FLINTS (N = 82)						
ONE	24	21	2	-	47	-
TWO	8	9	-	9	26	34.62%
THREE	3	1	-	3	7	42.86%
FOUR or FIVE	-	-	-	2	2	100%

* Eliminating double count for two used end-scraper/burins.

TABLE 4.16   TOOL-TYPE GROUPS BY SINGLE AND MULTIPLE
WORKED MATERIALS

| TOOL-TYPE GROUPS | TOOLS WITH A SINGLE WORKED MATERIAL | | | | | | | |
	BONE + ANTLER	UHM*	WOOD	DRY HIDE	PLANT	UNDEVEL., ABRADED, UNFAMIL.	TOTAL	DRY HIDE AS % OF TOTAL
A) RETOUCHED TOOLS (N = 78)								
END-SCRAPERS	1	-	-	8	-	-	9	88.89%
BECS	1	3	-	-	-	-	4	-
BURINS	3	1	1	4	-	-	9	44.44%
SIDE-RETOUCHED BLADES	-	-	1	3	-	-	4	75.00%
NOTCHES AND DENTICULATES	-	1	1	3	-	2	7	42.86%
SPLINTERED PIECES	-	1	1	10	-	-	12	83.33%
SIDE-SCRAPERS	1	-	-	5	-	-	6	83.33%
DIVERSE RETOUCHED	-	-	3	5	-	1	9	55.56%
TOTALS	(6)	(6)	(7)	(38)	-	(3)	(60)	(63.33%)

* UHM = Unspecified harder material (e.g., bone, antler, reeds).

TABLE 4.16   (continued)

TOOL-TYPE GROUPS	TOOLS WITH A SINGLE WORKED MATERIAL							
	BONE + ANTLER	UHM*	WOOD	DRY HIDE	PLANT	UNDEVEL., ABRADED, UNFAMIL.	TOTAL	DRY HIDE AS % OF TOTAL

B) UNRETOUCHED FLINTS (N = 82)

RETOUCHED-RIDGE PIECES	-	-	-	9	-	1	10	90.00%
SCARRED PIECES	2	2	3	12	-	1	20	60.00%
ORDINARY UNRE-TOUCHED PIECES	5	3	5	24	1	2	40	60.00%
TOTALS	(7)	(5)	(8)	(45)	(1)	(4)	(70)	(64.29%)

TOOL-TYPE GROUPS	TOOLS WITH MULTIPLE WORKED MATERIALS**											MULTIP. MAT'LS TOOLS AS % OF OVERALL TOTAL
	B+U	W+B	W+U	H+B	H+A	H+B +A	H+W	H+W +B	H+U	TOTAL	DRY HIDE AS % OF TOTAL	

A) RETOUCHED TOOLS (N =78)

END-SCRAPERS	-	-	-	1	-	-	1	-	1	3	100%	25.00%
BECS	-	1	-	-	-	-	-	-	-	1	-	20.00%
BURINS	-	-	-	1	-	1	-	-	2	4 .	100%	30.77%
SIDE-RETOUCHED BLADES	-	-	-	-	-	-	1	1	1	3	100%	42.85%
NOTCHES AND DENTICULATES	-	-	-	-	-	-	-	-	-	-	-	-
SPLINTERED PIECES	-	-	1	-	-	-	1	-	-	2	50.00%	14.29%
SIDE-SCRAPERS	-	-	-	1	-	-	-	-	1	2	100%	25.00%
DIVERSE RETOUCHED	-	-	-	1	2	-	-	-	-	3	100%	25.00%
TOTALS	-	(1)	(1)	(4)	(2)	(1)	(3)	(1)	(5)	(18)	(88.89%)	(23.08%)

B) UNRETOUCHED FLINTS (N = 82)

RETOUCHED-RIDGE PIECES	-	-	-	-	1	-	-	-	-	1	100%	9.09%
SCARRED PIECES	-	-	1	-	-	-	2	-	-	3	66.67%	13.04%
ORDINARY UNRE-TOUCHED PIECES	1	1	2	-	-	-	3	-	1	8	50.00%	16.67%
TOTALS	(1)	(1)	(3)	-	(1)	-	(5)	-	(1)	(12)	(58.33%)	(14.63%)

* B = Bone; A = Antler; U = Unspecified harder material; W = Wood; and H = Dry hide.

TABLE 4.17   PROPORTION OF PIECES WITH MULTIPLE WORKED MATERIALS
AMONG TOOLS WITH MORE THAN ONE IUZ

NUMBER OF IUZs	SINGLE BONE + ANTLER	WORKED UHM*	WOOD	MATERIALS DRY HIDE	OTHER	TOOLS W/ MULTIPLE WORKED MATERIALS	TOTAL	% OF TOTAL WITH MULTIPLE WORKED MAT'LS
A) RETOUCHED TOOLS (N = 76**)								
ONE	4	6	5	20	3	-	38	-
TWO	2	-	1	9	-	6	18	33.33%
THREE	-	-	-	6	-	4	10	40.00%
FOUR	-	-	1	1	-	3	5	60.00%
FIVE	-	-	-	-	-	3	3	100%
SIX or SEVEN	-	-	-	2	-	-	2	-
B) UNRETOUCHED FLINTS (N = 82)								
ONE	5	5	6	26	5	-	47	-
TWO	2	-	1	16	-	7	26	26.92%
THREE	-	-	1	2	-	4	7	57.14%
FOUR	-	-	-	1	-	0	1	-
FIVE	-	-	-	-	-	1	1	100%

* UHM = Unspecified harder material (e.g., bone, antler, reeds).

** Eliminating double count for two used end-scraper/burins.

TABLE 4.18   TOOL-TYPE GROUPS BY GREATEST RELATIVE USE DURATION

TOOL-TYPE GROUPS	SHORT (couple minutes)	MODERATE (few to ± 20 min.)	LONG (up to 90 min.)	VERY EXTENDED (over 90 min.)	UNCERTAIN
A) RETOUCHED TOOLS (N = 78)					
END-SCRAPERS	1	2	8	1	-
BECS	2	3	-	-	-
BURINS	2	6	5	-	-
SIDE-RETOUCHED BLADES	-	3	4	-	-
NOTCHES AND DENTICULATES	1	1	2	-	3
SPLINTERED PIECES	1	9	4	-	-
SIDE-SCRAPERS	-	3	4	1	-
DIVERSE RETOUCHED	-	9	2	-	1
TOTALS	(7)	(36)	(29)	(2)	(4)
B) UNRETOUCHED FLINTS (N = 82)					
RETOUCHED-RIDGE PIECES	-	5	4	1	1
SCARRED PIECES	-	10	11	-	2
ORDINARY UNRE-TOUCHED PIECES	1	26	16	1	4
TOTALS	(1)	(41)	(31)	(2)	(7)

TABLE 4.19   TOOL-TYPE GROUPS DISPLAYING IUZs INVOLVED
                     IN CURATION AFTER USE

TOOL-TYPE GROUPS	IUZs DISRUPTED BY BREAKS OR BURINS (EDGE NOT REUSED)	IUZs DISRUPTED BY RETOUCH (EDGE NOT REUSED)	IUZs MODIFIED THEN REUSED
A) RETOUCHED TOOLS (155 IUZs)			
END-SCRAPERS	1	4	7
BECS	-	-	-
BURINS	3	2	3
SIDE-RETOUCHED BLADES	2	2	2
NOTCHES AND DENTICULATES	-	1	-
SPLINTERED PIECES	-	6	2
SIDE-SCRAPERS	-	5	3
DIVERSE RETOUCHED	3	4	1
TOTALS	(9)	(24)	(18)
B) UNRETOUCHED FLINTS (128 IUZs)			
RETOUCHED-RIDGE PIECES	1	6	2
SCARRED PIECES	3	4	2
ORDINARY UNRE-TOUCHED PIECES	2	3	-
TOTALS	(6)	(13)	(4)

TABLE 4.20   USE OF BURIN TYPES

BURIN TYPE	NUMBER OF PIECES			NUMBER OF INDEPENDENT USE ZONES				
	UNUSED	USED	TOTAL	BONE/ANTLER	UHM*	WOOD	DRY HIDE	GRIT (GRIP)
17. END-SCRAPER/BURIN	1	2	(3)	2	1	-	4	-
27, 29. DIHEDRAL BURINS	1	5	(6)	4	1	-	2	-
30. ANGLED BURIN ON A BREAK	6	2	(8)	-	-	-	5	-
38, 39. TRANSVERSAL BURINS	6	2	(8)	1	1	-	2	1
40, 41. MULTIPLE BURINS	1	1	(2)	1	-	-	-	-
43. CORE-SHAPED BURIN	-	1	(1)	-	-	1	-	-
TOTALS	(15)	(13) 46.43%	(28)	(8)	(3)	(1)	(13)	(1)

* UHM = Unspecified harder material (e.g., bone, antler, reeds).

TABLE 4.21   INDEPENDENT USE ZONES ON SPLINTERED PIECES (PIECES ESQUILLEES)

USE IN RELATION TO ESQUILLEE RETOUCH *	UHM** in TRANSVERSE ACTION	WOOD in TRANSVERSE ACTION	WOOD in LONGITUDINAL ACTION	DRY HIDE in TRANSVERSE ACTION	DRY HIDE in LONGITUDINAL ACTION	TOTAL NO. OF IUZs
BEFORE	-	-	-	3	3	6
AFTER	1	1	-	-	2	4
UNCERTAIN	1	1	2	-	3	7
TOTALS	(2)	(2)	(2)	(3)	(8)	(17)

* BEFORE: Micropolish terminates abruptly at esquillée retouch; therefore, use preceded retouch.
  AFTER: Micropolish found on edge bearing esquillée retouch; therefore, use followed retouch.
  UNCERTAIN: No definite relation between micropolish and esquilée retouch.

** UHM = Unspecified harder material (e.g., bone, antler, reeds).

TABLE 4.22   SUMMARY OF USE PATTERNS OF TOOL-TYPE GROUPS

TOOL-TYPE GROUPS	TOTAL STUDIED	N & % USED	N and % USED IN 2 OR MORE TASKS	N and % USED IN 3 OR MORE TASKS	MAJOR SINGLE ACTION	N & % w/ MULTIPLE ACTIONS
A) RETOUCHED TOOLS (N = 78)						
END-SCRAPERS	21	12 57%	11 92%	8 67%	trans-verse	6 50%
BECS	27	5 19%	2 40%	1 20%	trans-verse	-
BURINS	28	13 46%	6 46%	3 23%	trans-verse	2 15%
SIDE-RETOUCHED BLADES	10	7 70%	5 71%	2 29%	trans. + longit.	4 57%
NOTCHES AND DENTICULATES	38	7 18%	1 14%	1 14%	trans-verse	1 14%
SPLINTERED PIECES	26	14 54%	3 21%	1 7%	longitu-dinal	2 14%
SIDE-SCRAPERS	14	8 57%	6 75%	2 25%	trans-verse	2 25%
DIVERSE RETOUCHED	28	12 43%	6 50%	3 25%	trans-verse	3 25%
TOTALS	(192)	(78) (41%)	(38) (51%)	(21) (27%)		(20) (26%)
B) UNRETOUCHED FLINTS (N = 82)						
RETOUCHED-RIDGE PIECES	14	11 79%	2 18%	1 9%	trans. + longit.	-
SCARRED PIECES	54	23 43%	14 61%	4 17%	trans. + longit.	6 26%
ORDINARY UNRE-TOUCHED PIECES	275	48 17%	19 40%	4 8%	trans. + longit.	8 17%
TOTALS	(343)	(82) (24%)	(35) (43%)	(9) (11%)		(14) (17%)

TABLE 4.22 (continued)

TOOL-TYPE GROUPS	MAJOR WORKED MATERIAL	OTHER WORKED MATERIALS	N and % WITH MULTIPLE WORKED MAT'LS	PREDOMINANT CURATED GROUPS
A) RETOUCHED TOOLS (N = 78)				
END-SCRAPERS	dry hide	bone/antler and UHM*	3 25%	XXX
BECS	UHM*	bone/antler and wood	1 20%	
BURINS	bone/antler, dry hide	UHM* and wood	4 31%	
SIDE-RETOUCHED BLADES	dry hide	wood, bone, and UHM*	3 43%	
NOTCHES AND DENTICULATES	dry hide	wood and UHM*	-	
SPLINTERED PIECES	dry hide	wood and UHM*	2 14%	X
SIDE-SCRAPERS	dry hide	bone/antler and UHM*	2 25%	X
DIVERSE RETOUCHED	dry hide	bone/antler and wood	3 25%	
TOTALS			(18) (30%)	
B) UNRETOUCHED FLINTS (N = 82)				
RETOUCHED-RIDGE PIECES	dry hide	antler	1 9%	X
SCARRED PIECES	dry hide	wood, UHM*, bone/antler	3 13%	
ORDINARY UNRE-TOUCHED PIECES	dry hide	wood, bone/antler, UHM*	8 16%	
TOTALS			(12) (17%)	

* UHM = Unspecified harder material (e.g., bone, antler, reeds).

TABLE 4.23   PROPORTIONS OF RETOUCHED AND USED PIECES BY MAJOR TYPES OF FLINT

			UNUSED		USED				NUMBER		OF			IUZ		% WITH 2 OR MORE
FLINT TYPES	TOTAL	% ALL PIECES	UNRET.*	RET.**	UNRET.*	RET.**	% RE-TOUCHED	% USED	1	2	3	4	5	6	7	IUZs
1. WHITE	60	11.28%	34	12	7	7	31.67%	23.33%	9	2	3	-	-	-	-	35.71%
2. YELLOW	50	9.40%	18	13	11	8	42.00%	38.00%	9	5	2	I	2	-	-	52.63%
3. BLUE-GREY	149	28.01%	64	23	29	33	37.58%	41.61%	32	17	8	3	2	-	-	48.39%
4. GREY-BLACK	29	5.45%	19	6	3	1	24.14%	24.14%	2	2	-	-	-	-	-	***
5. BANDED GREY	22	4.14%	13	4	3	2	27.27	22.73	3	1	1	-	-	-	-	***
6. IVORY-BROWN	89	16.73	41	23	16	9	26.97	28.09	15	7	2	1	-	-	-	40.00%
7. DIVERSE	133	25.00	72	32	13	16	36.09	21.80%	15	10	1	1	-	1	1	48.28%

* UNRET. = Unretouched.   ** RET. = Retouched.   *** Insufficient number of cases to give meaningful percentages.

TABLE 4.24   TOOL-TYPE GROUPS BY FLINT TYPES

	1. WHITE		2. YELLOW		3. BLUE-GREY		4. GREY-BLACK		5. BANDED GREY		6. IVORY-BROWN		7. DIVERSE	
TOOL-TYPE GROUPS	TOTAL	USED	TOTAL	USED	TOTAL	USED	TOTAL	USED	TOTAL	USED	TOTAL	USED	TOTAL	USED
END-SCRAPERS	2	1	1	1	5	4	1	-	1	1	3	1	7	3
BECS	3	-	8	3	6	1	3	-	-	-	4	1	3	-
BURINS	3	1	2	1	9	6	1	-	-	-	6	1	7	4
SIDE-RETOUCHED BLADES	-	-	-	-	9	6	-	-	-	-	-	-	1	1
NOTCHES AND DENTICULATES	7	3	3	1	4	1	2	1	-	-	10	1	13	1
SPLINTERED PIECES	1	-	2	1	15	10	-	-	3	-	3	2	2	1
SIDE-SCRAPERS	2	1	2	-	2	2	-	-	1	1	3	1	4	3
DIVERSE RETOUCHED	2	1	3	1	7	4	-	-	1	-.	3	2	11	3
TOT. RETOUCHED	(20)	(7)	(21)	(8)	(57)	(34)	(7)	(1)	(6)	(2)	(32)	(9)	(48)	(16)
RETOUCHED-RIDGE PIECES	-	-	3	2	8	7	-	-	2	1	-	-	1	1
SCARRED PIECES	7	2	6	2	15	7	2	1	2	-	11	6	11	5
ORDINARY UNRE-TOUCHED PIECES	33	5	20	7	69	15	20	2	12	2	46	10	73	7
TOTAL UNRE-TOUCHED	(40)	(7)	(29)	(11)	(92)	(29)	(22)	(3)	(16)	(3)	(57)	(16)	(85)	(13)

TABLE 4.25   BLADES AND BURIN SPALLS BY FLINT TYPES

	1. WHITE	2. YELLOW	3. BLUE-GREY	4. GREY-BLACK	5. BANDED GREY	6. IVORY-BROWN	7. DIVERSE	TOTAL
BLADES	6	2	19 43.18%	2	-	9	6	44
BURIN SPALLS	2	2	18 50.00%	-	5	4	5	36

TABLE 4.26   NUMBER OF INDEPENDENT USE ZONES PER FLINT TYPE BY WORKED MATERIAL

FLINT TYPES	BONE/ ANTLER	UHM*	WOOD	DRY HIDE	OTHER	TOTAL
1. WHITE	1	3	3	15 68.18%	-	22
2. YELLOW	5	6	9	15 38.46%	4	39
3. BLUE-GREY	12	12	11	68 60.18%	10	113
4. GREY-BLACK	-	-	-	5 83.33%	1	6
5. BANDED GREY	1	-	1	5 62.50%	1	8
6. IVORY-BROWN	5	2	6	22 57.89%	3	38
7. DIVERSE	7	2	8	35 61.40%	5	57

*UHM = Unspecified harder material (e.g., bone, antler, reeds).

TABLE 4.27   NUMBER OF INDEPENDENT USE ZONES PER FLINT TYPE BY USE DURATIONS

FLINT TYPES	SHORT (couple minutes)	MODERATE (few to about 20 min.)	LONG (up to 90 min.)	VERY EXTENDED (over 90 min.)	UNCERTAIN	TOTAL
1. WHITE	1	13	6	-	2	22
2. YELLOW	4	22	8	1	4	39
3. BLUE-GREY	14	56	33	1	9	113
4. GREY-BLACK	-	1	3	-	2	6
5. BANDED GREY	-	5	2	-	1	8
6. IVORY-BROWN	2	20	14	-	2	38
7. DIVERSE	4	24	23	2	4	57

TABLE 4.28   FLINT TYPES INVOLVED IN CURATION AFTER USE

FLINT TYPES	PIECES WITH IUZ DISRUPTED BY BREAKS OR BURINS (EDGE NOT REUSED)	PIECES WITH IUZ DISRUPTED BY RETOUCH (EDGE NOT REUSED)	PIECES WITH IUZ MODIFIED THEN REUSED
1. WHITE	2	3	2
2. YELLOW	-	1	-
3. BLUE-GREY	9	24	13
4. GREY-BLACK	-	-	-
5. BANDED GREY	-	-	1
6. IVORY-BROWN	1	4	-
7. DIVERSE	3	4	4

TABLE 4.29   PROPORTIONS OF RETOUCHED AND USED FLINTS AMONG THE TECHNOLOGICAL CLASSES

TECHNOLOGICAL CLASSES	TOTAL	% ALL PIECES	UNUSED		USED		% RE-TOUCHED	% USED	NUMBER	OF		IUZs				% WITH 2 OR MORE IUZs
			UNRET.*	RET.**	UNRET.*	RET.**			1	2	3	4	5	6	7	
FLAKES	305	57.33% (77.63%)	107	91	53	54	47.70%	35.08%	56	30	13	4	2	1	-	47.17%
SMALL FLAKES***	108	20.30%	97	4	6	1	4.60%	6.48%	6	1	1	-	-	-	-	25.00%
BLADES	44	8.27%	12	7	6	19	59.09%	56.82%	10	8	2	2	2	-	-	60.00%
BLADELETS	17	3.20%	16	-	1	-	-	5.88%	1	-	-	-	-	-	-	-
BURIN SPALLS	36	6.77%	17	4	14	1	13.89%	41.67%	9	5	1	-	-	-	-	40.00%
CORES	9	1.69	7	1	1	-	11.11%	11.11%	1	-	-	-	-	-	-	-
DEBRIS	13	2.44	5	6	1	1	53.85%	15.85%	2	-	-	-	-	-	-	-

* UNRET. = Unretouched.   ** RET. = Retouched.   *** under 18 x 24 mm.

TABLE 4.30   NUMBER OF INDEPENDENT USE ZONES PER TEHCNOLOGICAL
CLASS BY WORKED MATERIAL

TECHNOLOGICAL CLASSES	BONE/ ANTLER	UHM*	WOOD	DRY HIDE	OTHER	TOTAL IUZs
FLAKES	20	20	31	101 (53.72%)	16	188
SMALL FLAKES**	-	1	-	9 (90.00%)	-	10
BLADES	5	2	7	40 (67.80%)	5	59
BLADELETS	-	-	-	1	-	1
BURIN SPALLS	6	-	-	13 (59.09%)	3	22
CORES	-	-	-	1	-	1
DEBRIS	-	2	-	-	-	2

* UHM = Unspecified harder material (e.g., bone, antler, reeds).

** Under 18 x 24 mm.

TABLE 4.31   TECHNOLOGICAL CLASSES INVOLVED IN CURATION AFTER USE

TECHNOLOGICAL CLASSES	PIECES WITH IUZ DISRUPTED BY BREAKS OR BURINS (EDGE NOT REUSED)	PIECES WITH IUZ DISRPUTED BY RETOUCH (EDGE NOT REUSED)	PIECES WITH IUZ MODIFIED THEN REUSED
FLAKES	8	22	13
SMALL FLAKES*	1	2	-
BLADES	4	4	5
BLADELETS	-	1	-
BURIN SPALLS	2	6	2
CORES	-	1	-
DEBRIS	-	-	-

* Under 18 x 24 mm.

TOOL-TYPE GROUPS	OBSV. TOTAL	EXP. TOTAL	OBSV. USED	EXP. USED	OBSV. WITH 1 IUZ	EXP. WITH 1 IUZ	OBSV. WITH 2 OR MORE IUZs	EXP. WITH 2 OR MORE IUZs
END-SCRAPERS	10		5		-		5	
BECS	12		-		-		-	
BURINS	15		5		4		1	
SIDE-RETOUCHED BLADES	4		3		2		1	
NOTCHES AND DENTICULATES	22		4		4		-	
SPLINTERED PIECES	11		9		6		3	
SIDE-SCRAPERS	10		6		2		4	
OTHER RETOUCHED	10		5		1		4	
TOT. RETOUCHED	(94)	(86)	(37)	(35)	(19)	(16)	(18)	(19)
RETOUCHED-RIDGE PIECES	3		3		2		1	
SCARRED PIECES	26		12		3		9	
ORDINARY UNRE-TOUCHED PIECES	120		20		13		7	
TOTAL UNRE-TOUCHED	(149)	(157)	(35)	(37)	(18)	(21)	(17)	(16)
CHI-SQUARE:		1.15		.22		.99		.11
df:		1		1		1		1
p:		.3		.65		.3		.75
SIGNIFICANT DIFFERENCE?:		NO		NO		NO		NO

NB: Expected totals are 46% of the appropriate totals in Table 4.12.

TABLE 4.33   OBSERVED AND EXPECTED FREQUENCIES OF WORKED MATERIALS
AMONG FLINTS BEARING CORTEX

WORKED MATERIALS	OBSERVED IUZs	EXPECTED IUZs*	CHI-SQUARE	df	p	SIGNIFICANT DIFFERENCE?
BONE/ANTLER	8	14				
UHM**	8	11				
WOOD	21	17				
DRY HIDE	79	76				
OTHER	13	11				
TOTAL	(129)	(129)	4.81	4	.3	NO

* Expected totals are 46% of the total IUZs for corresponding
worked materials in Table 4.1.

** UHM = Unspecified harder material (e.g., bone, antler, reeds).

TABLE 4.34   OBSERVED AND EXPECTED FREQUENCIES OF FLINT TYPES
AMONG FLINTS BEARING CORTEX

FLINT TYPES	OBSERVED USED	EXPECTED USED*	CHI-SQUARE	df	p	SIGNIFICANT DIFFERENCE?
1. WHITE	5	6				
2. YELLOW	12	9				
3. BLUE-GREY	21	28				
4. GREY-BLACK	4	2				
5. BANDED GREY	2	2				
6. IVORY-BROWN	16	12				
7. DIVERSE	12	13				
TOTAL	(72)	(72)	6.33	6	4	NO

* Expected totals are 46% of the "Used" column in Table 4.23.

TABLE 4.35   OBSERVED AND EXPECTED FREQUENCIES OF LOCAL VS. IMORTED
FLINT TYPES AMONG PIECES BEARING CORTEX

FLINT TYPES	OBSERVED WITH CORTEX	EXPECTED WITH CORTEX*	CHI-SQUARE	df	p	SIGNIFICANT DIFFERENCE?
1. WHITE	26	28				
6. IVORY-BROWN	46	41				
TOTAL LOCAL FLINTS	(72)	(69)				
2. YELLOW	29	23				
3. BLUE-GREY	54	69				
4. GREY-BLACK	20	13				
5. BANDED GREY	9	10				
TOTAL IMPORTED FLINTS	(112)	(115)	.21	1	.65	NO

* Expected totals are 46% of the "Total" column in Table 4.23.

TABLE 4.36   OBSERVED AND EXPECTED FREQUENCIES OF THE TECHNOLOGICAL CLASSES
AMONG FLINTS BEARING CORTEX

TECHNOLOGICAL CLASSES	TOTAL OBSERVED w/ CORTEX	TOTAL EXPECTED* w/ CORTEX	CHI^2	df	p	SIGNIFICANT DIFFERENCE?	OBSERVED USED w/ CORTEX	EXPECTED** USED w/ CORTEX	CHI^2	df	p	SIGNIFICANT DIFFERENCE?
FLAKES	173	139					53	49				
SMALL FLAKES	26	49					1	3				
BLADES	20	20					13	12				
BLADELETS	5	8					-	-				
BURIN SPALLS	7	17					4	7				
CORES	8	4					1	-				
DEBRIS	4	6					-	1				
TOTALS	(243)	(243)	30.8	6	<.001	YES	(72)	(72)	4.02	6	.7	NO

* Expected totals are 46% of the "Total" column in Table 4.29.

** Expected totals are 46% of the "Used" column in Table 4.29.

TABLE 4.37   DISTRIBUTION OF FLINTS AND USED TOOLS BY METER SQUARES

SQUARE	TOTAL FLINTS		WITH RETOUCH*		USED		PIECES WITH THREE OR MORE IUZs		TOOLS WITH MULTIPLE WORKED MATERIALS		TOOLS WITH MULTIPLE ACTIONS		CURATED PIECES	
G26	42		13		11		2		-		3		3	
G27	123		49		40		7		6		8		14	
H27	60		19		21		6		3		5		5	
I27	42		17		11		3		2		4		3	
G28	86		28		26		5		7		4		6	
H28	45		22		17		3		2		3		3	
TOTAL FOR CAVE:	(398)	75%	(148)	73%	(126)	81%	(26)	93%	(20)	83%	(27)	84%	(34)	76%
G31	11		8		3		-		1		-		1	
G32	12		8		3		1		1		1		2	
H32	7		4		-		-		-		-		-	
G33	17		8		4		-		1		-		-	
H33	58		17		13		-		1		1		4	
G34	16		5		4		1		-		3		3	
H34	11		4		3		-		-		-		1	
TOTAL FOR TERRACE:	(132)	25%	(54)	27%	(30)	19%	(2)	2%	(4)	17%	(5)	16%	(11)	24%

* Retouched tool types and retouched-ridge pieces.

TABLE 4.38   DISTRIBUTION OF USED FLINTS BY WORKED MATERIALS
AND METER SQUARES

SQUARE	BONE/ ANTLER		UHM*		WOOD		DRY HIDE	
G26	3		-		-		8	
G27	4		2		8		32	
H27	2		3		4		16	
I27	1		1		1		9	
G28	4		9		8		10	
H28	2		2		3		11	
TOTAL FOR CAVE:	(16)	67%	(17)	81%	(24)	80%	(86)	83%
G31	2		1		-		1	
G32	1		-		1		2	
H32	-		-		-		-	
G33	3		-		1		-	
H33	2		3		3		8	
G34	-		-		-		4	
H34	-		-		1		2	
TOTAL FOR TERRACE:	(8)	33%	(4)	19%	(6)	20%	(17)	17%

* UHM = Unspecified harder material (e.g., bone, antler, reeds).

NB: In the case of a used flint with multiple worked materials, the
     piece was counted once under each relevant category of material.

TABLE 4.39   DISTRIBUTION OF USED FLINTS BY TOOL-TYPE GROUPS AND METER SQUARES

TOOL-TYPE GROUPS	G26	G27	H27	I27	G28	H28	CAVE TOTAL	%	G31	G32	H32	G33	H33	G34	H34	TERRACE TOTAL	%
END-SCRAPERS	1	3	3	2	1	2	(12)	100%	-	-	-	-	-	-	-	-	-
BECS	-	1	2	-	1	-	(4)	80%	1	-	-	-	-	-	-	(1)	20%
BURINS	1	3	-	2	2	2	(10)	77%	1	-	-	1	1	-	-	(3)	23%
SIDE-RETOUCHED BLADES	-	2	1	-	3	-	(6)	86%	-	-	-	-	1	-	-	(1)	14%
NOTCHES AND DENTICULATES	-	2	-	-	1	3	(6)	86%	-	-	-	-	-	1	-	(1)	14%
SPLINTERED PIECES	-	3	3	1	3	4	(14)	100%	-	-	-	-	-	-	-	-	-
SIDE-SCRAPERS	-	1	-	1	3	1	(6)	75%	-	-	-	-	-	1	1	(2)	25%
OTHER RETOUCHED	2	4	-	-	-	-	(6)	50%	-	2	-	-	3	1	-	(6)	50%
TOT. RETOUCHED	(4)	(19)	(9)	(6)	(14)	(12)	(64)	(82%)	(2)	(2)	-	(1)	(5)	(3)	(1)	(14)	(18%)
RETOUCHED-RIDGE PIECES	1	3	1	1	1	3	(10)	91%	1	-	-	-	-	-	-	(1)	9%
SCARRED PIECES	1	7	4	2	3	1	(18)	82%	-	1	-	1	2	-	-	(4)	18%
ORDINARY UNRE-TOUCHED PIECES	5	11	7	3	8	2	(36)	77%	-	-	-	2	6	1	2	(11)	23%
TOTAL UNRE-TOUCHED	(7)	(21)	(12)	(6)	(12)	(6)	(64)	(80%)	(1)	(1)	-	(3)	(8)	(1)	(2)	(16)	(20%)

TABLE 4.40   DISTRIBUTION OF PIECES BY FLINT TYPES AND METER SQUARES

SQUARE	1. WHITE TOTAL	USED	2. YELLOW TOTAL	USED	3. BLUE-GREY TOTAL	USED	4. GREY-BLACK TOTAL	USED	5. BANDED TOTAL	BREY USED	6. IVORY-BROWN TOTAL	USED	7. DIVERSE TOTAL	USED	TOTALS N	USED
G26	7	2	6	2	12	4	-	-	3	-	5	2	9	1	42	11
G27	18	6	24	11	36	16	2	-	9	1	9	3	25	3	123	40
H27	4	2	3	1	24	8	4	2	3	1	6	3	16	4	60	21
I27	4	-	1	1	11	4	5	-	-	-	6	2	15	4	42	11
G28	11	1	11	3	24	10	15	2	3	1	4	2	18	7	86	26
H28	9	2	1	-	17	10	1	-	2	1	1	-	14	4	45	17
TOTAL FOR CAVE:	(53)	(13)	(46)	(18)	(124)	(52)	(27)	(4)	(20)	(4)	(31)	(12)	(97)	(23)	(398)	(126)
G31	3	-	3	1	1	1	1	-	-	-	2	1	1	-	11	3
G32	-	-	-	-	3	2	-	-	-	-	5	1	4	-	12	3
H32	1	-	-	-	2	-	-	-	-	-	2	-	2	-	7	-
G33	-	-	-	-	4	1	-	-	1	1	5	2	7	-	17	4
H33	2	-	1	-	10	4	-	-	-	-	33	6	12	3	58	13
G34	1	1	-	-	2	1	1	-	1	-	7	1	4	1	16	4
H34	-	-	-	-	2	-	-	-	-	-	3	2	6	1	11	3
TOTAL FOR TERRACE:	(7)	(1)	(4)	(1)	(24)	(9)	(2)	-	(2)	(1)	(57)	(13)	(36)	(5)	(132)	(30)

TABLE 4.41   DISTRIBUTION OF FLINTS WITH DAMAGED
                        USE-WEAR POLISHES

SQUARE	OBSERVED WITH DAMAGED POLISHES*	EXPECTED WITH DAMAGED POLISHES**
G26	3	
G27	7	
H27	9	
I27	2	
G28	8	
H28	3	
TOTAL FOR CAVE:	(32)	(31)
G31	1	
G32	2	
H32	–	
G33	–	
H33	4	
G34	1	
H34	1	
TOTAL FOR TERRACE:	(9)	(10)

  * Pieces bearing an IUZ whose intentional use-wear
    polish ends abruptly with microchipping or by
    abrasion.

 ** Expected totals are 7.7% (41/532) of the "Total"
    column of Table 4.37.

TABLE 4.42   FUNCTIONAL STUDIES OF CHIPPED-STONE TOOL ASSEMBLAGES
BY THE HIGH-POWER METHOD

LOWER PALAEOLITHIC

  Hadar Formation: Afar, Ethiopia (Beyries and Roche 1981)

  Thomas Quarries: Casablanca, Morocco (Beyries and Roche 1982)

  Koobi Fora: Kenya (Keeley and Toth 1981)

  Swanscombe, Hoxne, Clacton: England (Keeley 1977, 1980)

MIDDLE PALAEOLITHIC

  Pech de l'Azé I & IV, Corbiac: Dordogne, France (Anderson 1980c;
                                        Anderson-Gerfaud 1981)

  Corbehem (Pas-de-Calais), Combe Grenal and Grotte Vaufrey (Dordogne),
  Marillac (Charente), Pié-Lombard (Alpes-Maritimes), Arcy-sur-Cure
  (Yonne): France (Beyries 1984)

  Mesvin IV: Belgium (Gysels and Cahen 1981)

UPPER PALAEOLITHIC

  Cassegros: Lot-et-Garonne, France (Vaughan 1983, and this volume)

  Pincevent: Seine-et-Marne, France (Cahen, Karlin et al., 1980; Moss
              1983a; Moss and Newcomer 1982)

  Verberie: Oise, France (Audouze et al., 1981)

  La Cotte de Saint-Brelade: Jersey Islands (Frame n.d.)

  Andernach (Rheinland-Pfalz), Zigeunerfels (Baden-Württemberg):
       West Germany (Vaughan 1985a, 1985b)

  Mikamine (Miyagi), Monsanru (Hokkaido): Japan (Kajiwara 1982;
                                        Serizawa 1982)

EPI-PALAEOLITHIC

  Meer II: Antwerpen, Belgium (Cahen 1980a, 1980b; Cahen, Karlin et al.,
           1980; Cahen and Keeley 1980; Cahen, Keeley et al., 1979;
           Keeley 1978a, 1982; Van Noten et al., 1980)

  Niederbieber: Rheinland-Pfalz, West Germany (Bosinski et al., 1982)

  Elkab: Belgium (Gysels 1981)

  La Tourasse: Haute-Garonne, France (Plisson 1982b)

  Pont d'Ambon: Dordogne, France (Célérier and Moss 1983; Moss 1981, 1983a)

TABLE 4.42   (continued)

MESOLITHIC

  Abu Hureyra, Mureybet: Euphrates Valley, Syria (Anderson-Gerfaud 1982,
                          1983; Coqueugniot 1983)
  El Wad, Ain Mallaha: Israel (Bueller 1983)
  Capsian sites: NW Africa (Beyries 1983; Beyries and Inzan 1982)
  Ringkloster, Ageroed V: Denmark (Jensen 1982, 1983)
  Mount Sandel: Northern Ireland (Dumont n.d.)
  Veerharen-De Kip: Belgium (Vermeersch 1982)

NEOLITHIC

  Abu Hureyra: Euphrates Valley, Syria (Moss 1978, 1980, 1983c)
  Franchthi Cave: Argolid, Greece (Perlès and Vaughan 1983)
  Aldenhovener Platte sites: Nordrhein-Westfalen, West Germany
                            (Vaughan 1985a)
  Blicquy: Belgium (Gysels 1981; Cahen and Gysels 1982, 1983)
  Somerset Level sites: England (Morris n.d.)

PREHISTORIC SITES IN THE AMERICAS

  Los Toldos, El Ceibo: Patagonia, Argentina (Mansur-Franchomme 1983a)
  Telarmachay: Junin, Peru (Vaughan 1982, 1985c)
  Labras Lake: Illinois, USA (Gerwitz 1980; Yerkes 1980, 1984)
  Cahokia Site (Illinois), Poverty Point (Louisiana): USA (Yerkes 1983)

Appendix B / Observations Concerning Two Nonuse Polishes on Flints From Cassegros

Two unusual micropolishes were noted on 100 flints from level 10 at Cassegros (56 retouched and 44 un-retouched pieces). In all, 144 occurrences of the polishes were recorded, which makes an average of one or two per piece, but as many as five special polish areas were found on one flint. The polishes were distributed in isolated or contiguous spots which varied in size from 0.1 mm (microscopic) to a couple of mm in diameter (macroscopic). In most cases (N = 113), the polish spots were ripply or undulating in cross-section (Plates 157, 158). In slightly less than half of the ripply polish spots (N = 51), the undulations were oriented diagonally to the nearest edge or ridge, as opposed to a parallel (N = 37) or a perpendicular orientation (N = 25) with respect to an edge or ridge. The second version of the special polish spots presented a totally flat cross-section (N = 28; Plates 159, 160). Regardless of cross-section, the surface of the special polish spots always had a highly smoothed texture that was very reflective or glossy and which was flawed sometimes only by random marks and striations from post-depositional or post-excavation damage (Plate 159). The "pattern of subparallel fine stripes" associated with the glossy spots investigated by D. Stapert (1976:38) under low magnification was not seen on any of the special polish spots from Cassegros, but such "stripes" may only be the undulating aspect of the ripply version of this polish as highlighted by the diagonal lighting normally employed with stereoscopic microscopes.

Optical microscopic examination of the unusual polishes on the Cassegros tools was conducted from 56x to 560x magnification, with usual viewing at 280x. In no instance did one of the polish spots appear lower than the surrounding flint surface. Rather, the ripply polish spots in particular seemed to be clearly sitting on top of the flint surface (Plates 157, 158), especially in one striking case where the polish looked like a drop of varnish which had been applied to the flint surface. (Repeated acetone baths did not remove the spot in question). The polish spots of flat cross-section appeared to be at least level with the surrounding flint surface if not slightly elevated above it (Plates 159, 160). In one isolated case, it was obvious that a flat polish spot was only the manifestation of a very smooth cleavage plane of a large quartz crystal in the flint matrix (Plate 165). However, crystal surfaces on flint fracture faces are not usually perfectly smooth, and they display geometriclike shapes not found among the special flat polish spots (cf. Plate 9), as seen, for example, on one Cassegros flint where a flat polish spot was contiguous to the surface of a large crystal, but the two features could be distinguished very easily (Plate 166). Therefore, optical observation up to 560x has shown the enigmatic polish spots on the Cassegros flints to be elevated above or level with the surrounding flint surface. This contrasts with observations made by F. Bordes (1950b:162) and by D. Stapert (1976:38) that under low magnification with the stereoscope such glossy spots appear depressed into the surface of the flint.

Whether microscopic or macroscopic in size, ripply or flat in cross-section, the unusual polish spots exhibited total randomness of location on the flints:

near edges, on ridges, within microscars, or in the middle of ventral and dorsal surfaces (see Stapert 1976:38 for a similar observation). There was no systematic relation whatsoever between the polish spots and edges or ridges which could possibly have been intentionally used or even affected by hafting. On two flints, spots of ripply polish were found superimposed over use-wear polishes from dry hide with added grit (Plate 162). Conversely, there were three unusual instances where the use-wear polishes from cutting dry hide with grit definitely appeared to have damaged previously formed ripply polish spots and thus to be superimposed over the special polish areas (Plates 163, 164). In comparing the special polish spots to other known microwear polishes, it is clear that the highly smoothed surface texture, the ripply and very flat topographies, the restricted size of the spots, and their random distribution over the flints do not resemble the features of any micropolish produced in the use and nonuse tests reported (see Part I) or by any other researcher.

A number of theories on the cause of the glossy polish spots have been advanced:

(1) *Friction between stones in the soil* (Evans 1872:510, 575; Shepherd 1972:120). But D. Stapert (1976:38) has discredited this model because the polish spots in his sample were found on flints from a wide variety of sediments (boulder-sand, sand, loess, etc.) and because the spots were larger on Upper Paleolithic pieces than on Middle Paleolithic flints which had been exposed to the hypothesized stone friction for a longer time.

(2) *Eolian action by fine-grained loess* (Bordes 1950b:162–163, 1967:45). It is very difficult to envision how eolian transport of fine-grained quartz particles could result in the formation of randomly distributed microscopic polish spots, particularly inside a cave.

(3) *Secondary deposition of silica on the flint surface* (Bordes 1950b:162; references in Stapert 1976: 30). This mechanism has been discounted both by Bordes (1950b:162) and by Stapert (1976:38) since such a deposit would not account for their observations made under low magnification that the glossy polish spots appeared to be depressed in comparison to the surrounding flint surface.

(4) *Root activity or the effects of lower organisms* (Stapert 1976:38). There is no evidence to demonstrate that living organisms form glossy patches on rocks (ibid: 41, note 5).

(5) *Abrasion by quartz grains in spring eddies* (Bordes 1950b:162; Meeks et al. 1982:330–32; Tixier 1958–1959:242–44). The examples from spring

sites are clearly the result of churning within sand-water eddies; but the resulting gloss covers wide areas of a tool if not its entire surface, and thus constitutes a different phenomenon.

(6) *Intentional utilization* (Vayson 1920:456, 489; Meeks et al. 1982:328). The presence of anomalous polish spots on *one* surface only of an edge (Vayson 1920:470) or in the middle of the ventral and/or dorsal surface of a flint cannot be accounted for by normal modes of stone-tool usage. Even hafting mechanisms of plant fibers, wood, bone, antler, hide strips, etc., cannot explain the surface features of the bright polish spots, at least as viewed on the Cassegros flints. As evidence for an anthropogenic origin, Meeks et al. (1982:328) cite the "ripple-markings" on the polish spots, which they take to be "of a type characteristic of unevenly applied pressure during tool use when found on human artifacts." To the contrary, the experimental and prehistoric *use* polishes presented in this volume underscore the *nonuse* origin of the ripply polish spots, particularly with respect to their ripply surface. And the random striations on the glossy spots examined by Meeks et al.—which they attributed to the "stones having been propelled by hand with a circular motion, during the period of gloss formation" (ibid:328)—could also have resulted from some natural or accidental factor which was not at all connected with the formation of the bright spots.

(7) *Curation practices* (Moss 1983a:81–83, ch. 8: Célérier and Moss 1983:103–5). Detailed observations of macroscopically visible "bright spots"—apparently similar to the ripply type described above—were conducted more recently by E. Moss on Final Paleolithic flints from Pont d'Ambon and Pincevent. On the Magdalenian flints from Pont d'Ambon the "polish g" (ripply type) was found particularly on retouched and unretouched pieces of "exotic" flint materials, was often covered by recognizable use polish, and was associated with intensively used tools. Moss attributes the enigmatic "polish g" to some kinds of curation practices by man such as storing and transporting flints in a leather bag along with bone and antler tools or possibly in a case made out of bone. Moss also reports seeing similar "bright spots" on a quartz hammerstone carried in a bag with other hammerstones and antler retouchers, and she hopes to arrive soon at experimental reproduction of her "polish g."

Experiments were performed to replicate W. Shepherd's model which proposes that the glossy polish spots on prehistoric flints are caused by friction between stones in the soil: "If two flints are rubbed together, the contact being maintained in the same small area, mirror-like facets may be formed in a very short time. . . . Fifty rubs on the same spot can produce the gloss (Shepherd 1972:120). The cortex surface of a small flint nodule was rubbed with considerable pressure for fifty short strokes on a small area of the ventral surface of a freshly knapped fine-grained flint. The same test was repeated on a different area of the same flint flake, but using a noncortex ridge from the nodule to rub. In neither test was a glossy spot found to result from the flint-on-flint contact. Rather, microscopic inspection of the rubbed areas revealed only patterns of intersecting striated polish of the same type that is caused by hammerstone percussion on a flint edge (Plate 113) or against a flint striking platform (Plates 114, 115). E. Moss (1983a:142) was also unable to produce "bright spots" by rubbing two flints together.

The tests were performed again, but with the addition of water onto the flint surfaces being rubbed. The result was glossy polish spots of the flat-surfaced variety (Plate 167), which were also detectable macroscopically. Rubbing glass onto a similarly moistened flint surface also produced a pronounced flat polish spot (Plate 168). This corroborates L. Keeley's observation that when cleaning flints in a solution in an ultrasonic cleaning tank "those parts of the implement in contact with the glass will, through their vibrations, pick up a smooth, glossy deposit of glass" (Keeley 1980:11, Plate 10).

Examination of one flat-type polish spot on a Cassegros flint at 1000x in the scanning electron microscope (Model JSM-U3) did not reveal wear patterns caused by scratches due to abrasion of the flint surface (Plate 169). Rather, the smooth surface of the polish would seem to indicate a surface alteration produced by a process of dissolution and reformation of silica gel, as P. Anderson-Gerfaud has proposed for the formation of use-wear polishes from contact with plant and animal materials. The slow but constant movements of various sorts occurring within archaeological sediments (e.g., Limbrey 1975; Rolfsen 1980) could induce the rubbing of a silicate rock against another silicate surface, which—within a semi-aqueous environment such as moist soils—should provide the silica, friction, and water that are needed to produce superficial flint dissolution and the formation of a layer of amorphous silica gel.

The question of what mechanism causes the ripply-type polish spots remains. At 2000x magnification the surface of a ripply bright spot on a Cassegros flint appears completely smooth and devoid of scratch patterns, in sharp contrast to the rough texture of the interior of a post-excavation microscar (Plate 170). Again, the formation of an amorphous silica gel seems to be the cause of the polish area. Since this type of bright spot usually appears 'sitting' on top of the flint surface like a drop of applied varnish, it could be hypothesized that a simple slow precipitation of silicates from a silica-saturated solution in the archaeological soils deposits a silica gel onto flints which happen to be located where conditions in the sedimentary matrix are appropriate for silica precipitation. The ripples could be due to the flow of the precipitate solution across the flint surface, just as stalactites and stalagmites usually exhibit an undulating, ripply surface.

These mechanisms are proposed only as models for further testing, since it is apparent that much more systematic and detailed research into the enigmatic glossy polish spots is necessary.

Bibliography

ABBREVIATIONS:

L'A.	L'Anthropologie
A.A.	American Antiquity
B.S.P.F.	Bulletin de la Société Préhistorique Française
C.N.R.S.	Centre National de la Recherche Scientifique
J.A.S.	Journal of Archaeological Science
J.F.A.	Journal of Field Archaeology
L.T.	Lithic Technology
P.P.S.	Proceedings of the Prehistoric Society
U.I.S.P.P.	Union Internationale des Sciences Préhistoriques et Protohistoriques
W.A.	World Archaeology

Ahler, S.
1971 *Projectile Point Form and Function at Rogers Shelter, Missouri.* Missouri Archaeological Society Research Series, no. 8. Columbia, Missouri: Missouri Archaeological Society.

Akoshima, K.
1980 An experimental study of microflaking, (in Japanese; English summary). *Kōkogaku Zasshi* 66(4):1−27.
n.d. Microflaking quantification. *The Human Uses of Flint and Chert: Papers from the Fourth International Flint Symposium.* G. Sieveking and M. Newcomer, eds., Cambridge, England: Cambridge University Press, in press.

Allain, J.
1979 L'industrie lithique et osseuse de Lascaux. *Lascaux inconnu.* A. Leroi-Gourhan and J. Allain, eds., Paris: C.N.R.S., pp. 87−120.
1983 Matériaux pour l'étude du "Magdalénien initial" et de ses origines. *B.S.P.F.* 80(5):135−39.

Allain, J., and R. Fritsch
1967 Le Badegoulien de l'Abri Fritsch aux Roches de Pouligny-Saint-Pierre (Indre). *B.S.P.F.* 64:83−94.

Ammerman, A., and M. Feldman
1974 On the 'making' of an assemblage of stone tools. *A.A.* 39: 610−16.

Anderson, P.
1980a A testimony of prehistoric tasks: diagnostic residues on stone tool working edges. *W.A.* 12(2):181−94.
1980b A scanning electron microscope study of microwear polish and diagnostic deposits on used stone tool working edges (abstract). *L.T.* 9(2):32−33.
1980c A microwear analysis of selected flint artifacts from the Mousterian of southwest France (abstract). *L.T.* 9(2):33.

Anderson-Gerfaud, P.
1981 Contributions méthodologiques à l'analyse des microtraces d'utilisations sur les outils préhistoriques. Thèse de 3ème cycle no. 1607, Institut du Quaternaire, Université de Bordeaux I, Talence.
1982 Comment préciser l'utilisation agricole des outils préhistoriques? *Cahiers de l'Euphrate* (Lyon) 3:149−64.
1983a A consideration of the uses of certain backed and "lustered" stone tools from Late Mesolithic and Natufian levels of Abu Hureyra and Mureybet (Syria). *Traces d'utilisation sur les outils néolithiques du Proche Orient.* M-C. Cauvin, ed., Lyon: Maison de l'Orient, pp. 77−105.
1983b L'utilisation de certains objets en céramique de Tell el-Oueili (Obeid 4): Rapport préliminaire sur les microtraces. *Rapport préliminaire sur les fouilles de Larsa (8ᵉ et 9ᵉ campagnes, 1978 et 1981).* J. L. Huot, ed., Paris: Aide à la Diffusion de la Pensée Française.

Anderson-Gerfaud, P., D. Helmer, and P. Reynolds
n.d. An experimental study of prehistoric plant-harvesting tools. *The Human Uses of Flint and Chert: Papers from the Fourth International Symposium on Flint.* G. Sieveking and M. Newcomer, eds., Cambridge, England: Cambridge University Press, in press.

Audouin, F., and H. Plisson
1982 Les ocres et leurs témoins au Paléolithique en France: Enquête et expériences sur leur validité archéologique. *Cahiers de Centre de Recherches Préhistoriques* (Université de Paris I) 8:33−80.

Audouze, F., D. Cahen, L. Keeley, and B. Schmider
1981 Le site Magdalénien du Buisson Campin à Verberie (Oise). *Gallia Préhistoire* 24(1):99−143.

Barton, R., and C. Bergman
1982   Hunters at Hengisbury: some evidence from experimental archaeology. *W.A.* 14(2): 237–48.

Beckhoff, K.
1970   "Schaber" oder "Kratzer." *Fruehe Menschheit und Umwelt.* Fundamenta Reihe A, Band 2. K. Gripp et al., eds., pp. 6–12.

Behm-Blancke, G.
1962– Bandkeramische Erntegeraete, zur Typologie
1963   der aeltesten Sicheln und Erntemesser. *Alt-Thueringen* 6: 104–75.

Betts, A.
1978   An experiment to examine some effects of agricultural implements on flints: Its results and implications (abstract). *Bulletin of the Institute of Archaeology* (University of London) 15: 241.

Beyries, S.
1981   Etude de traces d'utilisation sur des empreintes en latex. *B.S.P.F.* 78(7):198–99.
1982   Comparaison de traces d'utilisation sur différentes roches siliceuces. *Tailler! pour quoi faire: Préhistoire et technologie lithique 2, Recent progress in microwear studies.* Studia Praehistorica Belgica 2. D. Cahen, ed., Tervuren: Musée royal de l'Afrique centrale, pp. 235–40.
1983   Fonction et mode d'utilisation d'une série de lames ocrées capsiennes. *Traces d'utilisation sur les outils néolithiques du Proche Orient.* M-C. Cauvin, ed., Lyon: Maison de l'Orient, pp. 135–39.
1984   Approche functionnelle de la variabilité des différents faciès du Moustérien. Thèse de 3éme cycle, Laboratoire d'Ethnologie, Université de Paris X, Nanterre.

Beyries, S., and M-L. Inizan
1982   Typologie, ocre, fonction. *Tailler! pourquoi faire: Préhistoire de technologie lithique 2, Recent progress in microwear studies.* Studia Praehistorica Belgica 2. D. Cahen, ed., Tervuren: Musée royal de l'Afrique centrale, pp. 313–22.

Beyries, S., and H. Roche
1981   Contribution du matériel lithique de la formation d'Hadar à la connaissance des premières industries: Technologie et traces d'utilisation. Paper presented at 10e Congrès de l'U.I.S.P.P., October 1981, Mexico City.
1982   Technologie et traces d'utilisation: application à des industries acheuléennes (Carrières Thomas, Casablanca, Maroc). *Tailler! pour quoi faire: Préhistoire et technologie lithique 2, Recent progress in microwear studies.* Studia Praehistorica Belgica 2. D. Cahen, ed., Tervuren: Musée royal de l'Afrique centrale, pp. 267–78.

Biberson, P., and E. Aguirre
1965   Expériences de taille d'outils préhistorique dans les os d'éléphant: motif des expériences. *Quaternaria* 7: 165–83.

Binford, L.
1973   Interassemblage variability: The Mousterian and the "functional" argument. *The Explanation of Culture Change: Models in Prehistory.* A.C. Renfrew, ed., London: Duckworth, pp. 227–64.

Binford, S.
1968   Variability and change in the Near Eastern Mousterian of Levallois facies. *New Perspectives in Archaeology.* L. Binford and S. Binford, eds., Chicago: Aldine, pp. 313–41.

Binford, L., and S. Binford
1966   A preliminary analysis of functional variability in the Mousterian of Levallois facies. *American Anthropologist* 68(2): 238–95.

Bonwick, J.
1898   *Daily Life and Origin of the Tasmanians.* Second edition. London: Sampson, Low, Marston and Co.

Bordaz, J.
1970   *Tools of the Old and New Stone Age.* Garden City, New York: Natural History Press.

Bordes, F.
1950a Principes d'une méthode d'étude des techniques de débitage et de la typologie du Paléolithique ancien et moyen. *L'A.* 54:19–34.
1950b Du poli particulier de certains silex taillés. *L'A.* 54:161–63.
1951   Le gisement du Pech de l'Azé-Nord. Campagnes 1950–1951. Les couches inférieures à *Rhinocerus Mercki. B.S.P.F.* 48: 529–38.
1957   Review of R. Joffroy, P. Monton, and R. Paris, La Grotte de la Grande Baume à Balot (Côte-d'Or) in *Revue Archéologique de l'Est de du Centre-Est* 3: 209–32. *L'A.* 61: 529–32.
1958   Nouvelles fouilles à Laugerie-Haute. Premiers résultats. *L'A.* 62: 205–44.
1961   *Typologie du Paléolithique ancien et moyen.* Publications de l'Institut de Préhistoire de l'Université de Bordeaux, Mémoire no. 1. Bordeaux: Delmas.
1965   Utilisation possible des côtés des burins. *Fundberichte aus Schwaben* 17: 3–5.
1967   Considérations sur la typologie et les techniques dans le Paléolithique. *Quartaer* 18: 25–55.
1966   *The Old Stone Age.* Trans. by J. Anderson. New York: McGraw-Hill.
1970a Observations typologiques et techniques sur le Périgordien supérieur de Corbiac (Dordogne). *B.S.P.F.* 67:105–13.
1970b Réflexions sur l'outil au Paléolithique. *B.S.P.F.* 67: 199–202.
1971   Essai de préhistoire expérimentale: Fabrication d'un épieu de bois. *Mélanges de préhistoire, d'archéocivilisation et d'éthnologie offert à André Varagnac.* Paris: Ecole Pratique des Hautes Etudes, VIème section.
1972   *A Tale of Two Caves.* New York: Harper and Row.
1973   Position des traces d'usure sur les grattoirs simples du Périgordien supérieur évolué de Corbiac (Dordogne). *Estudios Dedicados al Professor Dr. Luis Pericot.* Barcelona: Instituto de Arquelogia y Prehistoria, Universidad de Barcelona, pp. 55–60.
1974a Bruised blades and flakes in the Upper Perigordian at

Corbiac, Dordogne, France. *Perspectives in Paleoanthropology, Prof. D. Sen Festschrift.* A. Gosh, ed., Calcutta, pp. 135–38.

1974b Notes de typologie paléolithique. *Zephyrus* (Salamanca) 25:53–64.

1975 Sur la notion de sol d'habitat en préhistoire paléolithique. *B.S.P.F.* 72:139–44.

1980a Question de contemporanéité: L'illusion des remontages. *B.S.P.F.* 77:132–33.

1980b Savez-vous remonter les cailloux à la mode de chez nous? *B.S.P.F.* 77:323–34.

Bordes, F., and M. Bourgon
1950 Le gisement du Pech de l'Azé-Nord, prise de date et observations préliminaires. *B.S.P.F.* 47:381–83.

1951 Le complèxe moustérien: Moustériens, Levalloisien, et Tayacien. *L'A.* 55:1–23.

Bordes, F., J-P. Rigaud, and D. de Sonneville-Bordes
1972 Des buts, problèmes et limites de l'archéologie paléolithique. *Quaternaria* 16: 15–34.

Bosinski, G., and J. Hahn
1972 Der Magdalénien-Fundplatz Andernach (Martinsberg). *Rheinische Ausgrabungen* 11: 81–257.

Bosinski, G., R. Braun, E. Turner, and P. Vaughan
1982 Ein spaetpalaeolithisches Retuscheurdepot von Niederbieber/Neuwieder Becken. *Archaeologisches Korrespondenzblatt* 12: 295–311.

Boucher de Perthes, J.
1847– *Antiquités celtiques et antédiluviennes.*
1864 *Mémoire sur l'industrie primitive et les arts à leur origine,* vols. 1, 2, and 3. Paris.

Bourgon, M.
1957 *Les industries moustériennes et pré-moustériennes du Périgord.* Archives de l'Institut de Paléontologie Humaine, mémoire no. 27. Paris: Institut de Paléontologie Humaine.

Breuil, H.
1910 Sur la présence d'éolithes à la base de l'Eocène parisien. *L'A.* 21: 285–408

Breuil, H., and R. Lantier
1965 *The Men of the Old Stone Age.* New York: St. Martin's Press.

Brézillon, M.
1973 L'outil préhistorique et le geste technique. *L'homme hier et aujourd'hui, Recueil d'études en hommage à André Leroi-Gourhan.* Paris: Cujas, pp. 123–32.

1977 *La dénomination des objets de pierre taillée.* Paris: C.N.R.S.

Brink, J.
1978a *An Experimental Study of Microwear Formation on Endscrapers.* National Museum of Man, Mercury Series no. 83. Ottawa: Archaeological Survey of Canada, National Museums of Canada.

1978b The role of abrasives in the formation of lithic use-wear. *J.A.S.* 5:363–71.

Briuer, R.
1976 New clues to stone tool function: Plant and animal residues. *A.A.* 41: 478–84.

Broadbent, N., and K. Knutsson
1975 An experimental analysis of quartz scrapers. Results and Applications. *Fornvaennen* 70:113–28.

Broderick, M.
1979 Ascending paper chromatographic technique in archaeology. *Lithic Use-Wear Analysis.* B. Hayden, ed. New York: Academic Press, pp. 376–83.

Brothwell, D.
1969 The study of archaeological materials by means of the scanning electron microscope: An important new field. *Science in Archaeology.* Second edition. D. Brothwell and E. Higgs, eds. London: Thames and Hudson, pp. 564–66.

Bruijn, A.
1958– Technik und Gebrauch der Bandkeramischen
1959 Feuersteingeraete. *Palaeohistoria* 6–7:213–24.

Bueller, H.
1983 Methodological problems in the microwear analysis of sampled tools from the Natufian sites of El Wad and Ain Mallaha. *Traces d'utilisation sur les outils néolithiques du Proche Orient.* M-C. Cauvin, ed. Lyon: Maison de l'Orient, pp. 107–25.

Cahen, D.
1980a Question de contemporanéité: L'apport des remontages. *B.S.P.F.* 77: 230–32.

1980b Pour clore le débat. *B.S.P.F.* 77: 234.

Cahen, D., ed.
1982 *Tailler! pour quoi faire: Préhistoire et technologie lithique 2, Recent progress in microwear studies.* Studia Praehistorica Belgica 2. Tervuren: Musée royal de l'Afrique centrale.

Cahen, D., and J. Gysels
1982 Technique et fonction de l'industrie lithique du groupe de Blicquy. *Notae Praehistoricae* (Tervuren) 2: 133–36.

1983 Techniques et fonctions dans l'industrie lithique du groupe de Blicquy (Belgique). *Traces d'utilisation sur les outils néolithiques du Proche Orient.* M-C. Cauvien, ed. Lyon: Maison de l'Orient, pp. 37–52.

Cahen, D., C. Karlin, L. Keeley, and F. Van Noten
1980 Méthodes d'analyse technique, spatiale et fonctionnelle d'ensembles lithiques. *Helinium* 20: 209–59.

Cahen, D., and L. Keeley
1980 Not less than two, not more than three. *W.A.* 12: 166–80.

Cahen, D., L. Keeley, and F. Van Noten
1979 Stone tools, toolkits, and human behavior in prehistory. *Current Anthropology* 20:661–83.

Cantwell, A-M.
1979 The functional analysis of scrapers: Problems, new techniques, and cautions. *L.T.* 8(1):5–11.

Cauvin, M-C, ed.
1983   *Traces d'utilisation sur les outils néolithiques du Proche Orient.* Lyon: Maison de l'Orient.

Célérier, G., and E. Moss
1983   L'abri-sous-roche de Pont d'Ambon à Bourdeilles (Dordogne), un gisement magdalénien-azilien. Microtraces et analyse fonctionelle de l'industrie lithique. *Gallia Préhistoire* 26(1):88–107.

Clark, J. G. D., and M. Thompson
1953   The groove and splinter technique of working antler in Upper Paleolithic and Mesolithic Europe. *P.P.S.* 20:148–60.

Clarke, D.
1976   Mesolithic Europe: the economic basis. *Problems in Economic and Social Archaeology.* G. Sieveking, J. Longworth, and K. Wilson, eds., London: Duckworth, pp. 444–81.

Clarke, W.
1914   Some aspects of striation. *P.P.S. of East Anglia* 1: 434–38.

Clayton, C., and R. Bradley
n.d.   The influence of flint microstructure on the formation of microwear polishes. *The Human Uses of Flint and Chert: Papers from the Fourth International Symposium on Flint.* G. Sieveking and M. Newcomer, eds., Cambridge, England: Cambridge University Press.

Collins, M.
1975   Lithic technology as a means of processual inference. *Lithic Technology.* F. Swanson, ed. The Hague: Mouton, pp. 15–34

Coqueugniot, E.
1983   Analyse tracéologique d'une série de grattoirs et herminettes de Mureybet, Syrie. *Traces d'utilisation sur les outils néolithiques du Proche Orient.* M-C. Cauvin, ed. Lyon: Maison de l'Orient, pp. 163–72.

Cotterell, B., and J. Kamminga
1979   The mechanics of flaking. *Lithic Use-Wear Analysis.* B. Hayden, ed. New York: Academic Press, pp. 97–112.

Crabtree, D.
1972   *An Introduction to Flintworking.* Occasional Papers of the Idaho State University Museum, no. 28. Pocatello: Idaho State University Museum.
1973   The obtuse angle as a functional edge. *Tebiwa* 16: 46–53.
1974   Grinding and smoothing of stone artifacts. *Tebiwa* 17:1–6.

Crabtree, D., and E. Davis
1968   Experimental manufacture of wooden implements with tools of flaked stone. *Science* 159:426–28.

Curwen, E. C.
1930   Prehistoric flint sickles. *Antiquity* 4:179–86.
1935   Agriculture and the flint sickle in Palestine. *Antiquity* 9:62–66.
1941   Some food-gathering implements: Study in Mesolithic tradition. *Antiquity* 15:320–37

Daniel, G.
1950   *A Hundred Years of Archaeology.* London: Duckworth.

D'Aujourd'hui, R.
1977a   Bedeutung und Funktion der Dickenbaennlispitzen, Mikroskopische Untersuchungen zur Funktionsdeutung von Silexgeraeten. *Verhandlungen der Naturforschungs-Gesellschaft Basel* 86(1–2):237–56.
1977b   Ein altpalaeolithischer Faustkeil aus Pratteln BL. *Festschrift Elisabeth Schmidt.* L. Berger, G. Bienz, J. Enwald, M. Joss, eds. Basel: Seminar fuer Ur- und Fruehgeschichte der Universitaet Basel, pp. 1–14.

Dauvois, M.
1974   Industrie osseuse préhistorique et expérimentation. *L'industrie de l'os dans la préhistoire.* H. Camps-Fabrer, ed., Aix-en-Provence: Editions de l'Université de Provence, pp. 73–84.
1976   *Précis de dessin dynamique et structural des industries lithiques préhistoriques.* Périgueux: Fanlac.
1977   Stigmates d'usure présentés par des outils ayant travaillé l'os. Premiers résultats. *Méthodologie appliquée à l'industrie de l'os préhistorique.* C.N.R.S. colloques internationaux no. 568. Paris: C.N.R.S., pp. 275–92.

Del Bene, T.
1979   Once upon a striation: Current models for striation and polish formation. *Lithic Use-Wear Analysis.* B. Hayden, ed. New York: Academic Press, pp. 167–77.

Del Bene, T., and P. Shelley
1979   Soapstone modification and its effects on lithic implements. *Lithic Use-Wear Analysis.* B. Hayden, ed. New York: Academic Press, pp. 243–57.

Diamant, S.
1979   A short history of sieving systems at the Franchthi Cave. *J.F.A.* 6:203–17.

Diamond, G.
1979   The nature of so-called polished surfaces on stone artifacts. *Lithic Use-Wear Analysis.* B. Hayden, ed., New York: Academic Press, pp. 159–66.

Driver, H.
1961   *Indians of North America.* Chicago: University of Chicago Press.

Dumont, J.
1982   The quantification of microwear traces: A new use for interferometry. *W.A.* 14 (2): 206–17
n.d.   A microwear analysis of the Mount Sandel artifacts. *The Human Uses of Flint and Chert: Papers from the Fourth International Symposium on Flint.* G. Sieveking and M. Newcomer, eds. Cambridge, England: Cambridge University Press, in press.

Elster, E.
1976   *The Chipped-Stone Industry of Anzabegovo.* Monumenta Archaeologica 1. Los Angeles: Institute of Archaeology Press, University of California at Los Angeles.

Evans, J.
1872 *The Ancient Stone Implements, Weapons and Ornaments of Great Britain.* New York: Appleton.

Eyman, F.
1964 The Teshoa, a Shoshonean woman's knife: A study of American Indian copper industries. *Pennsylvania Archaeologist* 34: 9–52.

Fernald, M.
1950 *Gray's Manual of Botany.* Eighth edition. New York: American Book Co.

Feustel, R.
1973 *Technik der Steinzeit.* Weimar: Bohlaus.
1974 *Die Kniegrotte, eine Magdalénien-Station in Thueringen.* Weimar: Bohlaus.

Fiedler, L.
1979 Formen und Technik neolithischer Steingeraete aus dem Rheinland. *Rheinische Ausgrabungen* 19: 53–190.

Flenniken, J., and E. Garrison
1975 Thermally altered novaculite and stone tool manufacturing techniques. *J.F.A.* 2: 125–31

Flenniken, J., and J. Haggerty
1979 Trampling as an agency in the formation of edge damage: An experiment in lithic technology. *Northwest Anthropological Research Notes* 13: 208–14.

Folk, R., and C. Weaver
1952 A study of the texture and composition of chert. *American Journal of Science* 250: 498–510.

Forde, C. D.
1963 *Habitat, Economy and Society.* London.

Frame, H.
n.d. Frugal flint: aspects of tool re-use at La Cotte de Saint-Brelade, Jersey. *The Human Uses of Flint and Chert: Papers from the Fouth International Symposium on Flint.* G. Sieveking and M. Newcomer, eds. Cambridge, England: Cambridge University Press, in press.

Gallagher, J.
1977 Contemporary stone tools in Ethiopia: Implications for archaeology. *J.F.A.* 4: 407–14.

Gendel, P., and L. Pirnay
1982 Microwear analysis of experimental stone tools: Further test results. *Tailler! pour quoi faire: Préhistoire et technologie lithique 2, Recent progress in microwear studies.* Studia Praehistorica Belgica 2. D. Cahen, ed. Tervuren: Musée royal de l'Afrique centrale, pp. 251–66.

Gerwitz, L.
1980 A microwear analysis of Labras Lake artifacts. *Investigations at the Labras Lake Site: Volume 1 –Archaeology.* University of Illinois at Chicago Circle, Department of Anthropology Reports of Investigations no. 1, pp. 265–317.

Gould, R.
1978 The anthropology of human resources. *American Anthropologist* 80: 815–35.

1980 *Living Archaeology.* Cambridge, England: Cambridge University Press.

Gould, R., D. Koster, and A. Sontz
1971 The lithic assemblage of the Western Desert Aborigines of Australia. *A.A.* 36: 149–69.

Grace, R., I. Graham, and M. Newcomer
n.d. The mathematical characterization of wear traces on prehistoric flint tools. *The Human Uses of Flint and Chert: Papers from the Fourth International Symposium on Flint.* C. Sieveking and M. Newcomer, eds. Cambridge, England: Cambridge University Press, in press.

Gramsch, B.
1966 Abnutzungsspuren an mesolithischen Kern- und Scheibenbeilen. *Ausgrabungen und Funde* 11 (3): 109–14.

1973 Gebrauchsspuren an Alt- und Mittelpalaeolithischen Silexartefakten. *Actes du 8e Congrès de l'U.I.S.P.P.,* vol. 2, Belgrade: U.I.S.P.P., pp. 137–40.

Grantz, G.
1969 *Home Book of Taxidermy and Tanning.* Harrisburg, Pennsylvania: Stackpole Books.

Greenwell, W.
1865 Notices of the examination of ancient grave-mills in the north riding of Yorkshire. *Archaeological Journal* 22: 97–117.

Griffin, P., and A. Estioko-Griffin
1978 Ethnoarchaeology in the Philippines. *Archaeology* 31 (6): 34–43.

Gunn, J.
1975 Dynamic typology: A model for functional typing of stone tools with an application to French Paleolithic burins. *L.T.* 4: 9–17.

Gysels, J.
1980 Microwear analysis: experiments and observations (abstract). *L.T.* 9: 33.

1981 Experimenteel gebruikssporen der zoek van het lithische materiaal van het epipaleolithische site Elkab en he neolithische site Blicquy. Thesis, Faculteit van de Letteren en de Wusbegeerte, Katholieke Universiteit te Leuven, Belgium.

Gysels, J., and D. Cahen
1981 Premiers résultats de l'analyse des traces microscopiques d'usure de quelques outils de Mesvin IV. *Notae Praehistoricae* (Tervuren) 1: 75–82.

1982 Le lustre des faucilles et les autres traces d'usage des outils en silex. *B.S.P.F.* 79 (7): 221–24.

Hallock, C.
1877 *The Sportsman's Gazetter and General Guide.* New York: Forest and Stream Publishing Co.

Hansen, J.
1978 The earliest seed remains from Greece: Paleolithic through Neolithic at Franchthi. *Berichte der deutschen botanischen Gesellschaft* 91: 39–46.

Hansen, J., and J. Renfrew
1978 Paleolithic-Neolithic seed remains at Franchthi Cave, Greece. *Nature* 271 (26 January): 349–52.

Haward, F.
1914 The problem of the eoliths. *P.P.S. of East Anglia* 1: 347–59.

Hayden, B.
1975 Curation: Old and new. *Primitive Art and Technology*. J. Raymond et al., eds. Calgary: Department of Archaeology, University of Calgary, pp. 47–58.
1977 Stone tool functions in the Western Desert. *Stone Tools as Cultural Markers*. R. Wright, ed. New Jersey: Humanities, pp. 178–88.
1978 Snarks in archaeology: Or, inter-assemblage variability in lithics (A view from the antipodes). *Lithics and Subsistence: The Analysis of Stone Tool Use in Prehistoric Economies*. Vanderbilt University Publications in Anthropology no. 20. D. Davis, ed. Nashville: Vanderbilt University, pp. 179–98.
1979a *Palaeolithic Reflections*. Australian Institute of Aboriginal Studies. New Jersey: Humanities.
1979b Snap, shatter, and superfractures: Use-wear of stone skin scrapers. *Lithic Use-Wear Analysis*. B. Hayden, ed. New York: Academic Press, pp. 207–29.
1980 Confusion in the bipolar world: Bashed pebbles and splintered pieces. *L.T.* 9: 2–7.

Hayden, B., ed.
1979 *Lithic Use-Wear Analysis*. Proceedings of the Conference on Lithic Use-Wear, Simon Fraser University, Burnaby (Vancouver), British Columbia, March 1977. New York: Academic Press.

Hayden, B., and J. Kamminga
1973a Gould, Koster, and Sontz on 'microwear': A critical review. *L.T.* 2: 3–8.
1973b Rejoinder. *L.T.* 2: 23.
1979 An introduction to use-wear: The first CLUW. *Lithic Use-Wear Analysis*. B. Hayden, ed. New York: Academic Press, pp. 1–13.

Heizer, R.
1951 The sickle in aboriginal Western North America. *A.A.* 16: 247–52.

Hester, T.
1976 Functional analysis of ancient Egyptian chipped stone tools: the potential for future research. *J.F.A.* 3: 346–51.

Hester, T., and L. Green
1972 A functional analysis of large bifaces from San Saba County, Texas. *Texas Journal of Science* 34: 343–50.

Hester, T., D. Gilbow, and A. Albee
1973 A functional analysis of 'Clear Fork' artifacts from the Rio Grande Plain, Texas. *A.A.* 38: 90–96.

Hester, T., and R. Heizer
1973 *Bilbliography of Archaeology 1: Experiments, Lithic Technology, and Petrography*. Addison-Wesley Module in Anthropology no. 29.

Hole, F., and K. Flannery
1967 The prehistory of southwestern Iran: A preliminary report. *P.P.S.* 33: 147–206.

Hole, F., K. Flannery, and J. Neeley
1969 *Prehistory and Human Ecology of the Deh Luran Plain*. Memoirs of the Museum of Anthropology, University of Michigan, no. 1. Ann Arbor, Michigan: Museum of Anthropology, University of Michigan.

Holley, G., and T. Del Bene
1981 An evaluation of Keeley's microwear approach. *J.A.S.* 8: 337–52.

Horniman Museum and Library
1929 *War and the Chase, A Handbook to the Collection of Weapons of Savage, Barbaric, and Civilized Peoples*. Second edition. London: London City Council.

Hulthén, B., and S. Welinder
1982 *A Stone Age Economy*. Theses and Papers in North European Archaeology 2. Stockholm: Institute of Archaeology, University of Stockholm.

Jacobsen, T.
1976 17,000 years of Greek prehistory. *Scientific American* 234 (6): 76–87.
1981 Franchthi Cave and the beginning of settled village life in Greece. *Hesperia* 50 (4): 303–19.

Jensen, H.
1982 A preliminary analysis of blade scrapers from Ringkloster, a Danish Late Mesolithic site. *Tailler! pour quoi faire: Préhistoire et technologie lithique 2, Recent progress in microwear studies*. Studia Praehistorica Belgica 2. D. Cahen, ed. Tervuren: Musée royal de l'Afrique centrale, pp. 323–27.
1983 A microwear analysis of unretouched blades from Ageroed V. *An Atlantic Bog Site in Central Scania*. Acta Archaeologica Lundensia, series no. 8, 12. L. Larson, Lund, pp. 144–52.

Johnson, L.
1978 A history of flint-knapping experimentation, 1838–1976. *Current Anthropology* 12: 337–59.

Jones, P.
1980 Experimental butchery with modern stone tools and its relevance for Palaeolithic archaeology. *W.A.* 12: 153–65.

Kajiwara, H.
1982 A microwear analysis of tanged scrapers from Mikamine site. (in Japanese; English summary). *Kōkogaku Zasshi* 68 (2): 43–81.

Kajiwara, H., and K. Akoshima
1981 An experimental study of microwear polish on shale artifacts. (in Japanese; English summary). *Kōkogaku Zasshi* 67 (1): 1–36.

Kamminga, J.
1977 A functional study of use-polished eloueras. *Stone Tools as Cultural Markers*. R. Wright, ed. New Jersey: Humanities, pp. 205–12.
1979 The nature of use-polish and abrasive smoothing on stone tools. *Lithic Use-Wear Analysis*. B. Hayden, ed. New York: Academic Press, pp. 143–57.

Kantman, S.
1970a Esquisse d'un procédé analytique pour l'étude macrographique des encoches. *Quarternaria* 13: 266–80.
1970b Essai d'une méthode d'étude des "denticulés" moustériens par discrimination des variables morpho-fonctionnelles. *Quaternaria* 13: 281–94.

1971   Essai sur le problème de la retouche d'utilisation dans l'étude du matériau lithique: Premiers résultats. *B.S.P.F.* 68: 200–204.

Keeley, L.
1974   Technique and methodology in microwear studies: A critical review. *W.A.* 5: 323–36.
1976   Microwear on flint: some experimental results. *Second International Symposium on Flint.* F. Engelen, ed. Maastricht: Nederlandse Geologische Vereniging, pp. 49–51.
1977   The functions of Paleolithic flint tools. *Scientific American* 237 (5): 108–26.
1978a   Preliminary microwear analysis of the Meer assemblage. *Les chasseurs de Meer.* Dissertationes Archaeologicae Gandenses no. 18. F. Van Noten, Brugge: De Tempel, pp. 73–86.
1978b   Microwear polishes on flint: Some experimental results. *Lithics and Subsistence: The Analysis of Stone Tool Use in Prehistoric Economies.* Vanderbilt University Publications in Anthropology no. 20. D. Davis, ed., Nashville: Vanderbilt University, pp. 163–78.
1980   *Experimental Determination of Stone Tool Uses: A Microwear Analysis.* Chicago: University of Chicago Press.
1982   Hafting and retooling: Effects on the archaeological record. *A.A.* 47: 798–809.

Keeley, L., and M. Newcomer
1977   Microwear analysis of experimental flint tools: A test case. *J.A.S.* 4: 29–62.

Keeley, L., and N. Toth
1981   Microwear polishes on early stone tools from Koobi Fora, Kenya. *Nature* 293 (no. 5832): 464–65.

Keller, C.
1966   The development of edge damage patterns on stone tools. *Man* 1: 501–11.

Keller, D.
1979   Identifying edge damage on surface occurring lithic artifacts: Some comments. *L.T.* 8:15–17.

Knudson, R.
1979   Inference and imposition in lithic analysis. *Lithic Use-Wear Analysis.* B. Hayden, ed. New York: Academic Press, pp. 269–81.

Korobkova, G.
1980   Ancient reaping tools and their productivity in the light of experimental tracewear analysis. *The Bronze Age Civilization of Central Asia. Recent Soviet Discoveries.* P. Kohl, ed., New York: Sharpe, pp. 325–49.

Kroeber, A.
1925   *Handbook of the California Indians.* Smithsonian Institution Bureau of American Ethnology, Bulletin no. 78. Washington, D.C.: Smithsonian Institution.

Lartet, E., and H. Christy
1864   L'homme fossile dans le Périgord. *Appendice à l'anncienneté de l'homme.* C. Lyell, ed. Paris, pp. 135–77.

Laville, H., J-P. Rigaud, and J. Sackett
1980   *Rock Shelters of the Perigord.* New York: Academic Press.

Lawn, B., and D. Marshall
1979   Mechanisms of microcontact fracture in brittle solids. *Lithic Use-Wear Analysis.* B. Hayden, ed., New York: Academic Press, pp. 63–82.

Lawrence, R.
1979   Experimental evidence for the significance of attributes used in edge-damage analysis. *Lithic Use-Wear Analysis.* B. Hayden, ed., New York: Academic Press, pp. 113–22.

Leguay, L.
1877   Les procédés employés pour la gravure et la sculpte des os avec les silex. *Bulletin de la Société d'Anthropologie de Paris,* 2ème série, 12: 280–96.

Lenoir, M.
1970   Le Paléolithique supérieur en surface devant la grotte de Lestruque, Commune de Soualève (Dordogne). *B.S.P.F.* 67: 71–78.
1971   Traces d'utlisation observées sur un nucléus à lamelles. *B.S.P.F.* 68: 69–70.
1978   Les grattoirs-burins du Morin et du Roc de Marcamps (Gironde). *B.S.P.F.* 75: 73–82.

Leroi-Gourhan, A.
1943   *L'homme et la matière.* Paris: Albin Michel.

Leroi-Gourhan, A. and M. Brézillon
1966   L'habitation magdalénienne no. 1 de Pincevent, près Montereau (Seine-et-Marne). *Gallia Préhistoire* 9: 263–385.

Le Tensorer, J-M.
1981   *Le Paléolithique de l'Agenais.* Cahiers de Quaternaire 3. Paris: C.N.R.S.

Levitt, J.
1979   A review of experimental traceological research in the USSR. *Lithic Use-Wear Analysis.* B. Hayden, ed., New York: Academic Press, pp. 27–38.

Limbrey, S.
1975   *Soil Science and Archaeology.* New York: Academic Press.

Lubbock, Sir John
1872   *Pre-historic Times.* Third edition. London: Williams and Norgate.

MacDonald, G., and D. Sanger
1968   Some aspects of microscopic analysis and photomicrography: Lithic artifacts. *A.A.* 33: 237–40.

Mallouf, R.
1982   An analysis of plow-damaged chert artifacts: The Brookeen Creek Cache (41HI86), Hill County, Texas. *J.F.A.* 9: 79–98.

Mandeville, M.
1973   A consideration of the thermal pretreatment of chert. *Plains Anthropologist* 18: 177–202.

Mandl, I.
1961   Collagenases and elastases. *Advance in Enzymology* 23: 164–264.

Mansur, M. E.
1982   Microwear analysis of natural and use striations: New clues to the mechanisms of striation formation.

Tailler! pour quoi faire: Préhistoire et technologie lithique 2, Recent progress in microwear studies. Studia Praehistorica Belgica 2, D. Cahen, ed., Tervuren: Musée royal de l'Afrique centrale, pp. 213–33.

Mansur-Franchomme, M. E.
1983a Traces d'utilisation et technologie lithique: Exemples de la Patagonie. Thèse de 3ème cycle no. 1860, Institut du Quaternaire, Université de Bordeaux I, Talence.
1983b Scanning electron microscopy of dry hide working tools: The role of abrasives and humidity in microwear polish formation. *J.A.S.* 10: 223–30.

Martin, H.
1923 *Recherches sur l'évolution du Moustérien dans le gisement de la Quina (Charente),* vol 2. Mémoires de la Société Archéologique et Historique de la Charente, vol. 14. Angoulême: Société Archéologique et Historique de la Charente.

Mason, O.
1891 Aboriginal skin-dressing. A study based on material in the U.S. National Museum. *Annual Report of the Smithsonian Institution for 1889,* pt. 2, pp. 553–89.

Massaud, J.
1972 Observations sur l'utilisation des burins multifacettés. *B.S.P.F.* 69: 231–34.

Masson, A., E. Coqueugniot, and S. Roy
1981 Silice et traces d'usage: Le lustré des faucilles. *Nouvelles Archéologiques du Musée d'Histoire Naturelle de Lyon* 19: 43–51.

Mauser, P.
1965 Die Interpretation steinzeitlicher Silexwerkzeuge nach modernen technologischen Gesichtspunkten. *Fundberichte aus Schwaben* 17: 29–42.

McGrath, K.
1970 A model for the use of ethnographic data in the analysis of prehistoric activities. Masters thesis, Department of Anthropology, University of Pennsylvania, Philadelphia.

Meeks, N., G. Sieveking, M. Tite, and J. Cook
1982 Gloss and use-wear traces on flint sickles and similar phenomena. *J.A.S.* 9: 317–40.

Moir, J.
1912 The natural fracture of flint and its bearing upon rudimentary flint implements. *P.P.S. of East Anglia* 1: 171–84.

Morris, G.
n.d. Microwear observation on Neolithic flint artifacts from Poitou-Charente (France) and the Somerset levels. *The Human Uses of Flint and Chert: Papers from the Fourth International Symposium on Flint.* G. Sieveking and M. Newcomer, eds., Cambridge, England: Cambridge University Press, in press.

Mortillet, G. de
1883 *Le Préhistorique. Antiquité de l'homme.* Paris: Reinwald.

Moss, E.
1978 A variation of a method of microwear analysis developed by L. H. Keeley and its application to flint tools from Tell Abu Hureyra, Syria (abstract). *Bulletin of the Institute of Archaeology* (University of London) 15: 238–39.
1980 Microwear analysis of burins from Tell Abu Hureyra (abstract). *L.T.* 9: 32.
1981 A role for microwear analysis in archaeology. *Third International Symposium on Flint.* F. Engelen, ed., Maastricht: Nederlandse Geologische Vereniging, pp. 88–90.
1983a *The Functional Analysis of Flint Implements – Pincevent and Pont d'Ambon: Two Case Studies from the French Final Paleolithic.* British Archaeological Reports, International Series, no. 177. Oxford: British Archaeological Reports.
1983b Some comments on edge damage as a factor in functional analysis of stone artifacts. *J.A.S.* 10: 231–42.
1983c The functions of burins and tanged points: Tell Abu Hureyra (Syria). *Traces d'utilisation sur les outils néolithiques du Proche Orient.* M-C. Cauvin, ed., Lyon: Maison de l'Orient, pp. 143–61.

Moss, E., and M. Newcomer
1982 Reconstruction of tool use at Pincevent: Microwear and experiments. *Tailler! pour quoi faire: Préhistoire et technologie lithique 2, Recent progress in microwear studies.* Studia Praehistorica Belgica 2. D. Cahen, ed., Tervuren: Musée royal de l'Afrique centrale, pp. 289–312.

Movius, H.
1968 Note on the history of the discovery and recognition of the function of burins as tools. *La Préhistoire, problèmes et tendances.* D. de Sonneville-Bordes, ed., Paris: C.N.R.S., pp. 311–18.

Movius, H., and N. David
1970 Burins avec modifications tertiaire du biseau, burins-pointe et burins du Raysse à l'Abri Pataud, Les Eyzies (Dordogne). *B.S.P.F.* 67: 445–55.

Movius, H., N. David, H. Bricker, and R. Clay
1968 *The Analysis of Certain Major Classes of Upper Paleolithic Tools.* American School of Prehistoric Research, Bulletin no. 26. Cambridge, Massachusetts: Peabody Museum, Harvard University.

Muller, H.
1903 Essais de taille du silex, montage et emploi des outils obtenus. *L'A.* 14: 417–36.

Mueller, S.
1897 *Nordische Altertumskunde.* Strasbourg: K. Truebner.

Newcomer, M.
1974 Study and replication of bone tools from Ksar Akil (Lebanon). *W.A.* 6: 138–53.
1977 Experiments in Upper Paleolithic bone work. *Méthodologie appliquée à l'industrie de l'os préhistorique.* C.N.R.S. colloques internationaux no. 568, Paris: C.N.R.S., pp. 293–301.

Newcomer, M., and F. Hivernel-Guerre
1974 Nucléus sur éclat: technologie et utilisation par différentes cultures préhistoriques. *B.S.P.F.* 71: 119–28.

Nilsson, S.
1838– *Skandinaviska Nordens Urinvanare.* Lund:
1843 Berlingska Boktryckeriet. (English edition: *The Primitive Inhabitants of Scandinavia.* 1868. London)

Odell, G.
1975 Micro-wear in perspective: A sympathetic response to Lawrence H. Keeley. *W.A.* 7:226–40.
1976 L'analyse fonctionnelle microscopique des pierres taillées, un nouveau système. *Actes du Congrès préhistorique de France, 20e Session, Martigues.* Paris: Société Préhistorique Française, pp. 385–90.
1977 The applicaiton of micro-wear analysis to the lithic component of an entire prehistoric settlement: Methods, problems and functional reconstructions. Ph.D. dissertation, Department of Anthropology, Harvard University, Cambridge, Massachusetts.
1978 Préliminaires d'une analyse fonctionnelle des pointes microlithiques de Bergumermeer (Pays-Bas). *B.S.P.F.* 75:37–49.
1979 A new improved system for the retrieval of functional information from microscopic observation of chipped stone tools. *Lithic Use-Wear Analysis.* B. Hayden, ed., New York: Academic Press, pp. 239–244.
1980a Toward a more behavioral approach to archaeological lithic concentrations. *A.A.* 45: 404–31.
1980b Butchering with stone tools: Some experimental results. *L.T.* 9: 38–48.
1981a The mechanics of use-breakage of stone tools: Some testable hypotheses. *J.F.A.* 8: 197–209.
1981b The morphological express at function junction: Searching for meaning in lithic tool types. *Journal of Anthropological Research* 37: 319–42.
1982a Some additional perspectives on appropriate models and analogies for hunter-gatherer populations. *A.A.* 47: 192–98.
1982b Emerging directions in the analysis of prehistoric stone tool use. *Reviews in Anthropology* 9: 17–33.
1983 Problèmes dans l'étude des traces d'utilisation. *Traces d'utilisation sur les outils néolithiques du Proche Orient.* M-C. Cauvin, ed., Lyon: Maison de l'Orient, pp. 17–24.

Odell, G., and F. Odell-Vereecken
1980 Verifying the reliability of lithic use-wear assessments by 'blind tests': The low-power approach. *J.F.A.* 7: 87–120.

Odell, G., R. Tringham, M. Roberts, B. Voyteck, and A. Whitman
1976 Microwear analysis (letter). *J.F.A.* 3: 239–40.

Olausson, D.
1980 Starting from scratch: The history of edge-wear research from 1838 to 1978. *L.T.* 9: 48–60.
1982– *Flint and Groundstone Axes in the Scanian*
1983 *Neolithic.* Scripta Minora 2. Lund: Archaeological Institute, University of Lund.

1983 Experiments to investigate the effects of heat treatment in use-wear on flint tools. *P.P.S.* 49:1–13.

Olausson, D., and L. Larson
1982 Testing for the presence of thermal pretreatment of flint in the Mesolithic and Neolithic of Sweden. *J.A.S.* 9: 275–85.

Owen, L., G. Unrath, and P. Vaughan, eds.
1982– Register of microwear analysts and their research.
1983 *Early Man News* (Tuebingen) 7–8:30–89.

Pant, R.
1979a Etude des traces d'utilisation des outils lithiques. *Les Dossiers de l'Archéologie* (Dijon) no. 36 (July–August): 86–89.
1979b Traces d'utilisation sur les outils du Paléolithique inférieur de la Caune de l'Arago à Tautavel. Thèse de 3ème cycle, Géologie du Quaternaire et Préhistoire, Université de Provence, Aix-en-Provence.

Payne, S.
1975 Faunal change at Franchthi Cave from 20,000 B.C. to 3000 B.C. *Archaeozoological Studies.* A. Classon, ed., New York: American Elsevier, pp. 129–31.

Perlès, C.
1976a Etude préliminaire des industries paléolithique de la grotte de Franchthi (Argolid, Grèce). *Résumés des Communications du 9e Congrès de l'U.I.S.P.P.,* Nice: U.I.S.P.P., p. 156.
1976b Rapport préliminaire sur les industries lithiques mésolithiques de la grotte de Franchthi (Argolid, Grèce). *Résumés des Communications du 9e Congrès de l'U.I.S.P.P.,* Nice: U.I.S.P.P., p. 239.
1979 Des navigateurs méditerranéens il y a 10,000 ans. *La Recherche* 10: 82–83.
1982 Les "outils d'Orville": des nucléus à lamelles. *Tailler! pour quoi faire: Préhistoire et technologie lithique 2, Recent progress in microwear studies.* Studia Praehistorica Belgica 2. D. Cahen, ed., Tervuren: Musée royal de l'Afrique centrale, pp. 129–48.

Perlès, C., and P. Vaughan
1983 Pièces lustrées, travail des plantes et moissons à Franchthi (Grèce) (Xème—IVème mill. B.C.). *Traces d'utilisation sur les outils néolithiques du Proche Orient.* M-C. Cauvin, ed., Lyon: Maison de l'Orient, pp. 209–24.

Peyrony, D., H. Kidder, and H. Noone
1949 Outils en silex émoussés du Paléolithique supérieur. *B.S.P.F.* 46:298–301.

Pfeiffer, L.
1910 Beitrag zur Kenntnis der steinzeitlichen Fellbearbeitung. *Zeitschrift fuer Ethnologie* 42: 839–95.
1912 *Die Steinzeitliche Technik.* Jena: G. Fischer.
1920 *Die Werkzeuge des Steinzeitmenschen.* Jena: G. Fischer.

Plisson, H.
1979 Etude des traces d'utilisation portées par les outils en silex. Maîtrise, Université de Paris I (Sorbonne), Paris.

1982a Une analyse fonctionnelle des outillages basaltiques. *Tailler! pour quoi faire: Préhistoire et technologie lithique 2, Recent progress in microwear studies.* Studia Praehistorica Belgica 2. D. Cahen, ed., Tervuren: Musée royal de l'Afrique centrale, pp. 241–44.

1982b Analyse fonctionnelle de 95 micro-grattoirs "tourassiens." *Tailler! pour quoi faire: Préhistoire et technologie lithique 2, Recent progress in microwear studies.* Studia Praehistorica Belgica 2. D. Cahen, ed., Tervuren: Musée royal de l'Afrique centrale, pp. 279–87.

1983a De la conservation des micro-polis d'utilisation. *B.S.P.F.* 80:74–77.

1983b An application of casting techniques for observing and recording of microwear. *L.T.* 12 (1): 17–21.

Plisson, H., and M. Mauger
n.d. Chemical and mechanical alteration of microwear polishes: An experimental approach. *The Human Uses of Flint and Chert: Papers from the Fourth International Symposium on Flint.* G. Sieveking and M. Newcomer, eds. Cambridge, England: Cambridge University Press, in press.

Pope, S.
1918 Yahi archery. *University of California Publications in American Archaeology and Ethnology* 13 (3): 103–52.

1923 A study of bows and arrows. *University of California Publications in American Archaeology and Ethnology* 13 (9): 329–414.

Poplin, F.
1972 Sur le dépeçage d'une hyène à l'aide d'un éclat de chaille. *B.S.P.F.* 66:113–17.

Pradel, L.
1966 Classification des burins avec notation chiffrée. *B.S.P.F.* 63:485–500.

1971 A new classification of burins. *Current Anthropology* 12:562–63.

1972– Nomenclature et possibilités fonctionnelles
1973 de l'outillage en pierre du Paléolithique en France. *Quartaer* 23:37–51.

1973a Stigmates d'accomodation et d'usage sur les burins moustériens de Fontmaure. *B.S.P.F.* 70:36–41.

1973b Traces d'usage sur les burins du Paléolithique supérieur. *B.S.P.F.* 70:90–96.

Purdy, B.
1974 Investigations concerning the thermal alteration of silica minerals: An archaeological approach. *Tebiwa* 17:37–66.

Ranere, A.
1975 Toolmaking and tool use among the Preceramic peoples of Panama. *Lithic Technology*. E. Swanson, ed. The Hague: Mouton, pp. 173–209.

Rau, C.
1864 Agricultural implements of the North American stone period. *Annual Report of the Smithsonian Institution for 1863*, pp. 379–80.

1869 Drilling in stone without metal. *Annual Report of the Smithsonian Institution for 1868*, pp. 392–400.

Ray, C.
1937 Probable uses of flint end-scrapers. *A.A.* 37:303–6.

Rigaud, A.
1972 La technologie du burin appliquée au matériel osseux de la Garenne (Indre). *B.S.P.F.* 69:104–8.

1977 Analyses typologiques et technologiques des grattoirs magdaléniens de la Garenne à Saint-Marcel (Indre). *Gallia Préhistoire* 20:1–43.

Rolfsen, P.
1980 Disturbance of archaeological layers by processes in the soil. *Norwegian Archaeological Review* 13: 110–18.

Rosenfeld, A.
1970 The examination of the use marks on some Magdalenian end-scrapers. *British Museum Quarterly* 35:176–82.

Rottlaender, R.
1975 The formation of patina on flint. *Archaeometry* 17: 106–10.

1976 Some aspects of the patination of flint. *Second International Symposium on Flint.* F. Engelen, ed. Maastricht: Nederlandse Geologische Vereniging, pp. 54–56.

Roy, S.
1983 Traces d'utilisation sur des outils a *posteriori* de Mureybit (Syrie): Méthodes d'étude. *Traces d'utilisation sur les outils néolithiques du Proche Orient.* M-C. Cauvin, ed., Lyon: Maison de l'Orient, pp. 25–30.

Rozoy, J-G.
1978 *Les derniers chasseurs.* Vols. 1,2, and 3. Charleville, France: J-G. Rozoy.

Sabo, D.
1980 Preliminary use-wear analysis of a Michigan chert. *The Michigan Archaeologist* 28 (3):55–72.

1982 The behavioral approach to lithics and the use of ethnographic analogy: A comment on Odell. *A.A.* 47:187–90.

Sankalia, H.
1964 *Stone Age Tools.* Poona, India: Deccan College.

Schiffer, M.
1976 *Behavioral Archaeology.* New York: Academic Press.

1979 The place of lithic use-wear studies in behavioral archaeology. *Lithic Use-Wear Analysis.* B. Hayden, ed., New York: Academic Press, pp. 15–25.

Seitzer, D.
1977– Form vs. function: Microwear analysis and its
1978 application to Upper Paleolithic burins. *Papers of the Archaeological Institute, University of Lund*, n.s. 2:5–20.

Semenov, S.
1964 *Prehistoric Technology.* Trans. by M. Thompson. Bath, England: Adams and Dart.

1970 The forms and functions of the oldest tools. *Quartaer* 21:1–20.

1971   A contribution to the question of certain Stone Age implements of Southeast Asia. *Soviet Anthropology and Archaeology* 10: 82–88.

1973   Fonctionologie du Paléolithique. *Actes du 8e Congrès de l'U.I.S.P.P.*, vol. 2. Belgrade: U.I.S.P.P., pp. 108–13.

Serizawa, C., ed.
1982   *Mosanru. A Palaeolithic Stone Industry Excavated from the Mosanru, Site, Hokkaido.* (in Japanese; English summary). Records of Archaeological Material no. 4. Sendai, Japan: Laboratory of Archaeology, Tohoku University.

Serizawa, C., H. Kajiwara, and K. Akoshima
1982   Experimental study of microwear traces and its potentiality. (in Japanese; English summary). *Archaeology and Natural Science* 14: 67–87.

Shackley, M.
1974   Stream abrasion on flint implements. *Nature* 248: 501–2.

Shafer, H., and R. Holloway
1979   Organic residue analysis in determining stone tool function. *Lithic Use-Wear Analysis.* B. Hayden, ed. New York: Academic Press, pp. 385–99.

Shepherd, W.
1972   *Flint. Its Origin, Properties and Uses.* London: Faber and Faber.

Shiner, J., and J. Porter
1974   Scanning electron microscopy and prehistoric stone tools. *Texas Journal of Science* 26: 284–86.

Sieveking, G., and M. Newcomer, eds.
n.d.   *The Human Uses of Flint and Chert: Papers from the Fourth International Flint Symposium.* Cambridge, England: Cambridge University Press, in press.

Smith, W.
1894   *Man the Primeval Savage.* London: Stanford.

Sollas, W.
1924   *Ancient Hunters.* London: Macmillan.

Sollberger, J.
1969   The basic tool kit required to make and notch arrow shafts for stone points. *Bulletin of the Texas Archaeological Society* 40: 231–40.

Sonnenfeld, J.
1962   Interpreting the function of primitive implements. *A.A.* 28: 56–65.

Sonneville-Bordes, D. de
1960   *Le Paléolithique supérieur en Périgord.* Bordeaux: Delmas.
1967   *La préhistoire moderne.* Périgueux: Fanlac.

Sonneville-Bordes, D. de, and J. Perrot
1953   Essai d'adaptation des méthodes statistiques au Paléolithique supérieur. Premiers résultats. *B.S.P.F.* 50:323–33.
1954–   Lexique typologique du Paléolithique
1956   supérieur. Outillage lithique. *B.S.P.F.* 51:327–35; 52: 76–79; 53:408–12, 547–59.

Sordinas, A.
1970   *Stone Implements from Northwestern Corfu, Greece.* Memphis State University Anthropological Research Center, Occasional Papers no. 4. Memphis, Tennessee: Memphis State University Anthropological Research Center.

Speth, J., and G. Johnson
1976   Problems in the use of correlation for the investigation of tool kits and activity areas. *Cultural Change and Continuity.* C. Cleland, ed. New York: Academic Press, pp. 35–57.

Speiss, A.
1979   *Reindeer and Caribou Hunters. An Archaeological Study.* New York: Academic Press.

Spurrell, F.
1884   On some Palaeolithic knapping tools and modes of using them. *Journal of the Royal Anthropological Institute of Great Britain and Ireland* 13: 109–18.

Stapert, D.
1976   Some natural surface modifications on flint in the Netherlands. *Palaeohistoria* 18:7–41.
1979   Zwei Fundplaetze vom Uebergang zwischen Palaeolithikum und Mesolithikum in Holland. *Archaeologisches Korrespondenzblatt* 9:159–66.

Steensberg, A.
1943   *Ancient Harvesting Implements.* Nationalmuseets Skrifter, Arkaeo-Historisk Raekke no. 1. Copenhagen: Nationalmuseet.

Steinbring, J.
1966   The manufacture and use of bone defleshing tools. *A.A.* 31: 575–81.

Strathern, M.
1969   Stone axes and flake tools: Evaluations from two New Guinea Highlands societies. *P.P.S.* 35: 311–29.

Stroebel, R.
1939   *Die Feuersteingeraete der Pfahlbaukultur.* Mannus Buecherei, Band 66. Leipzig: C. Rabitzsch.

Sturge, W.
1914   The chronology of the Stone Age. *P.P.S. of East Anglia* 1: 43–105.

Taute, W.
1981   Mesad Mazzal, ein Siedlungsplatz des praekeramischen Neolithikums suedlich des Toten Meeres (Vorbericht). *Beitraege zur Umweltgeschichte des Vorderen Orients.* Beihefte zum Tuebinger Atlas des Vorderen Orients, Reihe A, Nr. 8. W. Frey and H-P. Uerpmann, eds. Wiesbaden: L. Reichert Verlag, pp. 236–56.

Tixier, J.
1955   Les abris sous roche de Dakhlat es-Saâdane (commune mixte de Bon-Saâda). I—industries en place de l'Abri B. *Libyca* 3:81–125.
1958–   Les industries lithiques d'Ain Fritissa (Maroc).
1959   *Bulletin d'Archéologie Marocaine* 3:107–248.

Tixier, J. (*continued*)
1963   *Typologie de l'Epipaléolithique du Maghreb.*
        Mémoires du Centre de Recherches
        Anthropologiques, Préhistoriques et
        Ethnographiques no. 2. Algers: Centre de
        Recherches Anthropologiques, Préhistoriques et
        Ethnographiques.

Torrence, R.
1979   Macrocore production at the Melos obsidian
        quarries. *L.T.* 8: 51–60.

Tringham, R.
1971   The function, technology, and typology of the
        chipped stone industry at Bilany, Czechoslovakia.
        Alba Regia, Annales Musei Stephani Regis 12:
        143–48.
n.d.(a) Analysis of the flaked stone assemblage from
        Sitagroi. *Sitagroi.* A. C. Renfrew and M. Gimbutas,
        eds. Institute of Archaeology Press, University of
        California at Los Angeles, in press.
n.d.(b) Analysis of the flaked stone tool industry at Divostin.
        Excavations of Divostin. A. McPherron and D.
        Srejović, eds., in press.

Tringham, R., G. Cooper, G. Odell, B. Voytek, and
A. Whitman
1974   Experimentation in the formation of edge damage: A
        new approach to lithic analysis. *J.F.A.* 1:171–96.

Tsirk, A.
1979   Regarding fracture initiations. *Lithic Use-Wear
        Analysis.* B. Hayden, ed. New York: Academic Press,
        pp. 83–96.

Unger-Hamilton, R.
1983   An investigation into the variables affecting the
        development and appearance of plant polish on flint
        blades. *Traces d'utilisation sur les outils néolithiques
        du Proche Orient.* M-C. Cauvin, ed. Lyon: Maison de
        l'Orient, pp. 243–50.
1984   The formation of use-wear polish on flint: Beyond the
        "deposit versus abrasion" controversy. *J.A.S.* 11:
        91–98.

Unrath, G.
1982   Die Funktionsbestimmung geschlagener
        Steinwerkzeuge an Hand ihrer mikroskopisch
        erkennbaren Gebrauchsspuren. Magisterarbeit,
        Geowissenschaftliche Facultaet,
        Eberhard-Karls-Universitaet, Tuebingen.

Vanderwall, R.
1977   The 'fabricator' in Australia and New Guinea. *Stone
        Tools as Cultural Markers.* R. Wright, ed. New Jersey:
        Humanities, pp. 350–53.

Van Noten, F.
1978   *Les chasseurs de Meer.* Dissertations Archaeologicae
        Gandenses no. 18. With contributions by D. Cahen,
        L. Keeley, and J. Moeyersons. Brugge: De Tempel.

Van Noten, F., D. Cahen, and L. Keeley
1980   A Paleolithic campsite in Belgium. *Scientific
        American* 242 (2): 48–55.

Vaughan, P.
1980   On experimental design and publication (abstract).
        L.T. 9:31.

1981a   Microwear analysis of experimental flint and
        obsidian tools. *Third International Symposium on
        Flint.* F. Engelen, ed. Maastricht: Nederlandse
        Geologische Vereniging, pp. 90–91.
1981b   Lithic microwear experimentation and the functional
        analysis of a Lower Magdalenian stone tool
        assemblage. Ph.D. diss., Department of
        Anthropology, University of Pennsylvania,
        Philadelphia (Publication no. 82–08, 050,
        University Microfilms International, Ann Arbor,
        Michigan).
1982   Anàlisis funcional preliminar de instrumentos líticos
        tallados de Telarmachay. Telarmachay: niveles
        precerámicos de occupación. D. Lavallée, M. Julien,
        J. Wheeler, *Revista del Museo Nacional* (Lima)
        46:128–33.
1983   La fonction des outils préhistoriques. *La Recherche*
        148 (October): 1226–34.
1985a   Funktionsbestimmung von Steingeraeten anhand
        mikroskopischer Gebrauchsspuren. *Germania* 63(2)
        (in press).
1985b   The burin blow technique: Creator or eliminator,
        J.F.A. 12 (in press).
1985c   Analyse tracéologique. Telarmachay, chasseurs et
        pasteurs préhistoriques de Andes. D. Lavallée, M.
        Julien, J. Wheeler, C. Karlin, Paris: Aide à la Diffusion
        de la Pensée Française, in press.

Vayson, A.
1920   La plus ancienne industrie de Saint-Acheul. *L'A.* 30:
        441–96.

Vermeersch, P., ed.
1982   *Contributions to the the Study of the Mesolithic of the
        Belgian Lowland.* Studia Praehistorica Belgica 1.
        Tervuren: Musée royal de l'Afrique centrale.

Walker, P.
1978   Butchering and stone tool function. *A.A.* 43:710–15.

Warren, S. H.
1905   On the origin of "eolithic" flints by natural causes,
        especially by the foundering of drifts. *Journal of the
        Royal Anthropological Institute of Great Britain and
        Ireland* 35:337–64.
1913   Problems of flint fracture. *Man* 13:37–38.
1914   The experimental investigation of flint fracture and its
        application to problems of human implements.
        *Journal of the Royal Anthropological Institute of
        Great Britain and Ireland* 44: 512–51.
1923a   The sub-soil flint flaking sites at Grays. *Proceedings
        of the Geologists' Association* 34:38–42.
1923b   Sub-soil pressure flaking. *Proceedings of the
        Geologists' Association* 34:153–75.

White, J. P.
1968a   Fabricators, outils écaillés, or scalar cores? *Mankind*
        6:658–66.
1968b   Ston Naip Bilong Tumbuna: The living Stone Age in
        New Guinea. *La préhistoire, problèmes et tendances.*
        D. de Sonneville-Bordes, ed. Paris: C.N.R.S., pp.
        511–16.
1969   Typologies for some prehistoric stone artifacts of the
        Australian New Guinea Highlands. *Archaeology and
        Physical Anthropology in Oceania* 4:18–46.

White, J. P., and D. H. Thomas
1972   What mean these stones? Ethnotaxonomic models and archaeological interpretations in the New Guinea Highlands. *Models in Archaeology.* D. Clarke, ed. London: Methuen, pp. 275–308.

White, J. P., N. Modjeska, and I. Hipuya
1977   Group definitions and mental templates, an ethnographic experiment. *Stone Tools as Cultural Markers.* R. Wright, ed. New Jersey: Humanities, pp. 380–90.

Wilmsen, E.
1968a   Functional analysis of flaked stone artifacts. *A.A.* 33:156–61.
1968b   Lithic analysis in paleoanthropology. *Science* 161: 982–87.
1970   *Lithic Analysis and Cultural Inference. A Paleo-Indian Case.* Anthropological Papers, University of Arizona, no. 16. Tucson: University of Arizona Press.

Wilmsen, E., and F. Roberts, Jr.
1978   *Lindenmeier, 1934–1974.* Washington, D.C.: Smithsonian Institution.

Witthoft, J.
1955   Worn stone tools from southeastern Pennsylvania. *Pennsylvania Archaeologist* 35:16–31.
1958   Indian methods of skin dressing and tanning. *Ohio Archaeologist* 8 (3):94–99.
1967   Glazed polish on flint tools. *A.A.* 32:383–88.

Woodbury, R.
1954   *Prehistoric Stone Implements of Northeastern Arizona.* Peabody Museum of American Archaeology and Ethnology, Harvard University, vol. 34. Cambridge, Massachusetts: Peabody Museum, Harvard University.

Yacabaccio, H., and L. Borrero
1982   Bergumermeer and modeling: A comment on Odell. *A.A.* 47:183–87.

Yellen, J.
1977   *Archaeological Approaches to the Present.* New York: Academic Press.

Yerkes, R.
1980   A microdrill from the Mississippian component at the Labras Lake site. *Investigations at the Labras Lake Site: Volume 1-Archaeology.* J. L. Phillips, R. Hall, and R. Yerkes, eds. University of Illinois at Chicago Circle, Department of Anthropology Reports of Investigations no. 1. Chicago: University of Illinois at Chicago Circle, pp. 318–24.
1983   Microwear, microdrills, and Mississippian craft specialization. *A.A.* 48:499–518.
1984   Activities and subsistence at Labras Lake: A microwear and contextual investigation of the Late Archaic: Late Woodland, and Mississippian components of a bluff-site on the American Bottom, Illinois. Ph. D., diss., Department of Anthropology, University of Wisconsin, Madison.

Zeiler, I.
1981   Burins magdaléniens avec modification tertiaire: La morphologie des biseaux et les traces d'utilisation. *B.S.P.F.* 78:44–51.

Index